SCHOOL OF ORIENTAL AND AFRICAN STUDIES

———————————————

Jordan Lectures in Comparative Religion

XVIII

The Louis H. Jordan Bequest

The will of the Rev. Louis H. Jordan provided that the greater part of his estate should be paid over to the School of Oriental and African Studies to be employed for the furtheranceof studies in Comparative Religion, to which his life had been devoted. Part of the funds which thus became available was to be used for the endowment of a Louis H. Jordan Lectureship in Comparative Religion. The lecturer is required to deliver a course of six or eight lectures for subsequent publication. The first series of lectures was delivered in 1951.

JORDAN LECTURES 1993

Tales of Faith

Religion as Political Performance in Central Africa

V.Y. MUDIMBE

William R. Kenan Professor of French, Comparative Literature and Classics, Stanford University, and Distinguished Research Professor, The Literature Program, Duke University

THE ATHLONE PRESS
London & Atlantic Highlands, NJ

First published 1997 by
The Athlone Press
1 Park Drive, London NW11 7SG
and 165 First Avenue,
Atlantic Highlands, NJ 07716

© V.Y. Mudimbe, 1997
British Library Cataloguing in Publication Data
*A catalogue record for this book is available
from the British Library*

ISBN 0 485 17418 9

Library of Congress Cataloging-in-Publication Data

Mudimbe, V. Y., 1941–
    Tales of faith : religion as political performance in Central
Africa / V. Y. Mudimbe.
        p.   cm. -- (Jordan lectures in comparative religion : 18)
    Includes bibliographical references.
    ISBN 0-485-17418-9
    1. Africa, Central--Religion.   2. Christianity--Africa, Central.
3. Religion and politics--Africa, Central.   I. Title.   II. Series.
BL2466.M83   1997
297.1'77'0967--dc21   97-10362
                                                                  CIP

Typeset by Bibloset
Printed and bound in Great Britain by
Cambridge University Press

To the memory of Michel de Certeau and Engelbert Mveng, s.j.

Bin ich ein Gott? Mir wird so licht!
Ich schau in diesen reinen Zügen
Die wirkende Natur vor meiner Seele liegen.
Jetzt erst erkenn ich, was der Weise spricht:
'Die Geisterwelt ist nicht verschlosen;
Dein Sinn ist zu, dein Herz ist tot!
Auf, bade, Schüler, unverdrossen
Die irdsche Brust im Morgenrot!'

Goethe, Faust, 439–46

Am I a God? Light grows this page –
In these pure lines my eye can see
Creative nature spread in front of me.
But now I grasp the meaning of the sage:
'The realm of spirits is not far away:
Your mind is closed, your heart is dead.
Rise, student, bathe without dismay
In heaven's dawn your mortal head.'

The Manner

The only way to blaze a trail to responsibility in one's adherences is by doing it oneself. The eternal truths find their temporal, mortal modality in this or that concrete word, pronounced as it vanishes into thin air, in this or that concrete unprecedented initiative, taken and undone all in the same moment. Word and initiative flash forth in the presence of a moment, and disappear. In this momentary birthplace of the truth, the exercise of the truthfulness we have just accomplished will take up its abode.

To restore all things to this native soil of credibility has been the method I have followed, in its simplest act and essential form. Do not ask me, then, where I speak from, who I am, and what audience I wish to help or harm. I am a human being like you, I shall die, and I was not born a functionary of the Truth nor a professional in the service of 'Christianity'. I write in order to doff my masks before they blot out my face.

Not being this, or not believing that, is unimportant. The only important thing is the manner of not being or not believing. The sharing that it initiates is located beneath allegiances, doctrinal allegations, and programmes. It founds and justifies them. As Kierkegaard put it:

Altogether equal in importance to the truth, indeed, even more important than the truth, is the manner in which it is accepted – and it would not be of much use to lead thousands to accept the truth, if, precisely by the manner in which they accepted it, they were to find themselves excluded from it.

Fabien Eboussi-Boulaga

Contents

structuralist, which were well exemplified in France in the 1950s and 1960s and incarnated a methodological discontinuity that, in terms of epistemology, blurred falsely transparent oppositions such as 'primitive' versus 'civilized'. Yet a major difference between the two models could be seen: on the one hand, in the Marxist primacy of history and the pertinence of its mode of production concept; and, on the other hand, the structuralist emphasis on synchrony, structures and binarism. These two approaches made thinkable (by this expression, I do not imply a genealogical filiation nor a causality at any rate) the possibility of pluralizing the world's representations through rigorous techniques and, thus, directly contributing to the progressive disqualification of the nineteenth-century epistemology, with its grand division between sciences of normality and abnormality. From the 1950s, it became usual to practise human and social sciences on the basis of new constituent premises: anything, anyone, any totality can then be described and understood as being its own system, presided by its own internal norms and, in principle, governed by its own rules. This is not a minor phenomenon nor a marginal happening. It meant a rupture with an ancient order and fissured the epistemological certainties and paradigms of an intellectual configuration. For example, Sally Falk Moore, in her recent *Anthropology and Africa* (1994), shows well the transformations of her discipline and how, since the 1960s, new objects and perspectives arise in African anthropology. Similar critical renewals can be observed in other disciplines (see Bates and Alii, 1993). To refer only to a few, let us note history (e.g. Vansina, 1961), sociology (e.g. Balandier, 1955), political science (e.g. Coleman and Halisi, 1983), philosophy (e.g. Crahay, 1965), theology and missiology. (e.g. Hastings, 1979).

It is precisely in this post-structuralist period that I would like to situate these lectures – more exactly, to make their fundamental objective *hic et nunc* explicit. How and why should I try to apprehend a particular quality of religious performances in its presentness which, in representations as well as in perceptions, manifests itself in the polarity and tension of a subject–object relationship, while asserting itself as pregnant with a possible transcendence? Traces of Heidegger, Jaspers and Sartre could be seen lingering in such an objective. Yet I see it also solidly predicated in today's reflection on – and search for – 'our' father's house, in which its many mansions would suit our differences, as Anthony Appiah would put it (1992).

In these lectures, I focus on texts as phenomena, and on phenomena as texts, considering all of them as signs that can be decrypted, understood and compared. I look for intertextual, intercultural connections and, whenever necessary, even interrogate extra-textual relations. Apropos religion and religious forms of experience, this project strives to bring together discourses that describe sociohistorical events and claim to decode and interpret the meaning of these events perceived as signs. In this sense, *Tales of Faith* is about representing certain things which, in their own right, are already – as anthropological, exegetical, historical, philosophical or theological discourses, to quote only the most used – representations of a given, a represented which is out there.

From an extremely critical angle, one might wonder whether such a perspective does not simply reduce itself to a reversed image of its own theatricality, but such a critique seems excessive for three reasons. First, the sources used are mostly respectable (which does not necessarily mean believable and still less true) but nevertheless submitted to the disciplinary exigencies of their time. Second, the representations conveyed and formulated should be considered as 'objectivist' in their own right. They are dependent on methods coming from particular intellectual frameworks inscribed within the history of a discipline with all that such an insertion supposes in terms of determinations and overdeterminations. From this viewpoint, it would be inappropriate to disqualify a priori Lévy-Bruhl's pronouncements because they do not fit completely within 'true' structuralism or, for example, to exclude evolutionists from the history of scientific anthropology and its interpretations because they would have contributed to the confrontation of racist ideologies. Finally, my presentation of *Tales of Faith* might be judged too controversial, aggravated by the weight of theoretical preoccupations. To this I would respond that what I am offering is not sheer fiction; it can sustain critical examination and, more importantly, can and should be checked against empirical studies, above all the experiential authority of serious Africa scholars and ongoing objectivist researches in the field. Despite its avowed status as a representation interrogating already highly worked and stylized representations, both in spirit and method it is far removed from metanarratives concerned, say, with the history of histories of philosophy (e.g. Lucien Braun), the antihistory of histories of literature (e.g. Deconstruction and Cie), or even – should I dare? – the possibility of a multivolume on 'anthropological theories and Africa', as Sally Falk Moore menaces in the foreword to her stimulating *Anthropology and Africa* (1994).

Originally, each lecture focused on a specific theme, namely, (1) the textual authority of a Faith looking for adequate expressions of its intelligence, a *Fides Quaerens Intellectum*, to use Saint Anselm's words; (2) the existential indetermination of religious beliefs and activity in the prose of everyday life; (3) the grand dichotomy – 'primitive' versus 'civilized' – as what is, or is no longer, at the heart of narratives promoting cultural and spiritual conversion; (4) the discursive practices of conversion and their predicaments; (5) finally, the phenomenon of acculturation as a figure of *métissage* – that is, cultural 'hybridation' witnessing to contemporary dynamics of dialogues between peoples and histories. These entries have been synthesized and reduced to four chapters, in which I comment on the dialogue itself and its opposite that are analogous to the paradoxical and always changing identity of any individuality understood as a transcendence of a *For-Itself* and a *For-Others*.

Created for the Louis H. Jordan Lectureship in Comparative Religion at the School of Oriental and African Studies of the University of London, the lectures were delivered in English during five separate sessions in May 1993. They were adapted slightly in French for a series of talks I gave during the same period, as Associate Director of Studies, in the seminars of Jean-Loup Amselle, Marc Augé, Jean Bazin, Elikia M'Bokolo and Emmanuel Terray, at l'Ecole des Hautes Etudes en Sciences Sociales in Paris. Although I have made changes and sometimes introduced important developments, the version published here fundamentally retranscribes the essentials of my original Jordan lectures, including their spoken style, rhythm, hesitations, and – alas – repetitions. Modifications are generally presented as concrete examples of cultural *métissage*, which explicate or articulate in other words what in the original lectures seemed too synthetic, a bit obscure, or at times somewhat esoteric. Occasionally, definitions of concepts and bibliographical information have been added, or paragraphs and illustrations expanded, as in the texts about Jean Ishaku and Alexis Kagame. The latter, in actuality, is a translation by Victor Provenzano of my 1981 'In Memoriam', published in the French journal *Recherche, Pédagogie et Culture*.

Here, I would like to recognize gratefully the input of both my British and French audiences. The sole major addition in this book is a systematic reference to a text I wrote in French on the prose of everyday life as a contribution to a special issue of *Social Sciences and Medicine* (**15B** 1981: 195–211). Published by Pergamon Press on the topic of medical anthropology, the issue derives from the proceedings of a conference on 'African Medical Systems as Systems of Thought, Causality, and Taxonomy', which took place at Cambridge University from 23–26 June 1980. Throughout my 1993 spring lectures in London and Paris, particularly during my exchanges with the audiences, this old article and, strangely enough, its ratiocinations proved useful as a key for correcting, grounding or, at any rate, clarifying ongoing intellectual modes of discursivity which, in anthropology, history, philosophy and theology accord themselves to African cultures, their virtues and predicaments. The article became such an important part of my reflection on *Tales of Faith* and exchanges with my audiences that I could not reasonably avoid mentioning it here. It goes without saying that I have seriously amended all my references to the original text.

I would also like to thank very much all those who contributed to the realization of these lectures and to their publication as a book. First of all, I think of the Committee of the Reverend Louis H. Jordan Lectureship at the University of London, which decided on the honour bestowed on me as the 1993 lecturer. I wish to thank in particular David Edwards, Richard Gray and Gerald Hawting. For their advice, encouragement and friendship, I am also deeply grateful to Christopher Davis, Louis Brenner, John Middleton and Murray Last. My entire research on *Tales of Faith* would not have reached the publication stage without the help and generosity of close collaborators: Priscilla Lane, who has served for many years as my personal assistant at Duke University, North Carolina; Isabelle Collignon, Doris Garraway, Katarina Kivel and Patricia Reefe who, at Stanford University, participated in different capacities in the completion of this book. Finally, my sincere thanks to my publisher for a superlative job.

I am dedicating this book to the memory of two companions of the road: Michel de Certeau and Engelbert Mveng, a Frenchman and a Cameroonian, indefatigable explorers of tales of faith.

Palo Alto, 11 August 1995

I

God's Inflections
On the Politics of Interpretation

> What may be contained or expressed, beyond
> Being, in the richer forms of representation of
> God or the Absolute is, in the beginning, only an
> empty word and only Being; this simple thing, that
> otherwise has no meaning, this emptiness, is there-
> fore most completely the beginning of Philosophy.
>
> Hegel

There are some risks in facing the complex domain of religion and the
religious, particularly for an agnostic, and especially when the objective
of the research is not the apprehension of their being but rather their
relation to, and expressions in the field of, politics. By politics, one
may simply understand that which in the *polis* – in our case the African
context – deals with community affairs and the norms for both everyday
life and the explicit and implicit forms of civil government. Briefly,
referring to the distinction made by G. Van Der Leeuw (1938: 23),
the purpose here is not to analyse religion and the religious from their
own viewpoint, according to which 'the religious man perceives that
with which his religion deals as primal, as originative or causal', but,
from the background of a reflective thought, to situate religion and the
religious as dimensions to be decrypted and understood in a political
context. Such a methodological position, that the real is to be described,
is close to that expounded by Edmund Husserl and noted by Maurice
Merleau-Ponty in the beginning of his *Phenomenology of Perception* :

The whole universe of science is built upon the world as directly experienced,
and if we want to subject science itself to rigorous scrutiny and arrive at a
precise assessment of its meaning and scope, we must begin to reawaken the
basic experience of the world of which science is the second-order expression.
Science has not and never will have, by its nature, the same significance *qua*
form of being as the world which we perceive, for the simple reason that it is

a rationale or explanation of that world. I am not a 'living creature' nor even a 'man', nor again even 'a consciousness' endowed with all the characteristics which zoology, social anatomy or inductive psychology recognize in these various products of the natural or historical process – I am the absolute source, my existence does not stem from my antecedents, from my physical and social environment; instead it moves out towards them and sustains them, for I alone bring into being for myself (and therefore into being in the only sense that the word can have for me) the tradition which I elect to carry on, or the horizon whose distance from me would be abolished if I were not there to scan it with my gaze. Scientific points of view, according to which my existence is a moment of the world's, are always both naive and at the same time dishonest, because they take for granted, without explicitly mentioning it, the other point of view, namely that of consciousness, through which from the outset a world forms itself round me and begins to exist for me. To return to things themselves is to return to that world which precedes knowledge, of which knowledge always *speaks*, and in relation to which every scientific schematization is an abstract and derivative sign-language, as is geography in relation to the countryside in which we have learnt beforehand what a forest, a prairie or a river is.

(Merleau-Ponty, 1989: VIII–IX)

The Concept of Religion

Let us thus accept any religion, its rituals and theatricality as perceptual phenomena. More specifically, two possible forms could be distinguished from the etymology of the word religion itself. As Cicero suggests in *De Natura Deorum* (2.28.72), the first, and the most ancient, advances the hypothesis that the word would have come from the verb *relegere*, 'bringing, putting together'. The second, as used by Lactantius (4.28) and Saint Augustine (*Retractationes* 1.13) indicates the verb *religare* as a possible origin. In Latin, *religare* means 'to be linked to one or several people' in the exact meaning coming out of such expressions as 'to sheave the wheat'. The first hypothesis would reduce the etymological meaning of the concept religion to whatever unites a group of individuals. The second, the favourite of contemporary etymologists, insists that there is in the etymon the root – *lig* – that reproduces the Latin *lex*, 'the law', which should be considered as a simple variation (Benveniste, 1973: 518–22). It follows that religion (*religio*) would have something in common with the law (*lex*), because both prescribe and establish not only collective norms of behavior but also well-specified duties and obligations that bind the members of a community. As Benveniste put it, '. . . the Latin *religio* . . . remains, in all western languages, the sole and constant word, for which no equivalent or substitute has been able to establish itself' (Benveniste, 1978: 518).

Beyond, or on this side of, the etymology of the word which, according to Benveniste, 'has been discussed since ancient times, and even then scholars were unable to agree, modern scholars remain no less divided' (1973: 518), one could, from a strictly anthropological perspective, suggest a minimal definition of religion. It would include *naturism*, that is, an explicit will to integrate one spiritually in the cosmic order; *fetishism*, or the desire to transcend and manipulate the culturally and conventionally separated orders of the sacred and the profane; and finally, *a cult of ancestors*, or a cult of sanctified models offered to a community as concrete and living examples of 'political' perfection (e.g. Thomas, 1969). Within this perspective, a traditional understanding of the concept might seem to be called into question. On the one hand, such a minimal suggestion appears to amplify the rule of a practice without explicitly signifying the binding theme of submission to the presence of a deity. Cicero and Lactantius bring together both the practice of religion and the bond of dependence that link the practitioner to God. On the other hand, this minimal definition may seem to respond too easily to the exigencies of politics as ultimate principles regulating the human community. Thus, following Sir James Frazer's advice:

There is probably no subject in the world about which opinions differ so much as the nature of religion, and to frame a definition of it which would satisfy every one must obviously be impossible. All that a writer can do is, first, to say clearly what he means by religion, and afterwards to employ the word consistently in that sense throughout his work. By religion, then, I understand a *propitiation* or *conciliation of powers superior to man* which are believed to direct and control the course of nature and human life. Thus defined, religion consists of two elements, a theoretical and a practical, namely, a belief in powers higher than man and an attempt to propitiate or please them. Of the two, belief comes first, since we must believe in the existence of a divine being before we can attempt to please him. (Frazer, 1922: 57–8, my emphasis)

In Sir James Frazer's definition – which I would like to accept – the notions of propitiation and conciliation of powers seem value laden. In fact, they voice something that is not observable, and give away a signification that might come from the mediation of the observer, unless it establishes itself as a completion of a dialogue between the practitioner (of what supposedly is a propitiation or conciliation of powers) and the analyst's perception of these systems. Thus, accepting Sir James Frazer's definition of religion, instead of underlining the propitiatory and conciliatory dimensions, I would understand religion as a performance, namely, as an acting, an abstract or concrete practice of representing something that seems to be beyond human control. Indeed, as noted by Sir James Frazer, the performance consists of two essential elements: a belief or theory and a practice. The two examples of Saint Anselm and Cerno Bokar Saalif Taal (1883–1940) illustrate this as they are performers in this specific sense. Saint Anselm's *Fides Quaerens Intellectum*, 'Faith Looking for Intelligence', written between 1033 and 1109 – in which he expounds what will become known as the ontologic argument (and that Saint Bonaventure, Duns Scott, Descartes and Leibniz will later rethink) – is fundamentally also a *fides ferens intellectum,* a 'faith fearing intelligence', as Koyré (1964) noted. In other words, it is a discourse on a belief looking for illumination and in this very process bearing witness to it and thus to a revelation, an uncovering and its foundation: God as *Lux* (Light) and *Veritas* (Truth). In his book, *The Religious Heritage and Spiritual Search of Cerno Bokar Saalif Taal* (1984), which superbly analyses the personal quest of *Le Sage de Bandiagara*, Louis Brenner describes the search and spiritual journey of a man who was convinced that 'people (should) activate their religious principles in their everyday lives' and that 'ordinary life can provide aids to one's search' (Brenner, 1984: 3): to look concretely for something foundational, an ultimate *ratio*, and, eventually, to accept and submit to its disclosure (revelation). The third and last illustration is Stefano Kaoze, who became the first Roman Catholic priest in Central Africa in 1917. At the beginning of the century, while still a Catholic seminarian, he published a brief text (1907–11) on Bantu psychology, in which he opposed African against Euro-Christian practices, considering the latter as fulfilment of the former, and thus explicitly indicating both the fatality of an evolution and the superiority of the Euro-Christian paradigms of faith. What is common in these three examples is, first of all, that Saint Anselm, Cerno Bokar Saalif Taal and Stefano Kaoze connect the practice of their lives to a belief, and their narratives are in reality performances referring to an external 'something': an incredible transcending everyday practice and its obvious rationality, a *Word* signifying both revelation and salvation. Thus, the body of the text by Saint Anselm, Cerno Bokar or Kaoze does not seem to belong to the text itself but to this something that is both its embodiment and justification. Hence, as intellectual performances, these texts transgress themselves for, as Jean-Luc Marion put it apropos any theological writing, 'the play from words to the Word implies that the theological writing is played in distance, which unites as well as separates the man writing and the Word at hand' (Marion, 1991: 1).

These three examples have something else in common: a language, or to use Saint Anselm's book as a metaphor, the *Fides Quaerens Intellectum* is, in actuality, a *Fides Quaerens Linguam* and a *Fides Quaerens Legem*. In fact, the narratives actualize reflective discourses that claim to unveil a hidden truth. As such, these discourses cannot be confused with familiarity discourses, that is, with our everyday life discursive practices. Indeed, these are first-level apprehensions of what we consider as human reality and experience. They sometimes proceed asyndetically and, in general, can be characterized as practices that systematically rely on the implicit, collectively shared by a cultural community. Such discursive practices need not be systematic, since they deal with the familiar, and thus any member of the community is always, at least in principle, capable of apprehending the unfinished sentence or the unsaid carried on by a gesture, a wink, or simply a silence. Then, in all communities there is a second-level discursive practice, a phenomenological one. In this case, an individual describes what (s)he perceives and literally maps the apparent disorder of the perceived. What this discourse renders does not seem to be the materiality, the otherness which is out there, but instead a flow, the functioning of the consciousness participating in a world, organizing and interpreting it. If so, what would be a convincing alternative? Should we emphasize another level, an objectivist one, that claims to bring together the discourses of sciences? Here, a theoretical model – say, in economics, geography, history or physics – claims that it can account for what is out there and offers the means of mastering it or, at least, of explaining how it works. The objectivist discourse does not reflect the reality it pretends to master. To use an Althusserian concept, it is a generality that modifies itself over time (Althusser, 1965); and, thus, from a scientific paradigm to another, it attempts new techniques and methods for mastering and rendering what is out here. In this sense, Collingwood's historical re-enactment principle (1946) could be – *mutatis mutandis* – compared to astrophysicists' successive models of mapping the geography and life of celestial bodies. In *Le Conflit des interprétations* (1969), Paul Ricoeur comments on another level – that of hermeneutics – which demonstrates a critical capability for interrogating the foundation and perspective of objectivist discourses. To clarify the singularity of this practice, hermeneutics should be understood as the totality of techniques and knowledge. In the history of a social formation and the life of a culture, this allows one to interpret meanings as opposed to semiology, which is a knowledge allowing one to classify social signs. On which level should one situate a discursive practice on religion? If we reinscribe the levels as points on a circle, specialists of religions and theologians would probably prefer the uncomfortable position situated tangentially between the objectivist practices of sciences and a theory of theories and practices. Thus, starting with language of familiarity and continuing clockwise, one would face, successively, the phenomenological, the objectivist and, finally, a theory of scientific practices.

Pierre Bourdieu has been advocating this concept of theory practices that might give to theoretical knowledge 'a solid basis by freeing it from distortions arising from the epistemological and social conditions of its production. It has nothing in common with the aim of rehabilitation which has misled most discourses on practice; it aims simply to bring to light the theory of practice which theoretical knowledge implicity applies and so to make possible a truly scientific knowledge of practice and of the practical mode of knowledge' (Bourdieu, 1990: 27).

If so, it becomes urgent to state the place from where I shall be looking at religious practices as political performances in and about Central Africa.

My field of perception [wrote Maurice Merleau-Ponty] is constantly filled with a play of colors, noises and fleeting tactile sensations which I cannot relate precisely to the context of my clearly perceived world, yet which I nevertheless immediately 'place' in the world, without ever confusing them with my daydreams. Equally constantly I weave dreams round things I imagine, people and things whose presence is not incompatible with the context, yet who are not in fact involved in it: they are ahead of reality, in the realm of the imaginary. If the reality of my perception were based solely on the intrinsic coherence of 'representations', it ought to be for ever hesitant and, being wrapped up in my conjectures on probabilities. I ought to be ceaselessly taking apart misleading syntheses, and reinstating in reality stray phenomena which I had excluded in the first place. But this does not happen. *The real is a closely woven fabric.* It does not await our judgment before incorporating the most surprising phenomena, or before rejecting the most plausible figments of our imagination. Perception is not a science of the world, it is not even an act, a deliberate taking up of a position; it is the background from which all acts stand out, and is presupposed by them. The world is not an object such that I have in my possession the law of its making; it is the natural setting of, and field for, all my thoughts and all my explicit perception. Truth does not 'inhabit' only 'the inner man' or more accurately, there is no inner man, man is in the world, and only in the world does he know himself. When I return to myself from an excursion into the realm of dogmatic common sense or of science, I find not a source of intrinsic truth, but a subject destined to the world.

(Maurice Merleau-Ponty, 1989: X–XI, my emphasis)

In my case, that is the real context in which I perceive religion as a performance. How, then, can I make sense of religion insofar as it is basically only from this background of my perception that I can name the seen and look for its signification which, to refer again to Maurice Merleau-Ponty, makes itself visible at the intersection of my experiences and those of other people, through the meeting of both?

Anthropology and Religion

Thus, naming – but to name, as Martin Heidegger taught us, is to bring into human presence, which implies to allow 'something' or 'someone' to be caught by a language. One might decide to do an ethnography of any religious performance by objectivizing it and, in so doing, conforming a practice and its language of familiarity to a supposed 'objective reality' that could more or less correspond to a social scientist's expectations. Here, instead of claiming to record performances and their meanings in an African social order, I would like to focus on an already given objectivist vision of African religious practices as it appears, trapped, between a social physics (that pretends to render an objective reality) and a social phenomenology (that claims to describe it faithfully). Sir E.E. Evans-Pritchard's *Theories of Primitive Religion* (1965) is a good example.

This booklet consists of a series of 1962 lectures, which distinguish three main domains in the field of 'primitive religions'. The first domain, that of psychological theories elaborated in the eighteenth and nineteenth centuries, analyses contributions by President Brosse and Auguste Comte of France on African fetishism; Max Muller of Germany, on the school illustrated by his solar theme theory as being the origin of human intuition about a divinity; in England, Herbert Spencer, a leading theorist of the primitivity concept in anthropology, and Edward Tylor, who correlated magic and superstition and, on the other hand, civilization and monotheism, arguing that there has been an evolution from the former to the latter; and, finally, in the United States, Robert H. Lowie, a specialist of Indian Crows, according to whom a religious behaviour would not exist among Indians but only a religious sentiment. These psychological theories, well illustrated by Evans-Pritchard, were sustained by two epistemological presuppositions. The first is a conditional question: If I were a horse, how would I behave among other horses? The second supposes an evolutionary paradigm: 'Primitive people' or 'first people' – as they are called today in the offical UN language – and their religions would manifest the genesis of human development and history.

The second domain is that of sociological theories. Thus, in France, in *La Cité antique*, Fustel de Coulanges tried to demonstrate that the Greek *polis* was organized according to the parameter of a lineage extended family. United in memory of its departed ones, such a family would first have established a cult of ancestors, then proceeded to divinize them, and ultimately invent the divine. Emile Durkheim, who still dominates the essentials of our sociological paradigms, considered primitive religion as a 'clan cult': There would be complementarity between totemism and segmentary systems, a point of coincidence between the divine and the clan, making totemism an elementary form of religion, and religion the basis of all human institutions. It is from this background that one can follow Marcel Mauss's and Henri Hubert's arguments, according to which gods should be understood as representations and projections of human communities' experiences.

The third domain is more complex because here the analysis of Evans-Pritchard seems to hesitate. In principle, the chapter is on Lévy-Bruhl's project and method, yet long passages refer to Vilfredo Pareto's *Trattato de sociologia generale*. A possible explanation is the relationship that Evans-Pritchard finds between logical and non-logical actions (and thought). The latter tension, established by Pareto, comes from peculiar methodological discriminations. As Evans-Pritchard notes:

There are in any societies 'residues' – for convenience we may call them sentiments – some of which make for social stability, and others for social change. Sentiments are expressed in behaviour and also in 'derivations' (what other writers call ideologies or rationalizations). Now most actions in which Pareto includes thought, which express these residues or sentiments are non-logico-experimental (non-logical, for short), and they must be distinguished from logico-experimental (for short, logical) actions. Logical thought depends on facts and not the facts on it, whereas non-logical thought is accepted a priori, and dictates to experience; and should it conflict with experience, arguments are evoked to re-establish accord.

(Evans-Pritchard, 1980: 92–3)

Evans-Pritchard's reading of Lévy-Bruhl is original. One therefore wonders why it has not created a major debate since, in its objective, it corrects Lévy-Bruhl's *Carnets* (in which the French philosopher recants his own theory) and shows the methodological soundness of a distinction between a given thought and its antecedent or its synchronically dissimilar. This would explain the purpose of a metaposition. The reason such a thesis has not provoked a reaction might be that those who know how to read carefully also know how to keep silent; and, in social and human sciences, those who shout against 'ethno-centrism' and other intellectual diseases are probably not always patient readers, missing such important issues that challenge facile, political agenda.

Evans-Pritchard organizes his argument by clearly distinguishing two questions in Lévy-Bruhl: the first, methodological; and the second, political. According to Evans-Pritchard, the French scholar would here, in terms of method, have chosen an original path opposing the anthropological tradition of his time, which supposedly was keen on promoting similarities between Westerners and non-Westerners instead of analysing differences. Thus, Lévy-Bruhl would have been one of the first to study and understand cultural difference in its own terms. Let me quote Evans-Pritchard himself:

His first two books about primitive people, translated into English under the titles of *How Natives Think* and *Primitive Mentality*, set forth the general theory of primitive mentality for which he became so well known. His later works were an amplification of it, though he seems in them also to have slowly modified his original views in the light of modern field reports, for he was a modest and humble man. At the end of his life he may have reversed his position, or at any rate considered doing so, if one may judge from his posthumous Carnets. Nevertheless, it was his views as set forth in the earlier books which constituted his distinctive theoretical contribution to anthropology, and it is therefore these I must discuss.

Like Durkheim, he condemns the English School for trying to explain social facts by processes to individual thought – their own – which are the product of different conditions from those which have molded the minds they seek to understand. They think out how they would have reached beliefs and practices of primitive people, and then assume that these people must have reached them by those steps. In any case, it is useless to try to interpret primitive minds in terms of individual psychology. The mentality of the individual is derived from the collective representations of society, which are obligatory for him; and these representations are functions of institutions. Consequently, certain types of representations, and therefore certain ways of thinking, belong to certain types of social structure. In other words, as social structures vary, so will the representations, and consequently the individual thinking. Every type of society has therefore its distinctive mentality, for each has its distinctive customs and institutions, which are fundamentally only a certain aspect of collective representations; they are, so to speak, the representations considered objectively. Lévy-Bruhl did not mean by this that the representations of a people are any less real than their institutions.

Now, one can classify human societies into a number of different types, but, says Lévy-Bruhl, considered in the broadest possible way, there are two major types, the primitive and the civilized, and there are two and opposed types of thought corresponding to them, so we may speak of primitive mentality and civilized mentality, for they are different not merely in degree, but in quality. *It will be observed that he wishes to emphasize the differences between civilized and primitive people; this is perhaps the most important single observation to be made about his theoretical standpoint, and is what gives it much of its originality. For various reasons most writers about primitive people had tended to lay stress on the similarities, or what they supposed to be the similarities, between ourselves and them; and Lévy-Bruhl thought it might be as well, for a change, to draw attention to the differences.* The criticism often brought against him, that he did not perceive how very like primitives we are in many respects, loses much of its force, once we recognize his intention: he wanted to stress the differences, and in order to bring them out more clearly, he spotlighted them and left the similarities in shadow. He knew that he was making a distortion – what some people like to call an ideal construct – but he never pretended to be doing anything else, and his procedure is methodologically justifiable.

(Evans-Pritchard, 1980: 79–80, emphasis mine)

Lévy-Bruhl's discussion of the *Law of mystical participation* is perhaps the most valuable, as well as being a highly original, part of his thesis. He was one of the first, if not the first, to emphasize that primitive ideas, which seem so strange to us, and indeed sometimes idiotic, when considered as isolated facts, are meaningful when seen as parts of patterns of ideas and behaviour, each part having an intelligible relationship to the others. He recognized that values form systems as coherent as the logical constructions of the intellect, that there is a logic of sentiments as well as of reason, though based on a different principle. His analysis is not like the just-so stories we have earlier considered, for he does not try to explain primitive magic and religion by a theory purporting to show how they might have come about, what is their cause or origin. He takes them as given, and seeks only to show their structure and the way in which they are evidence of a distinctive mentality common to all societies of a certain type.

(Evans-Pritchard, 1980: 86, my emphasis)

It would be pointless to go back to the original and focus on what René Girard, in summing up a tradition, sees as a confusion of categories in a primitive interpretation of phenomena (Girard, 1987: 62). For me what is important is the objectivation of Lévy-Bruhl's arguments by Evans-Pritchard. To involve Lévy-Bruhl's texts would demand that we face the texts in themselves as well as the procedures already objectifying information coming from missionaries and travellers who claimed to translate concrete everyday experiences of natives' languages of familiarity, and Lévy-Bruhl's particular history as a philosopher, as a remarkable student of German philosophy, especially of Jacobi and Hegel. This had an impact on how Lévy-Bruhl read anthropologists and travelers' reports on 'primitives'. To sum up my point: Evans-Pritchard read an objectifying interpretation in Lévy-Bruhl – an interpretation codified by both the Hegelian perspective of his preceding studies and his correspondents' narratives – which constructed a vision from other objectifying interpretations projected by real native informants. Subordination and deviation – visible when one goes from the so-called African 'something' to the savant discourse of Lévy-Bruhl – manifests a native performance and, through mutations, becomes a 'hyper-refined theoretical' model on cultural differences. The second question in Evans-Pritchard's narrative is more political. In order to explain the reason and pertinence of Lévy-Bruhl's loaded concepts, such as prelogical representations, collective mentality and participation, etc. – all of which were important in his philosophy of cultures – Evans-Pritchard, a close friend of the French philosopher, has a set of amazing confidences. First one notes an intellectual accord between the anthropologist and the philosopher:

Lévy-Bruhl was a mere armchair theorist who, like the rest of his French colleagues, had never seen a primitive man, far less talked to one. I think I may claim to be one of the anthropologists here or in America who spoke up for him, not because I agreed with him, but because I felt that a scholar should be criticized for what he has said, and not for what he is supposed to have said. My defence had therefore to be exegetical, an attempt to explain what Lévy-Bruhl meant by his key expressions and concepts which evoked so much hostility: *prelogical, mentality, collective representations, mystical, and participations.* This terminology makes, at any rate for a British reader, his thought obscure, so that one is often in doubt, of what he wished to say.

Lévy-Bruhl calls 'prelogical' those modes of thought (magico-religious thought, he did not distinguish between magic and religion) which appear so true to primitive man and so absurd to the European. He means by this word something quite different from what his critics said he meant it. *He does not mean that primitives are incapable of thinking coherently but merely that most of their beliefs are incompatible with a critical and scientific view of the universe. They also contain evident contradictions. He is not saying that primitives are unintelligent, but that their beliefs are unintelligible to us.*

(Evans-Pritchard, 1980: 81, my emphasis)

Then Evans-Pritchard proceeds to explain how Lévy-Bruhl was 'not speaking of an individual's ability, or inability, to reason, but of the categories in which he reasons'. More explicitly, Lévy-Bruhl 'is speaking, not of a biological or psychological difference between primitives and (Westerners), but of a social one' (1965: 82). But how do we define this social feature insofar as African communities are concerned? Is Evans-Pritchard referring to the concept of state, nation, segmentary or lineage organizations? Briefly, can we say that in the vocabulary as well as in the grids that it allows, such a position does not seem to indicate a discontinuity from the evolutionary theories of the late eighteenth century and those of the nineteenth century? Cultural deviation is posited in Evans-Pritchard's reading of Lévy-Bruhl as a key prescribing that which elsewhere, in popular writings for example, is still described as monstrosity. The 'prelogical mentality', or the 'mystical' and 'collective representations' of the so-called primitive people, would go in this sense, as Evans-Pritchard notes:

The representations of primitive people have a quality of their own, namely the quality of being mystical, which is quite foreign to our own representations, and therefore we may speak of primitive mentality as something *sui generis*. The logical principle of these mystical representations is what Lévy-Bruhl calls the law of mystical participation. The collective representations of primitive people consist of a network of participations which, since the representations are mystical, are mystical also. In primitive thought, things are connected so that what affects one is believed to affect others, not objectively but by mystical action (though primitive man himself does not distinguish between objective and mystical action). Primitive people, indeed, are often more concerned about what we would call the supra-sensible or, to use Lévy-Bruhl's term, mystical relations between things than about what we would call the objective relations between them. To take the example I have used before, some primitive people participate in their shadows, so what affects their shadows affects them. Hence it would be fatal for a man to cross an open space at midday, because he would lose his shadow. Other primitive people participate in their names, and they will therefore not reveal them, for were an enemy to learn a name, he would have the owner of it also in his power.

(Evans-Pritchard, 1980: 85)

Both Lévy-Bruhl and Evans-Pritchard are psychologizing and deter-mining the difference between primitive and non-primitive in terms of a fundamental psychological structure: mystical versus rational. No lateral resemblances can stand any further apart from essentialist ones, which were given at the foundation of presuppositions. Theses had silently established an evolutionary model which marked Lévy-Bruhl's hypothesis and inscribed themselves in Evans-Pritchard's reading. In fact, Evans-Pritchard was introduced to them as a student and by choosing anthropology, as his own work testifies, he accepted the separation of an ancestral memory, a historical one, from its confrontations with synchronic cultures extending into the present both the representations of the beginnings and their apparent irrationality. In Evans-Pritchard's reading, one may sense the presence of mute values and the signs and density of cultural values. Hence, it is difficult to know from which hidden terror and from whom – Lévy-Bruhl or Evans-Pritchard – a justification like the following is coming:

Lévy-Bruhl, it is now, I think, unanimously agreed among anthropologists, *made primitive people far more superstitious*, to use a commoner word than prelogical, *than they really are*; and he made the contrast more glaring between their mentality and ours by presenting us as more positivistic than most of us are. From my talk with him I would say that in this matter he felt himself in a quandary. *For him Christianity and Judaism were also superstitions, indicative of prelogical and mystical mentality, and on his definitions necessarily so. But, I think in order not to cause offense, he made no allusion to them. So, he excluded the mystical in our own culture as rigorously as he excluded the empirical in savage cultures.* This failure to take into account the beliefs and rites of the vast majority of his fellow countrymen vitiates his argument. And he himself, as Bergson naughtily observed, in constantly accusing primitive man of not attributing any event to chance, accepted chance. He thereby placed himself, on his own showing, in the prelogical class.

However, this does not mean that, in his sense of the word, primitive thought is more 'mystical' than ours. The contrast Lévy-Bruhl makes is an exaggeration, but, all the same, primitive magic and religion confront us with a real problem, and not one imagined by the French philosopher. Men with long experience of primitive people have felt confounded by it; and it is true that primitives often, and especially in misfortunes, attribute events to supra-sensible forces where we, with our greater knowledge, account for them by natural causation, or seek to do so. But, even so, *I think that Lévy-Bruhl could have posed the problem to better advantage. It is not so much a question of primitive versus civilized mentality as the relation of two types of thought to each other in any society, whether primitive or civilized, a problem of levels of thought and experience.* It was because Lévy-Bruhl was dominated, as were almost all writers of the period, by notions of evolution and inevitable progress that he did not appreciate this.

(Evans-Pritchard, 1980: 91, my emphasis)

The facile dichotomy, *us* versus *them*, predicated by evolutionist paradigms, transforms itself radically: in *us* as well as in *them* there are at least two types of thought, mythical and non-mythical, each one being governed by its own internal order. Thanks to Evans-Pritchard's exegesis, one can now see how Lévy-Bruhl reflects himself in some of the major theses of Lévi-Strauss, *The Savage Mind* (1962, 1966). Let us note only those comparing magic and science as 'two parallel modes of acquiring knowledge', which, on the one hand, 'require the same sort of mental operations', and on the other, 'differ not so much in kind as in the different types of phenomena to which they are applied' (Lévi-Strauss, 1966: 13). It follows that there is no reason not to postulate a theory of causation proper to magic and different from that of science, and to consider the former – and, indeed, performances such as witchcraft – as 'natural philosophy' (Evans-Pritchard, 1955).

It becomes imperative to distinguish Lévy-Bruhl's inscription in the interpretative context of a given intellectual configuration from the discontinuity implied by both his method promoting differences instead of similarities and his conceptual distinctions apropos societies.

The discourses on primitive religion presented by Evans-Pritchard, including his own analysis, witness to an intellectual configuration. They construct and magnify a supposedly primitive religious space of performance, and in themselves they constitute an interpretation of interpretations. Furthermore, they are interwoven in contradictory objectivist discourses which, in their specific content, play and replay other objectivist knowledges and are all invented and political performances, too.

From Evans-Pritchard's reading, all these objectivist discourses on primitive religions – the psychological, the sociological or that of Lévy-Bruhl – are witnesses to politics in the etymological sense of the word. That is, they are comments on the *polis* as city and locus of the analyst's culture. Within the framework established by Evans-Pritchard, one can follow and describe its expressions by noting the transformation

that takes place in the reconversion of methodological grids accounting
for cultural differences from psychological to sociological theories to
Lévy-Bruhl's hypothesis. On the other hand, there is an epistemological
genealogy: from the time of President Brosse to that of Auguste Comte,
Max Muller, Herbert Spencer, Edward Tylor and Robert Lowie, the
paradigms of discourses seem to obey a biological model (religion
and its practices are seen as parts of a living organism) and thus
confuse biology and cultures. In historical descriptions, religion and
its practices are seen as parts of an evolving totality and are apprehended
as organisms that have a beginning, an evolution, and possible transmu-
tations subsumed in betterments: animism, polytheism, monotheism. In
the sociological domain, from Fustel de Coulanges to Vilfredo Pareto,
a socioeconomic model imposes itself. Religion belongs to a social
structure, more exactly to a cultural superstructure. This is the area
in which discourses are products of a dialectical tension between
an ideological signalization and a tradition of speculative practices,
a tension relying on an organization of production and power *vis-à-vis*
discursive practices. The reconversion – which is actually a rupture –
from a psychological to a sociological model and then to Lévy-Bruhl's
anthropological paradigm, exerts an influence upon the way we read
the reality of African religions today. The traditional readings are not
rendered as part of a cultural order *sui generis* but, indeed, as signs and
proofs of something else, namely, epistemological categories unfolding
from an intellectual configuration completely alien to the cultural spaces
they claim to reflect. As paradoxical as it may seem, Evans-Pritchard's
Lévy-Bruhl might be one of the best signs of a recent general and
fundamental mutation of history and its interpretations of non-Western
religions and cultures.

The broader sequence of paradigms is well known: the evolution of
ideas illustrated by Frazer and Tylor; Lévy-Bruhl's research on primitive
mentality; the Vienna school with its presuppositions on non-Western
practices, using diffusion as a key to, and argumentation for, the most
positive religious features; and, finally, functionalism that explicitly
transfers the concept of African religion into the domain of politics.
For Radcliffe-Brown, for example, religion was just an adjunctive
element to a social structure; and most functionalist works from the

1920s to the 1950s focus on such paradigms as 'ancestor worship' and its energetic impact in terms of authority (Fortes, Colson) and witchcraft (Evans-Pritchard, Wadel Marwick) as a mode of solving social tension. In Francophone countries, the power of Lévy-Bruhl was immense. Placide Tempels, a Belgian Franciscan and a Catholic missionary, was his disciple when he arrived in the Belgian Congo in the 1930s.

The 'Primitive': For a Semiotics of Absence

Primitive as an anthropological concept for what is 'pertaining to a preliterate or tribal people having cultural or physical similarities with their early ancestors' is 'no longer in technical use', states the unabridged second edition of *The Random House Dictionary of the English Language* (1987). This seems more like a good wish than a fact. The anthropological lexicon might somehow have marginalized the word, but its semantic web still dominates the configuration of the discipline and its object. Through complex chains of conceptual equivalences, its cognates have been routinized and now belong to the general intellectual vocabulary of any well-educated Western fellow. In fact, *primitive* transcends the semantic values of such common adjectives as aboriginal, crude, savage, simple, uncivilized, unsophisticated, unrefined, etc. But more clearly than these, *primitive* essentially conveys the basic notion of genesis and its immediate implications, already well-attested in the Latin *primitivus*, a synonym of *primigenus* 'original', 'first born', 'that comes first'. However, in this evocation of primordiality, there are two subtle, complementary – yet opposed – signifieds: one of 'absence', instigated by the notion of primogeniture, which simply implies that the primary comes after or from nothing; the second, one of a 'presence', is established in that the pristine actualizes a qualitatively simple *post-genesis* event or form that is strictly relative to a 'something', which in this case would be a nothing commencing a succession of events. This paradoxical polysemy is perceptible in a number of technical usages. In logic, for instance, one qualifies as primitive a proposition which, in a deductive system, is not inferred from another proposition. In linguistics and philology, primitive designates any initial form from which another element derives through morphological or historical transformation. Finally, in biology as well as in mathematics, one faces the same ambiguous value of a genesis signifying simultaneously both a presence and an absence: primitive designates a variety considered as primordial and very slightly developed, or an algebraic or geometrical paradigm functioning as a referential basis for derived forms.

In anthropology and sociology, primitiveness was initially used in the sense of the eighteenth-century German *Naturvölker*, which marks a reference to both nature and an absolute genesis, and thus its two main constitutive elements, simplicity and archaism. The *Lalande* synthesizes well this problematic (1962: 824–7). One of the clearest definitions of primitive is given by Emile Durkheim in the beginning of *Les Formes élémentaires de la vie religieuse*:

> Nous disons d'un système religieux qu'il est *le plus primitif* qu'il nous soit donné d'observer quand il remplit les deux conditions suivantes: en premier lieu *il faut qu'il se rencontre dans des sociétés dont l'organisation n'est dépassée par aucune autre en simplicité; il faut, de plus, qu'il soit possible de l'expliquer sans faire intervenir aucun élément emprunté à une religion antérieure* . . . . Dans le même sens, nous dirons de ces sociétés qu'elles sont primitives, et nous appellerons primitif l'homme de ces sociétés.
>
> (Durkheim, 1; my emphasis)

> [We say that a religious system is *the most primitive* that we can observe when it obeys the following two conditions: first, *it must be found in the simplest societies in so far as organization is concerned; moreover, it should be possible to explain this system without reference to any element from an anterior religion* . . . . In this same sense, we shall say that these societies are primitive, and we shall call primitive its members.]

Sir James Frazer's monumental work (see e.g. 1963) is predicated on a similar understanding that defines primitiveness on the basis of antiquity and structural simplicity. Lévy-Bruhl was the first to oppose it and, in *Les Fonctions mentales dans les sociétés inférieures*, explicitly argued against Frazer's principle of simplicity – in the evolution of thought as well as matter, the simplest always comes first chronologically. Lévy-Bruhl notes that languages spoken in 'primitive' societies might be 'more primitive' than English, yet witness to a real complexity and, subsequently, the concept of simplicity should not be confused with that of undifferentiatedness. A similar understanding can be found in Carl Gustav Jung's work:

Primitive mentality, he writes, differs from the civilized chiefly in that the conscious mind is far less developed in scope and intensity. *Functions such as thinking, willing, etc. are not yet differentiated; they are pre-conscious*, and in the case of thinking, for instance, this shows itself in the circumstance that the primitive does not think *consciously*, but that thoughts *appear*. The primitive cannot assert that he thinks; it is rather that 'something thinks in him'.

(1980: 153)

Interestingly enough, in the specialized vocabulary of anthropology, primitive and primitiveness are deemed inadequate from the beginning. Durkheim considers primitive an almost unavoidable term but lacking in precision. Lévy-Bruhl – apropos who is primitive? – states that 'by this *improper* yet almost *indispensable* term (of primitive), we mean to designate the members of the simplest societies that we know'. The same ambivalence can still be found even in the most significant writings of contemporary anthropology, for example, Evans-Pritchard and Lévi-Strauss. In Evans-Pritchard's introduction to *Theories of Primitive Religion* (1980), an opposition intervenes between the 'Victorian prosperity and progress' and 'people living in small-scale societies'; and, more importantly, there is a distinction between the logical and chronological meaning of the word primitive:

Some people today find it embarrassing to hear people described as primitives or natives, and even more so to hear them spoken of as savages. But I am sometimes obliged to use the designations of my authors, who wrote in the robust language of a time when offense to the people they wrote about could scarcely be given, the good time of Victorian prosperity and progress, and, one may add, smugness, our pomp of yesterday. But the words are used by me in what Weber calls a value-free sense, and they are etymologically unobjectionable. In any case, the use of the word 'primitive' to describe people living in small-scale societies with a simple material culture and lacking

literature is too firmly established to be eliminated. This is unfortunate, because
no word has caused greater confusion in anthropological writings, as you will
see, for it can have a logical and a chronological sense and the two senses have
sometimes not been kept distinct, even in the minds of good scholars.

(1980: 18-19)

From a slightly different perspective, Claude Lévi-Strauss begins
his discussion of 'The Concept of Archaism in Anthropology' by first
situating the primitive against the object of the historian, and then
vis-à-vis the Western industrial and cultural expansion:

Despite all its imperfections, and the deserved criticism which it has received, it
seems that *primitive*, in the absence of a better term, has definitely taken hold in
the contemporary anthropological and sociological vocabulary. We thus study
'primitive' societies. But what do we mean by this? Taken in its broad sense,
the expression is clear enough. First, we know that 'primitive' denotes a vast
array of non-literate people, who are thus not accessible through the research
methods of the conventional historian. Second, they have only recently been
affected by the expansion of industrial civilization, and, because of their social
structure and world view, the concepts of economics and political philosophy
regarded as basic to our own society are inapplicable to them. But where shall
we draw the line of demarcation?

(1963: 101)

This is an excellent question, indeed: where do we draw a convincing
separation between what is primitive and what is not? Lévi-Strauss
refers explicitly to Pharaonic Egypt and ancient China. One might also
bring in, for example, the Aztec, Inca and Maya civilizations and thus
confront the completely relative pertinence of the two criteria used,
those of literacy and economics. Lévi-Strauss marshals some strong
facts that would probably have flabbergasted some nineteenth-century
anthropologists: 'A primitive people is not a backward or a retarded
people; indeed, it may possess, in one realm or another, a genius for
invention or action (e.g. sociological planning of traditional Australian
communities), that leaves the achievements of civilized people far
behind'; 'nor do primitive people lack history, although its development often eludes us' (1963: 102). Finally, the logic of his own
argument leads Lévi-Strauss to the curious distinction postulated by
Marcel Mauss between 'conventionally designated primitives' and

'true primitives' and, ultimately, to a very simple conclusion: 'The important thing is to help anthropology to disengage itself from the philosophical residue surrounding the term *primitive*. A true primitive society should be harmonious, a society, so to speak, at one with itself' (1963: 117). Briefly, 'a true primitive society' cannot be but an invented, constructed, and pure perfection. As Lévi-Strauss himself qualified it in *Tristes Tropiques*:

(Anthropology) leads to something other than the revelation of a Utopian state of nature or the discovery of the perfect society in the depths of the forest; *it helps us to build a theoretical model of human society, which does not correspond to any observable reality, but with the aid of which we may succeed in distinguishing between what is primordial and what is artificial in man's present nature* and in obtaining a good knowledge of a state which no longer exists, which has perhaps never existed, and which will probably never exist in the future, but of which it is nevertheless essential to have a sound conception in order to pass valid judgment on our present state.

(1977: 446–7, my emphasis)

Here, then, is the paradox. In the brief history of anthropology, the terms 'primitive' and 'primitiveness' have always been articulating two antinomic values, 'presence' and 'absence': 'presence', in the anteriority of small-scale societies having simple social and economic organizations; and 'absence', in what the preceding qualification implies as lack, including illiteracy and the cultural and social undifferentiated-ness of absolute beginnings. One thus wonders how Sir Evans-Pritchard could claim to manipulate such concepts in a value-free sense. Claude Lévi-Strauss was right in reducing these concepts to 'a theoretical model' that we could thematize as being a sort of *nothingness* in the Sartrean sense. In fact, the primitive or original matter would be functioning like a *Being-In-Itself*, in which a *Being-For-Itself* would be simultaneously collapsing and reflecting itself as a suscitated presence, as consciousness. This image is important. It allows us a radical correction of our introductive definition from the *Random House Dictionary*, and a more rigorous conceptualization of the primitive as a representation which, in any given culture, signifies its own genesis with its paradoxical qualities of 'absence' and 'presence'.

Let us go a bit further by looking at two other concepts – midnight and zero – and how well they exemplify the ambivalent values of primitiveness of any genesis.

Why does the day begin at midnight? The response is easy: it is a Roman legacy – a curious one – that makes the West the only culture in which the alternation of days and nights, yesterdays and tomorrows is based on a bipartition of the night. For ancient Egyptians, Greeks and, likewise, most non-Western people, the day begins at dawn or at sundown, and such a division seems pretty natural insofar as it obeys the visible course of the solar disc. Georges Dumézil explains the Roman custom:

Rome herself had adopted the middle of the night and from this concept flowed religious or civil rules that the erudite Romans, first among them Varro, collected. We read in Macrobius (Saturnalia, 1.3: 6–8):

As for the custom of the Roman people, noted by Varro, of counting the days from midnight to midnight, there are many illustrative examples . . . . The rites and practices of auspication conform to this way of calculating. In fact, one rule requires that the magistrates take the omens and perform the act for which they took them within one day. So, taking the omens after midnight and performing the act after sunrise, they are reputed to have taken the omens and acted the same day. By the same token, the plebeian tribunes are not permitted to be away from Rome an entire day. So, when they leave after midnight and return after the lighting of the first torch, but before midnight, it is not considered a full day's absence.

In the eighty-fourth *Roman Question*, Plutarch wonders why the Romans began the day at midnight and his response is interesting, though insufficient. According to him, the Roman State was first of all essentially military. After all, in the battle most of the plans are made 'in advance' during the night, daybreak being the time of execution, night that of preparation. But, this specific and quite practical consideration would probably not have sufficed to cut the night ritually and juridically into two parts, and to attach the second part to the following day. The reason is rather a religious one and results directly from the mythology of Aurora subjacent to the Matralia rites as we understand them.

(Dumézil, 1980: 108)

The *Matralia*, a ritual and festival honoring Aurora or *Mater Matuta*, the goddess of dawn, was celebrated on 11 June, in preparation for the summer solstice and the crisis symbolized by the longest day of the year. This ritual was thus antithetical to the *Divalia* which, under the patronage of a different goddess, *Diva Angerona*, marked the winter solstice on 21 December, and prepared for *angusti dies*, the shortest day. In fact, the two festivities expressed the same expectation and prayer for regular, equal and successive days and nights. We should note that to the tense rapport between Aurora and Angerona, between the positively excessive represented by the summer solstice (the longest day of the year) and the negatively excessive represented by the winter solstice (the shortest day), there is another symmetrical opposition: a bad versus a good darkness, a negative versus a positive part of the night, before versus after midnight. In other words, the day must succeed the night and, in mythic representations, this signifies that Aurora – the good and benevolent goddess – should follow carefully and bring to finition the Sun, the *alterius proles*, the product of someone else's body – that is, a being conceived before her presence. This rather confusing point in Roman theology is expressed beautifully by Dumézil:

The Matralia:

These rites imply: (1) that there is a 'bad', but also a 'good' Darkness, one the enemy of the day, expelled from the sky by Aurora, the other pregnant with the Sun, transmitting to Aurora the luminous infant being born; and (2) that Aurora is not the mother of the Sun, but his adoptive mother. Alone she is incapable of producing him; she gathers him up after he has been prepared and brought into the world by 'the other' – *alterius proles – by the good Darkness who is incapable of accompanying him in the life she has just given him.* In other words, in the couple each of the two – those whom the Vedic hymns willingly call 'the two sisters' – is indispensable for the accomplishment of the common act. *For Aurora to be able to take charge of the Sun, the Night must first perform her office of pregnant and parturient female. For the Night's maternity to be fruitful, Aurora must be ready to take her place.* The Roman concept of day does no more than translate this theologem: *the second part of the nocturnal darkness, carrying within it the sun to be born, is inseparable from the day that follows; it is in fact the first part of the day.*

(Dumézil, 1980: 109, my emphasis)

The Roman theory of the bipartition of the night inherited by the West, and now expanded almost all over the world, is remarkable in how it posits midnight as the paradigm of an absence which is

also a presence – that is, an exemplification of a primitiveness. The
Roman mythical representation spells it out very clearly: The tension
between solstices duplicates itself in the opposition and length of
days and nights which, in turn, reproduces itself in the two parts
of the night, midnight being something like an absolute reference. It
functions simultaneously as a negative and positive point of disjunction:
its *before* is a *minus*, dangerous by the absence of the sun and also by
such negative manifestations as ominous lightnings and the demons
which, as Christianity would want, then haunt the world, its *after* is a
plus and incarnates a positive climate: a newborn light ascends slowly
but steadily, the solar disc becomes a sign of life and all its promises.
Briefly, and much more importantly, midnight, symbolically zero in our
common representation is, to this day, an absolute cultural as well as
juridico-religious paradigm: the day begins at midnight.

The zero by its lack of referentiality and absence of a monosemic
positive signified might, *mutatis mutandis*, illustrates the complementary values of 'presence' and 'absence' in a more abstract way.
In *Signifying Nothing* (1987), Brian Rotman notes the conflictual
perceptions we may have of a zero, either as a sign symbolizing the
absence of other signs, or as a sign given for a primitive and ambiguous
positivity in the order of numbers.

The etymology of zero, via 'cypher' from the Hindu *sunya* (= void), clearly
recalls its intimate and long-standing connection both to the idea of an empty
meaningless character and to the notion of 'nothing' or no thing. In any event,
there is no doubt that, as a numeral, the mathematical sign zero points to the
absence of certain other mathematical signs, and not to the non-presence of
any real 'things' that are supposedly independent of or prior to signs which
represent them. At any place within a Hindu numeral the presence of zero
declares a specific absence: namely, the absence of the signs $1, 2, \ldots, 9$ at
that place. Zero is thus a sign about signs, a meta-sign, whose meaning as a
name lies in the way it indicates the absence of the name $1, 2, \ldots, 9$. Thus, zero
points to the absence of certain signs either by connoting the origin of quantity,
the empty plurality, or by connoting the origin of ordering, the position which
excludes the possibility of predecessors. These connotations constitute zero's
role as a meta-sign formulated in terms of, but separate from and exterior to,
the proto-numbers. But zero also occurs within the domain of 'number' in direct
arithmetical contact with ordinary numbers. In such equations as $0 = 0$, $1 - 1$
$= 0$, $3 + 0 = 4 - 1$, $3 (2 - 2) = 0$, and so on, zero appears explicitly as a number

among numbers, having the same status as, operating on the same plane as, and
interchangeable with, the other numbers.

(Rotman, 1993: 12–13)

To conclude provisionally this preliminary to a possible semiotics
of absence, I would like to emphasize that our three concepts – the
primitive, *midnight* and *zero* – share a number of characteristics that
one could refer to, in order to meditate on their '*ipse-ity*'. First of all,
they are all signs actualizing in their own being a 'nothing', which can
mysteriously transmute itself into 'a something'; secondly, this sign –
or more exactly, this signifier – is an untenable paradox in the prose of
the world, a signifier like others and, at the same time, a metasignifier
thanks to which all the others get their nature: people *vis-à-vis the
primitive*, hours *vis-à-vis midnight*, numbers *vis-à-vis zero*. Thirdly,
these signs or signifiers incarnate contradictory virtues and are qualified
by two antithetical adjectives. In fact, they are absolute negations of a
void, and yet relative insofar as they inscribe themselves as genesis
moments in a chronological or logical order of succession for cultures,
hours and numbers. The three features could be united and reduced to
the scandal actualized by zero – a sign that Christianity opposed for
quite a long time since signifying a nothing, which is not an absolute
and definitive absence.

Observe, finally, that zero is an origin at a very primitive, parsimonious and
minimally articulated level of sign formation. Signification codes difference,
hence the need for more than one sign. How to produce, with the minimum of
ad hoc extra-semiotic means, two 'different' signs? Answer: let there be a sign
– call it 1 – and let there be another sign – call it 0 – indicating the absence
of the sign 1. Of course, such a procedure *produces* the difference it appears
subsequently to describe; and the use of absence to manufacture difference in
this way is a viable sign practice only through the simultaneous introduction
of a syntax: a system of placing signifiers in linear relation to each other in
such a way that it allows signs to be interpretable in terms of the original
absence/presence signified by 0.

The sign 1 can be anything. If 1 is one and 0 is zero and the syntax is the
standard positional notation for numbers, then what results, as the limiting
case of the system, is the two-valued descendant of the Hindu decimal system.
Leibniz, who spent much time formulating the rules for binary arithmetic, was
deeply impressed by the generative, infinitely proliferative principle inherent

in such zero-based binarism: so much so that he refracted the binary relation between 1 and 0 into an iconic image for the Old Testament account of creation *ex nihilo*, whereby the universe (the infinitude of numbers) is created by God (the unbroken 1) from the void the cypher 0). Again, if 1 signifies the presence of a current in a circuit and 0 signifies the absence of such a current and the syntax is 2-valued Boolean algebra, then what emerges is the binary formalism with which the logic and language of all present-day computer programs are ultimately written.

(Rotman, 1993: 105–7)

The primitive seems a mystery, a metaproblem, as Gabriel Marcel would have said. We could suggest that it was one of the basic canons in Western representation – most explicitly so since the end of the eighteenth century, if we accept Michel Foucault's hypothesis on the reappropriation and reformulation of genealogy and chronology in such disciplines as biology, economics and linguistics, to which we could, without hesitation, also add anthropology. In fact, this new science rethinks the West by focusing on *the primitive*, that West which, as Jean-Luc Nancy wrote at the very threshold of *The Birth to Presence* (1993),

is precisely what designates *itself as limit, as demarcation, even when it ceaselessly pushes back the frontiers of its imperium* . . . . By the turn of a singular paradox, the West appears as what has its planetary, galactic, universal vocation limitlessly to extend its own delimitation. It opens the world to the closure that it is. This closure is named in many ways (appropriation, fulfillment, signification, destination, etc.); in particular, it is named 'representation'. *Representations is what determines itself by its own limit*. It is the limitation for a subject, and by this subject, of what 'in itself' would be neither represented nor representable.

(1993: 1, my emphasis)

Aesthetic of Invocation versus Aesthetic of Virtuosity

As noted earlier, Placide Tempels arrived in Central Africa as a disciple of Lévy-Bruhl prepared to work on the cultural and religious metamorphosis of *the primitive*. Some years later, with his acclaimed

Bantu Philosophy (1944), Tempels became the defender of indigenous systems of thought for the implementation of an enlightened colonial rule that would respect and promote the most positive elements of African traditions. The Franciscan missionary is not, strictly speaking, an accident. He is a voice that can be localized from Evans-Pritchard's 1965 reading of Lévy-Bruhl. Tempels' conditions of possibility are in the intellectual cadre that, in the 1920s, makes diffusionism and functionalism pertinent in anthropology and progressively marks the social sciences (Copans, 1974 and 1975). This gradual transformation ultimately led to Claude Lévi-Strauss' generalized relativism (1958, 1962, 1966) in the late 1940s and throughout the 1950s.

Three recent publications will help us to localize the change of scene and its intensity: Sally Falk Moore's survey of the history of African Anthropology (1994), Dismas Masolo's Afrocentric suppositions in a historical presentation of the practice of philosophy in Africa (1994), and Eric de Rosny's prescriptions (1981, 1982) for a new *pastorale* of conversion.

In *Anthropology and Africa* (1994), Sally Falk Moore qualifies a history of the practice of anthropology apropos Africa. An expansion of her 'Changing Perspectives on a Changing Africa: The Work of Anthropology', a chapter published in *Africa and the Disciplines* edited by Robert Bates (1993), the book brings together the principal trends of twentieth-century African anthropology, which is exactly her objective for publishing it:

In the writing of this . . . essay I have needed to control a desire to write detailed commentaries on the ethnographic contents and theoretical perspectives of many of the books mentioned. Much more could also have been said about the persons who devoted their lives to this field. Indeed, I am well aware of the vast materials over which I had to pass quickly. By necessity, I have omitted many authors and works all together. But anyone who wants a substantial start in the anthropology of Africa will get a clear idea about previous scholarship and about what to read next from reading this work. I particularly hope that it will be read in Africa.

(Moore, 1994: VII)

It is fair to say that such an enterprise is marked by the promise in which it inscribes itself: a history and a discourse claim to transcend geographical distances and reflect on questions and dramas of a disciplinary practice. Some important moments are emphasized: the beginning, before 1920; the middle colonial period, 1920–1940; the later colonial period to 1960; and after, the African independence. From our endlessly relived debate on the pertinence of cultural translations and incommensurability of human experiences, Moore dwells on the strangeness of 'scientific' annulations of distance and how, in their limits, they have made possible new supplemental horizons, briefly, less foreign renderings of African human contexts, lives and histories. These moments can be reduced to a number of sets of names and anthropological trends: at the end of the nineteenth century, Tylor and Morgan; then in America, the period of Boas, Kroeber and Herskovits; in Britain, the era of Malinowski followed by that of Radcliffe-Brown, Evans-Pritchard and Fortes; and finally, in France, by that of Delafosse, Griaule, Balandier and the structuralists.

Moore's *Anthropology and Africa* presents three main features: first of all, it is a clear and dependable presentation of anthropology's 'changing perspectives on a changing scene' with the explicit ambition of 'identifying, understanding and comparing what were conceived of as real "traditions"; and addressing the changing current African experience' (1994: 131). Secondly, using the metaphor of the snake biting its own tail, the author questions the pertinence of what she calls 'meta-anthropology' (as, for example, actualized in the United States by Clifford and Marcus). Indeed, the relationship between knowledge and power seems a major issue in the colonial exercise as well as in the development of anthropology. Later on, apropos the 'Colonial Library', I shall come back to this particular point – with reference to my *Invention of Africa* (1988) – and meditate on how good analytical intentions might lead to disastrous results. In fact, the confusion of a healthy autocritical stance in the history of a discipline and ethical predicaments, as well illustrated for instance by Leila Abu-Lughod (1986), Gérard Leclerc (1972) or Peter Rigby (1985), cannot be reduced to a sheer accident. The dependence of anthropology on the expansion of Europe overseas and vice versa testifies to both a political and an intellectual saga, despite the fact – and this is a different major issue – that we could, after Foucault, note that there is a certain position of the Western *ratio* that was constituted in its history and *provides a foundation for the relation it can have with all other societies*, even with the society in which it historically appeared. Obviously, *this does not mean that the colonizing situation is indispensable to ethnology*: neither hypnosis, nor the patient's alienation within the fantasmatic character of the doctor, is constitutive of psychoanalysis; but just as the latter can be deployed only in the calm violence of a particular relationship and the transference it produces, so *ethnology can assume is proper dimensions only within the historical sovereignty* – always restrained, but always present – of *European thought and the relation that can bring it face to face with all other cultures* as well as with itself.

(Foucault, 1970: 377, my emphasis)

In short, apropos the power–knowledge relationship in the practice of African anthropology, it does not matter if a particular study represents a colonial representation or not. What is significant is that a given work, in its enunciation, might performatively unveil the truth of colonialism and its obscure ambiguities. In any case, I should finally add that Sally Falk Moore's book is an excellent guide that brings anthropology and Africa comprehensively together.

D.A. Masolo's *African Philosophy in Search of Identity* (1994) shares much with Sally Falk Moore's overview. First, it concerns the fate of a discipline – this time philosophy – its controverted intellectual foundation in colonial time and its post-colonial destiny; second, both Moore's and Masolo's books intend to be introductions to academic knowledges and their performances; third, both emphasize reason and its genealogy as a way of apprehending what is out there in its proper and tropic materiality. For Moore, it is the object of anthropology; for Masolo, the practice of philosophy in a new space – that is, in the reapprehension of an intellectual genealogy. Here, we could finger a difference between the two projects. Moore elaborates on the discipline in itself, and from its historical background evaluates concrete discursive practices. Masolo, on the other hand, chooses to interrogate the very reason that makes his discourse possible, qualifying his own reading as 'a reconstructivist term which symbolizes many aspects of the struggle of the people of African origin to control their own identity'. In this specific sense, Masolo distances himself from Moore and plays dangerously on an 'afrocentricity' perspective.

Afrocentricity conceives its goal from a position that claims to render a genuine reality of an African history and its cultures. In this sense, the political pan-Africanism of Kwame Nkrumah or the cultural prescriptions of Senghor's *Négritude* are Afrocentric. Their best expressions would be, in the Kenyan-born Ali Mazrui's proposition of three legacies accounting for the present-day African identities: the African past or traditions; the imports of Islam and Christianity; and the upsurge of a modernity which, since colonization, would have radically transformed African spaces and cultures. There is in the United States today a different understanding of Afrocentricity. Its proponents perceive themselves as disciples of the late Sheik Anta Diop, a Senegalese nuclear physicist and Egyptologist who spent his life demonstrating cultural connections between Black Africa and the Mediterranean basin. The most well-known of these theorists is Molefi Asante of Temple University. On the whole, their perspective seems to essentialize African cultures, reducing the complexity of histories to some metaphors and their variations. In this transposition that is an *Ubertragung* in a Freudian operation, the real self is lost in a magnificent negation. The contradictory, negotiated, and perpetually recommenced enunciation about oneself – and whose truth is always and already in the apprehension of oneself as a being-for-other – ceases to indicate the intricacy of an existence (of any existence), of a culture (of any culture) as projects. The condition for being oneself as self-conciousness is to apprehend oneself as a self that does not and cannot coincide to itself. As Sartre would have put it: 'A freedom which wills itself freedom is in fact a being-which-is-not-what-it-is and which-is-what-it-is-not, and which chooses as the ideal of being, being-what-it-is-not and not-being-what-it-is' (1956: 798). Yet, in the American context, with its essentialist presuppositions concerning ethnic entities structured from a dubious hypothetical notion of an absence of anything, an absolute blank (see e.g. Hacker, 1994; Todd, 1994), any sane person may indeed wonder if, for African-Americans, the Afrocentricity supposition is not politically a rational choice. But that is a different issue.

Finally, should we not rethink the obvious, by which I mean the diversity of knowledge in cultural variations in the interpretation of human experiences?

Recent arguments by Eric de Rosny in *Les Yeux de ma Chèvre* (1981) and *L'Afrique des Guérisons* (1992) hold concretely that Lévy-Bruhl's so-called prelogical mentality is, in actuality, a reasonable fiction to the point that, using a fatigued expression, the irrational is in its own right rational. Independently from Lévy-Bruhl's recantation in *Les Carnets*, does this contradiction not simply signify that any ensemble of beliefs could be perceived as constituting a system with its own norms and rules? The French Jesuit missionary, Eric de Rosny, arrived in Cameroon in 1957 and served for many years as the director of an institute of economic and social development in Abidjan, Ivory Coast. In the 1970s, he began meeting and listening to a '*nganga*', an African traditional healer, and writing down his impressions. 'In ten years, from 1970 to 1980, I have inhabited this book as if it were a house, giving to its dimensions more and more width . . . . I have written down on paper my observations, with the certainty that I have to communicate them.' Initiated and introduced into what one might call – after Evans-Pritchard – a 'natural philosophy', Eric de Rosny simply notes: 'Two arguments pushed me to converting my past essays into a new book. Moreover, I could see a *nganga* operating on me to the point that "my eyes were opened" by one of them; and, indeed, I wanted them to be known by the largest public possible. Simultaneously, I was forced by my immediate milieu, particularly by a *Douala* friend, to speak out: and yourself, he told me one day, what do you think of all that?' (de Rosny, 1981: 9–10).

This is a major symbol. To the classical 'if I were a horse' principle (which a priori or a posteriori can justify the usefulness of a fieldwork), Eric de Rosny opposes the 'how I became a horse'. Initiated by a 'master of the night', the French Jesuit proclaims the order of his newly discovered system: 'What is beyond normal vision and knowledge of ordinary mortals; that is the other side of things, the world of secret intentions and hidden projects' (de Rosny, 1981: 64). Here, the awareness of the witness simultaneously asserts (see also de Rosny, 1992) a cultural relativism and the confidence of a believer in 'those who have received the gift of perceiving invisible realities and who have an impressive power that allows them to act on health, sickness to the advantage or the disadvantage of normal human beings' (de Rosny, 1981: 64). Is

confrontation between these concepts basically actualizes the paradoxes of a system which transcends the violence and tension in presence. The past and the present, the normative and the exotic, and the civilized and the savage can be illuminated as comparative *oeuvres* in the nakedness of a now (a *maintenant*) challenging all boundaries. Let me illustrate this by summarizing Robert Plant Armstrong's work on *The Powers of Presence* (1981), a *tour de force* that combines a deep knowledge of aesthetics in general, African arts, and a very rare philosophical eclecticism. The aim of the study is double: to understand and examine how 'the work of art is a presence and that it abides in power', and also to reveal and show 'the conditions of the work's subjectivity and the varieties of its powers'. On the way to these goals, the reader is treated to an extremely exciting interpretation of the nature of art. The central idea of the book can be summed up in the following quotation:

The powers of the work of affecting presence are the powers of *being* subject. And the work is a subject because it exists in that estate of intending something which is a capability alone of a sentient being. Yet that work is also a subject because it has the power to execute itself as a subjective estate of being upon its witness.

(1981: 124)

The six chapters can be grouped into three parts, the first comprising an analysis of the powers of invocation and what Armstrong calls the powers of the analogic. It deals with the contrasts between work of art *in invocation*, which tends to exist 'in an ambient time', in performance, and work of art *in virtuosity*, which is determined by space alone. Thus, we have the aesthetic of invocation versus the aesthetic of virtuosity. In the first, works 'are conceived to be physical loci of extra-mortal energies – e.g. an important mask – which may be so strong that they can and often do vitiate or destroy the piece which hosts them' (1981: 12). On the contrary, according to the author, 'the aesthetic of virtuosity originates in the freeing of the work of affecting presence from dependence upon the energies of gods and other external sources' (1981: 12). Two main themes appear from this opposition: one concerns the relationships between 'differing virtuosities' and 'differing artistic movements'; the other is about humans as subjects of a complex and 'expanding repertoire of behavioural options'. In his analysis of the powers of the analogic, Armstrong emphasizes the significance of humans' analogic estates and their externalization. He states that 'human history has been the history of human exploitation of the potentialities of spatial and temporal analogies' (1981: 24), and thus he can address the status of works and the powers of the analogic.

Part two comprises three chapters: one on the 'Powers of the Mythologemic' and two on the 'Powers of the Mythoform'. An essential paradigm inspired by Jung's philosophy introduces the analysis: 'The mythic is the universe of our consciousness' enactment of certain general, highly abstract, universal and generative dynamics of being human' (1981: 48). This perspective allows the author a clear distinction between *mythologems* ('thematic and dynamic nodules of consciousness which exist recurringly and powerfully among man's behavioural options') and *mythoforms* ('a culturally specific dynamic of time–space-process'). Accordingly, he presents a careful specification of types of powers. Concretely, the mythologemic dimension explains the relationship that a 'literate' observer or analyst can establish between *Galatea*, a Raphael *Madonna and Child*, and an *Anyi maternity*. On the other hand, a focus on Yoruba sculptural works gives to the observer a precise sense of the Yoruba mythoform with its specific dynamics, Pan-African features, and some characteristics that are common to ancient non-industrial cultures. From the dialectic between mythologems and mythoforms, Armstrong addresses major questions on the 'universality of the systematic nature of consciousness and the pervasion of the human consciousness by the aesthetic', the notion of the conservation of consciousness, and the archetypality of the sorcerer.

The final part of the book discusses the powers of celebration on the basis of a separation between primary works ('those which present the mythoformal and the mythologemic forthrightly', e.g. *Tar Baby*) and secondary works ('those in which the mythic tends to hide rather than to stand forthrightly in its purity'). In short, on the one side there is a kind of general, universal and mythic illumination of a piece; on the other, one would contemplate the localized and particularized biography of a work of art. On the whole, this final chapter is a key to the author's theory on *the work of affecting presence*, which is posited at the intersection of six powers of cognition: metaphysical, epistemic, formal (culturally defined physical properties), mythologemic, mythoformal and analogic.

In fact, Armstrong's book can be viewed as a refutation of traditional interpretations of primitive art and mentality. Within this well-organized theoretical framework, new orders of linkage and differentiation can be studied between Yoruba or Kongo sculptures and Lipschitz's *Prometheus* and Van Gogh's *Wheat Field*, for example; and one easily agrees that Armstrong has inaugurated new and very original avenues in aesthetics. The only contention I have is with Armstrong's assumption about African works of art. He distinguishes 'classical' from 'non-classical' pieces and chooses to rely on 'non-canonical' pieces. I do not dispute the artistic character and value of Dogon masks, Yoruba sculptures, or Lega figures, yet I wish he could have addressed the question *why these pieces are works of art*. What is called African art includes a wide range of objects introduced into a Western historicizing and classificatory frame. When and how did these objects, which were perhaps not art at all, become art and take on both an aesthetic character and a potentiality for reproducing artistic forms?

Robert F. Thompson considers Armstrong's book as 'the culmination of what will go down in history as one of the most distinguished trilogies in the history of aesthetics'. He is right. This super book brilliantly completes *The Affecting Presence: An Essay in Humanistic Anthropology* (1971) and *Wellspring: On the Myth and Source of Culture* (1975). It is a stimulating, cogently argued, and intelligently organized volume, which brings enormous erudition and exciting perspectives to bear on African works of art, demonstrating beyond doubt how art is the child of both science and myth, and proceeds and unveils itself simultaneously as system, poetry and revelation.

God's inflections narrate the politics of readings that claim to fulfil them as knowledge, mediation or vision. These performances reflect memories of the past as conceived from the present: things and events take place, lodging themselves in rational grids and their proper determinations. But can we really interrogate them from the angle we perceive them, and expect a good image for their comprehension?

II

Erasing the Difference of Genesis

> Le paganisme peut être valablement interprété
> comme une négation têtue, de la part de l'indigène,
> de la 'vérité' dominante en tant que la dite
> vérité n'en est qu'une parmi plusieurs, et que
> les techniques disciplinaires visant à l'imposer ne
> l'imposent point, en définitive.
>
> Achille Mbembe, *Afriques indociles,* 211

One might imagine a theoretical map of African religious activities at the beginning of this century, more accurately between 1900 and 1920 – the most systematic period of European evangelization – and compare it to its transformation between 1950 and 1960 when this expansion and its foundation are being questioned. On the first map, one clearly distinguishes the side of origins or paganism (which ultimately will get the new name, of traditional religions) and, on the other hand, the side of the future signified in the conquering privileges of Christian missions. Anthropologists and historians tell us that we could understand the tension between these two poles in a more general grid, in which four sets of concepts would be opposed: *orality* versus *writing, spatiality* versus *temporality, alterity* versus *identity, unconsciousness* versus *consciousness.* These concepts characterize two types of society: on the one hand, traditional or 'primitive' and, on the other, historical. Commenting on the historian's writing and ethnological orality and referring to Ampère's use of ethnology, Michel de Certeau (1988: 209–10) specified the models by qualifying only the first terms of the sets: *orality* ('communication within a primitive, savage or traditional society'), *spatiality* ('the synchronic picture of a system that has no history'), *alterity* ('the difference which a cultural break puts forward'), and *unconsciousness* ('status of collective phenomena, referring to a significance foreign to them and given only to knowledge originating elsewhere'). In these qualifications, which reproduce Lévi-Strauss' grand dichotomy between *cold* and *hot* societies, is a thesis we face in that each of the four guarantees and calls for the other three.

Cold Society	*Hot Society*
Orality	Writing
Spatiality	Temporality
Alterity (Otherness)	Identity
Unconsciousness	Consciousness

Thus, in 'primitive society, a timeless land as it were is displayed before the observer's eye . . . . it is taken for granted that speech circulates without its users knowing what unspoken rules it obeys. It is thus the task of ethnology to articulate these rules in writing and to organize this space of the other into a picture of orality' (de Certeau, 209).

Let us note a number of problems. First of all, whether properly founded conceptually, or articulated from the a prioris of functionalism and structuralism, these models could be read from the solidity of the naivest evolutionary grids at the end of the nineteenth century that justify colonization, Christianization and anthropology. According to these models, the primitive difference must be transcended in the language of the same and its culture. This is illustrated by the following diagram from my book *The Invention of Africa* (1988):

	Premises	**Mediators**	**Aims**
Status	Primitiveness	Conversion	Civilization
Symbols	Pagan (evil)	Christianity	Christian (positive)
or signs	Naked (child)	Education	Civilized (adults)
	Cannibal (beast)	Evolution	'Evolué' (human being)
Method	Anthropological Presuppositions	Missiology, applied anthropology, Pedagogy	Colonial sciences

The basic attitudes that arbitrarily relate these essentially unrelated qualities – paganism, nakedness, cannibalism – are those that assign all cultural differences to the single category of savagery; and one trait as it distinguishes a savage from a European becomes an index to the existence of the other traits which are part of the syndrome of savagery (Hammond and Jablow, 1977: 36–7).

The characteristics in this model function with the same efficiency as the conceptual traits of de Certeau's traditional society: each one guarantees the necessity of the other three and can be seen as an index to them. Moreover, in the play of oppositions, which makes it possible to define and understand them as linked in relations of necessity, the set of a cold society, in its otherness and visibility, is given a genetic power thanks to which the second set, that of a hot society, becomes the invisible paradigm for structuring knowledge and history.

The controversy that Michel de Certeau's exposition of ethnological orality can give rise to could be re-evaluated (but not necessarily suppressed) if we bring back into the discussion two main affirmations of Lévi-Strauss in *The Savage Mind* (1966): first, the opposition between abstract science (that of engineering) and *the bricolage,* which seems to dominate mythical thought; and, second, that it would be sounder to consider mythical thought as well as its concrete science as 'prior' rather than primitive (1966: 16).

Paganism is theoretically mapped in continuity with a theory of representation, which explicitly posits, on the one side, an empirical body of knowledge and beliefs of genesis and, on the other, an analytic of finitude concerned with the historicity and orders of differences, which come from the particular historical experience of the theory. Thus, from one side to the other, the movement was perceived, theorized, and actually carried out at the beginning of the twentieth century in very tight chain policies. Catholic bishops in Africa, for example, write explicit *instructions* to their priests and religious aides on how to conquer the difference of paganism and convert it.

The polarity spatialized by the empiricity of the conversion map seems to imply the existence of a physical void between paganism, mythical thought and orality and, on the other hand, Christianity, a science of the abstract and historicity. Even if we were to hypothesize such a radical tension, as Michel de Certeau did, common sense observation would lead one to wonder about the pertinence of this deviation. Firstly, as generally accepted today, there is no human society without history and historicity. The ambiguous efficiency of both is well-portrayed in manipulations of the past that each generation relives, as if to prove their fictitious nature and that history is always history for someone – that is, a contemporary stage from which one's past is invented, recreated and renegotiated. Secondly, as to the separation between orality and writing, mythical thought and the science of the abstract, and the implied superiority of the latter that often goes unquestioned, one may remember Lévi-Strauss' statement: 'It was in Neolithic times that man's mastery of the great arts of civilization – of pottery, weaving, agriculture and the domestication of animals – became firmly established. No one today would any longer think of attributing these enormous advances to the fortuitous accumulation of a series of chance discoveries or believe them to have been revealed by the passive perception of certain natural phenomena' (Lévi-Strauss, 1966: 13–14). The argument is there and leads to the only possible conclusion: The dichotomy (*concrete, mythical* versus *abstract, scientific*) is problematic when it reduces the first set to a primitive genesis incapable of conceiving functional modes of observation, classification and interpretation. Finally on the basis of our minimal definition of religion, one would agree with Aylward Shorter when he states in his *African Christian Theology – Adaptation or Incarnation* (1977) that 'talk of "Black Theology" or "African Theology" is excellent, but it must mean a contribution to other theologies. If it is meant to be exclusive, then it ceases to be theology. No single culture has a monopoly of God, just as no single culture has a monopoly of human experience' (1977: 132). This quotation exemplifies an evolution of ideas carried out in the interlocking of anthropological, religious and political grids and models accounting for the African difference (Hastings, 1979).

The fundamental concepts for indexing difference (orality, spatiality, otherness, and unconsciousness) have receded progressively with the general disqualification of the reigning paradigms, which used to classify all forms of difference in the first part to this century. As suggested by Michel Foucault: 'A vast shift has led the human sciences from a form more dense in living models (e.g. biology and economics) to a more saturated with models borrowed from language.

But,' adds Foucault, 'this shift was paralleled by another: that which caused the first term in each of the constituent pairs (function, conflict, signification) to recede, and the second term (norm, rule, system) to emerge with a corresponding greater intensity and importance: Golden, Mauss, Dumézil may be taken to represent, as near as it makes no difference, the moment at which the reversal took place within each of the models' (1970: 360) – that is, concretely, Golden in his reinterpretation of the functional model leading to the primacy of localized norms; Mauss, with that of conflict to which he opposes the immanence of individual and specific rules; and, finally, Dumézil with his rethinking of the signification of models and his emphasis of the generality of the system. Thus, it becomes possible to speak of, analyse and understand every culture, individual and language from the rationality of their own norms, internal rules, and within the logic of their own systems. In African studies, the shift meant a radical passage from mapping the difference of an 'invented' genesis to the mapping of cultural individualities; just as in anthropology, Luc de Heusch comes after Evans-Pritchard and Lévy-Bruhl; and in missionary studies, Fabien Eboussi-Boulaga follows Alexis Kagame and Vincent Mulago, and these are, in time, after G. Parrinder, J.V. Taylor and Placide Tempels.

I have meditated elsewhere (1994) on the missionary activity, its generosity, and political ambiguities. Let me use some signs. On 22 April 1878, a contingent of White Fathers, the disciples of the French Cardinal de Lavigerie, left the port of Marseille. Their destination was Central Africa. They reached Ujiji on 22 January 1879 and, on 25 November of the same year, organized the first Catholic mission in Burundi. Other caravans followed. Scheutists in 1888, Sisters of Charity in 1892, Jesuits in 1893, Trappists in 1893, 'White' Sisters in 1895, Franciscans in 1896, Fathers of the Sacred Heart in 1897, Norbertines in 1898, Redemptorists in 1899, etc. In this movement one immediately reads a mission, that of converting pagan cultures and spaces to Christianity. There is thus a unity in the ideal: it works to confine the 'pagan' in a difference, just as it expresses itself as the promotion of a new law that would negate the difference. If the movement or, more exactly, the missionary activity, finds its unity in a unique purpose, this seems to be so only because of an exterior and more general purpose:

the necessity of converting backward cultures and introducing them into the Hegelian perspective of history. Thus, a bipolar structure – the primitive versus the civilized – which indicates first of all a basic statement (the conversion of African space and time, and its insertion into human history) paradoxically also seems to negate the plurality of a conquering Catholicism. If there is a Christian unity that transcends the difference between a Jesuit and a Franciscan for example, does it mean that their missionary work is not submitted to particular doctrinal styles and spiritualities that might organize differently the mastery of African cultural alterities? I am suggesting that a plurality of spiritual vocations partitioned the religious experiences of converting Central African spaces along charismatic lines, at the very moment that, in the name of the mission, it wanted to erase the African difference by reducing it to the uniformity of a paradigmatic Catholicism.

Christianity, for instance, crumbles into a plural discourse when one takes into account the competition between Catholics and Protestants. The 1885 Berlin Act acknowledges freedom of religion. Leopold II, the king of the newly declared 'Free State of Congo', prefers to have his own fellow Belgian Catholic peoples missionizing in his newfound kingdom. Along with the Gospel, they teach their converts how to despise Protestants: 'Protestants do not know how to pray; they close their eyes and sleep instead of praying' Catholic children used to sing in Kasai. Protestant youths would react with other songs, ridiculing 'the Catholic missionaries who wear women's clothes' and Catholics, in general, 'papists, who celebrate idols'. The plural discourse, indeed, comments on the theoretical originality of Catholicism and Protestantism. Insofar as the latter is concerned, the various ideological structures of Methodists, Anglicans and Baptists also display a diversity of discourse, doctrine and situations. On the other hand, the ideological monolithism seen in both African Protestantism and Catholicism has its best symbolic sign in their own projects of religious conversion and, most visibly, as we shall see in the next section on missionizing, in their political procedures for reproducing both their objectives and their mission.

There is also a Black Islam or Black world of Islam according to a specialist, Vincent Monteil (1964). He distinguishes it from four other

Islamic areas: Arabic, Turkish, Indo-Iranian and Malayo Indonesian. In his 1982 study on African Muslims, another specialist, René-Luc Moreau, indicates that of the 435,250,000 inhabitants of the continent, 190,892,000 are Muslims and thus represent 44 per cent. Their culture might seem fundamentally different from those of Islamic North Africa or the Middle East, yet despite linguistic and political barriers, the faithful define themselves throughout Africa as members of God's *Umma*, sole and unique community. Their cultural impact is immense in three linguistic areas: that of *Ki-swahili,* spoken on the Eastern side of the continent by some 50 million people; the *Hausa*, spoken in West Africa (Nigeria and Niger) by 35 million people; and the *Pular* and its dialects used throughout the West Coast. Indeed, Arabic is not only an appropriate means of communication, but even where it is not known it is considered a sacred medium, the best key to *al-Charî'a*, the Law, and God's language. One should also note the International Islamic Conference, a political structure that coheres all the Islamic countries existing in the world today. Among them, 21 are from Africa: Algeria, Burkina-Faso, Cameroon, Comores, Djibouti, Gambia, Gabon, Guinea, Guinea-Bissau, Egypt, Libya, Mali, Mauritania, Morocco, Niger, Senegal, Somalia, Uganda, Sudan, Tchad and Tunisia.

Missionizing

Bernard Salvaing recently published (1994) an interpretive historical account of Christian missionaries on the West Coast, focusing on their contacts with the Ewes, Edos, Fons, Ibos, Ijaws and Yorubas from 1840 to 1891. Imaginative, multidimensional, and extremely well documented, the book analytically explores three main aspects of Christian missionizing: its doctrinal and historical basis, the everyday life of missionaries, and their vision and perception of the African milieu and its inhabitants.

Three main religious societies participated in the missionizing: The Church Missionary Society (CMS) implanted in Yorubaland since 1842, The Wesleyan Methodist Missionary Society (WMS) on the coast almost at the same period, and the French La Société des Missions

Africaines de Lyon (SMA), which began its activities in Dahomey in 1861. Salvaing describes a process and its reasons, insisting on an important point of method. He avoids including his personal positions in the exposé and, more importantly, his method has been to situate statements and facts in the context of the period, the African as well as the European, and restitute everything concerning the missionaries to a wider perspective that would thus justify occasional references to other categories of Europeans. Such an option which, in actuality, is a prudent yet strong criticism of traditional historical practices, constitutes a thesis in itself. As Pierre Bourdieu puts it apropos such a method: 'Even the most strictly constative scientific description is always open to the possibility of functioning in a prescriptive way, capable of contributing to its own verification by exercising a theory effect through which it helps to bring about that which its declares.' Salvaing chooses to follow his intuition, offering a maximum of angles of views and bringing together the most sympathetic visions on conversion with highly negative opinions of some colonization theoreticians and missionaries. On the other hand, let us note that Salvaing's work integrates the most up-to-date techniques of historical practices with a systematic art of suspicion, as we shall see later on.

The entry to the research unfolds the doctrinal and political premises of the missionizing activities: Henry Venn's (CMS) critique of Western cultural arrogance and his emphasis on Christianity based on a profound respect for the 'native'; his direct participation in the evangelization process and promotion of a real elite, as already remarkably demonstrated by Jacob F.A. Ajayi's work on Christian missions in Nigeria, go along well with his support of commerce, civilization and, indeed, the primacy of the British empire. In the same vein, the basic principles of Methodist missions (WMS) include two complementary directives: the condemnation of colonization motivations before the 1830s and the humanist postulation of Christianity as a necessary and sufficient means for African development. The specific case of Augustin Planque (SAM), a Catholic priest, could serve as a good index to a complex intellectual climate. His perception of Africa evolves from very negative presumptions to an enlightened position which, with a typical French distrust of the English, opposes the excessive dependence of British missionaries on local auxiliaries, yet strongly encourages the constitution of an indigenous clergy. In other words, Planque, by his own life, *writes* well the prose of the mission in its complexity and contradictions. In particular, he not only incarnates the conjunction of Mère Javouhey's or Livingston's determination and generosity, but also the colonial interventionism as expressed simultaneously in theology and imperialist programmes. Two conflicting paradigms meet here and conflict with each other: a negative one equals Africans to an absolute evil – *furca, furax, infamis, iners, furiosa ruina* as R. Burton put it; and a positive one, which assigns itself the ambiguous role of translating the negativity symbolized by the evil into the ineffable delight of God's children.

The everyday life of missionaries is filled with an impressive list of tasks that directly or indirectly concern their mission: such material and organizational activities as health care, construction of buildings, education and catechizing, and the formation of a native clergy, etc. Salvaing rightly insists on some highly difficult issues: domestic slavery, polygamy, and the competition among Churches. The first two are internal to local cultures. They are perceived and described by missionaries as completely incompatible with the Christian spirit. As a consequence, the missionaries develop their pastorale in a double strategy: an impeccable and vigorous action against pagan customs conceived as an exposition of horror and lack of humanity and, on the other hand, a systematic articulation of the major steps toward conversion as a process of gradual introduction into God's Kingdom. Incarnating redemption, in its religious and secular meaning, the mission also had to translate in convincing arguments the paradox of its own division (Catholics versus Protestants, CMS versus WMS, etc.) and, more significantly, its claims for a divine superiority *vis-à-vis* Islam. One might doubt the profound motivations of missionaries. Their spirit of sacrifice is nevertheless unquestionable, and admirable. Salvaing comments on the high death rate presented by statistics and emphasizes three possible explanations: (a) in average, death seems due to tropical diseases, the male missionary passing away in the two years following his arrival in Africa; (b) the mortality rate of females is higher than that of their male counterparts – for the Protestant churches, that of their husbands – and this discrepancy could be accounted for by pregnancies and/or depression and terror; (c) apart from few exceptions, well-educated missionaries, at least until the end of the nineteenth century, did not live very long in missions, and one wonders whether this is related to their familial background, their formation, or their more sophisticated minds and sensitivity.

The third and longest part of Salvaing's research deals with the missionaries' vision of Africa and Blacks. Divided into logical chapters, it successively presents 'the African milieu', 'Blacks' personality', and 'fetishism', the latter including a discussion of fetishism and its nature, the human sacrifice phenomenon, and Abomey customs. On the whole, Salvaing confirms here an already well-known representation, as attested by punctual as well as general studies of the contacts between Europe and Africa since the end of the fifteenth century. We face a postulation already given and understood as an a priori evidence justifying the European mission: white versus black, order versus disorder, and heaven versus hell. Retrospectively, Salvaing's analysis permits an obvious translation of ancient knowledge, in which the African side renders the negative materiality of human destiny. This destiny is illustrated by the research of Jean Pirotte, where he analyses Belgian missionaries' journals published between 1889 and 1940 and national stereotypes and racial preconceptions during those centuries. What is fascinating in Salvaing's contribution resides in what we could call the ideological apportionment of missionaries' groups, an enlightened humanism and optimism of certain Methodists and, on the other hand, the extreme pessimism and intransigence of some Catholics.

Indeed, it must be acknowledged that the shadow of a method and its tradition always marks such a work of historical interpretation. The presuppositions of the *Ecole des Annales* might account for the innovative and elaborate perspective of Salvaing's research. It clearly differentiates this book from yesterday's even iconic oeuvre such as Henri Brunschwig's *L'Avènement de l'Afrique noire* (1963), in which African history strictly coincides with the conqueror's venue; and 'African civilization' between 1840 and 1880 is encapsulated in comments on 'palm oil', 'French factories', the constitution of 'the Gold

Coast from 1843 to 1874', 'the genesis of Nigeria', and 'slave-trade and exchange in the Indian Ocean'. Salvaing's book is, in its own right, a challenge to conflicting nineteenth-century representations and a well-informed transdisciplinary outlook. It transcends particular anthropological and historical monographs, organizes its findings, and forges comparisons on the basis of highly varied and reliable sources, English and French, European and African. The representation of Africa and missionary activities that it brings to light is a fluctuating one made of subtle shades, contradictory, discontinuous, and sometimes contiguous layers of explanation. Even on human sacrifice, instead of following a tradition that reduces it to a sheer monstrosity and without celebrating the practice, Salvaing cautiously lists a series of justifications – from the most anthropological (the theme of expiation by death) to the most theological (the presence of Satan).

Finally, one should note the remarkable critical vigilance of Salvaing. Throughout the narrative, Salvaing refers to and uses texts as witnesses to be interrogated and carefully checked and questioned. His project is not to assimilate in one vision the oppositions manifested in CMS documents versus the WMS or the SMA, but to hold them in a higher tension signified by his discourse. And it is this affirmation of a going beyond the relative claims a knowledge that assures its independence from scrutinized texts on missionizing in nineteenth-century Africa. Thus, on the ambiguous and ritualistic declensions of savagery and anti-women practices, Salvaing does not hesitate, for comparison purposes, to bring into discussion the negative preconceptions concerning America's Indians, Saint Jean-Marie Vianney's sermons, and their castigation of French women's depravations, Jean Delumeau's physiology of Western theological discourse and its aberrations as depicted in *La Peur en Occident* (1978). The entries to the general conclusion – which include the thought of missionaries and its specificity, the vices of French people, the legacy of discovery, slave trade, and European racism – speak well and convincingly to an original research, and sum up remarkably the whole book as a strong demonstration of the following statement made by P. Duviols apropos the religious conversion of Indians in colonial Peru: 'A dogma of our epoch, the *de jure* axiom according to which each culture has a right to its own existence, has transformed our mentality to the point that what in former times was considered as the saga for implementing the Faith among Barbarians might seem to today's anthropologist to be just a cultural genocide.'

The Retreat Policy

In 1898, Victor Roelens, who was appointed an Apostolic Administrator of the Vicariate of Higher Congo by Rome some years earlier, invited Father Huys to build and conceive a minor seminary that would prepare native candidates for the Catholic priesthood. Stefano Kaoze, the first to be ordained, became a priest on 21 July 1917. The project and its procedures are exemplary of a conversion pact. They all refer back to a rationality of practice and a paradigm of action in which coexist a will to know and the necessity of extending it in the name of both Christianity and progress. Commenting on Christian formalities of philosophical practices in the eighteenth century, Michel de Certeau recently said that

it seems that 'enlightened' practice is organized along the lines of formalities which were of religious nature before being taken up as postulates of a morality. What it produces still obeys the principles of what is replaces. The pattern is the same for the three great stages of ethics which can be designated by the privileged reference: politics, conscience, progress. These moments refer to historical experiences of Christianity and bear the mark of religious forms whose very archeology they establish, whether it be an ecclesiology, a spirituality or pietism, or a messianism of a people elected by God for a universal mission.

(de Certeau, 1984)

In the African context, the religious structures which translate ideological discourses that fuse with political performances are the clearest. Religious enterprises, in their organization as well as in their aims, render a colonial activity in all its political formalities to the point that the politics of conversions re-enact at once the three stages of ethics: *politics* of development, while reactualizing the postulates of evolutionism, negate and transcend cultural specificities in the name of history; *conscience*, reduced to the Christian paradigm that brings together the light of revelation and the universal mission of 'the enlightened'; and, finally, *progress*, already predicated in the concept of politics: the Christian civilization discovers in its own being and nature a form of conquest, as Michel de Certeau put it, binding reason to the ability to transform man through the diffusion of the Enlightenment (1988).

From the beginning, one of the major keys to the policy of conversion is the constitution of a native clergy. If evangelization confronts cultures to transform, then the constitution of a local clergy means and indicates its most important condition of success, namely, the articulation of the enlightenment pact in concrete human beings (see e.g. Ajayi, 1965; Salvaing, 1994). In Central Africa, the candidates to this corps are chosen when very young from among the most promising children in the local community, preferably from an already Christian family. In the seminary, completely cut off from the rest of the world and their families, they go through three main stages. The first and minor seminary lasts between seven and eight years, depending on the region. During the first two years, they complete and revise subjects taught in primary schools, such as arithmetic, calligraphy, drawing, geography and history, etc. But the main emphasis includes catechism and Christian religion. During the following six years of the minor seminary each week includes at least five hours of religion, six of Latin language, literature and Roman institutions (and in rare seminaries, five hours of ancient Greek). Apart from very general surveys in anatomy, botany and zoology, systematic courses in European geography and history, in particular, articulated the horizons of an exemplary civilization and its roots.

A concrete illustration follows: My usage of French as a means of communication and creation is inscribed in such a process. I had been alphabetized in an African language, Swahili, and it was only in second or third grade that I learned my first French words. I was seven or eight years old then when, by necessity, it became my first language at school, besides my two familial languages: Songye through my father, and Luba, the language of my mother. Indeed, in the seminary we were supposed to function as native speakers of French. For more than seven years, I lived, thought, and dreamed without interruption in French. It was indeed the language of our ordinary communication and schooling. More importantly, it was also the language of spirituality. I should add that, for me personally, it was also the mediation by which I was first introduced to other African languages than my own – Bemba, Sanga, Kinyarwanda, Kikongo and Lingala – and throughout my education to European languages such as English, Flemish, German, Italian, Spanish and Portuguese.

The pre-eminent status and role of French (in education, administration, churches and public life, etc.) as the official language was exaggerated. No one could rigorously pretend that the adjective 'francophone' meant what its etymology spelled out: 'speaking French'. In fact, a mere 40 per cent of the 30 million inhabitants of the country could qualify as francophone in the 1960s. Thus, in the minor seminary, what was conveyed with a systematic teaching of French – the language of the master – was a solid aristocratic programme of cultural conversion. It had its enemies. Some conservative colonials, for example, feared that with Black people speaking French it would become impossible to express themselves freely. In the Eastern Congo, at least in the Vicariate of Bishop Roelens, the White Clergy, believing that French would turn the seminarians into corrupt and immodest citizens, decided to use Swahili, an African language, as a mediation in teaching all the subjects: arithmetic, geography and history, etc. Only late in their education – during the last years of secondary school – were students taught an instrumental French. Thus, for years, in Central Africa one could meet African priests who were more fluent in Latin than French.

As for the major seminaries, they were always located far from the minor seminary. The education averaged six years: two completely devoted to the study of Thomist and scholastic philosophy (particularly ontology, criteriology, logic, theodicy, cosmology, psychology and ethics), and four to the main domains of Christian theology. Each week, and more scrupulously than at the minor seminary, regular lectures introduce the candidates to correct 'table manners', 'ways' of walking, speaking and interacting with (fellow) Blacks and with White colonizers and missionaries. When studying philosophy, the candidate, now at least in principle well-introduced to a Western intellectual configuration, is

encouraged, under the supervision of a missionary advisor, to find and
work on an empirical field of research, in short, a 'primitive' hobby.
Thus, for example, Stefano Kaoze, in the 1910s chose Bantu psychology
and provided an account that confirmed Lévy-Bruhl's theses. Later on,
Alexis Kagame looked at the history of Rwanda and re-read Father
Tempels with an Aristotelian grid; and, after he left the seminary,
Joseph Kiwele's interest in African musical arrangements led him to
the invention of his 'Missa Katanga', in which the native Katangese
rhythmic structures are submitted to, and submerged by, the spiritual
economics of the Gregorian chant. The hobby is a test: it allows the
religious master to evaluate the candidates's depth of Westernization
and Christianization and how he can formulate original procedures for
converting the pagan culture of his own milieu. Just before the last
year of theology, that is, after the fifth year in the major seminary, the
candidate is sent to practise real missionizing. He generally lives as the
only Black in a European community. For one year, he will be observed,
tested and even aggressed by his fellow White 'confrères'. His contacts
with his fellow Black people are scrutinized and he is submitted to a
strict discipline. He has to correspond perfectly to the post-Tridentine
model of a cleric and to the paradigm of a future missionary among
his own people in politics of conversion, Christian conscience, and
human progress. If he succeeds in this ultimate test, he will return to
the seminary for the last year of theology. This is followed by a solitary
retreat which, according to the region, varies between one week and ten
or fifteen days and after which, if his bishop decides so, he is ordained
as a Catholic priest, becoming a living proof and a concrete example
(by his mind, body and purpose) of a Christian *politics, conscience*
and *progress*; thus, a living scripture, a docile body actualizing the new
Enlightenment pact.

'Docile Bodies'

This expression from Michel Foucault's *Discipline and Punish* (1979)
designates well the ideal African cleric produced during the colonization

era. As Foucault notes, 'La Mettrie's *L'Homme-machine* is both a materialist reduction of the soul and a general theory of dressage, at the center of which reigns the notion of 'docility', which joins the analysable body to the manipulable body. A body is docile that may be subjected, used, transformed and improved' (Foucault, 1979: 136).

Chosen young, submitted to specific norms that should mark the triumph of a Christian representation over the pagan, these young African bodies signified the metamorphosis of a complex desire: the unattainable perfection of conversion speaking about itself in two different languages, that of the conqueror and the submitted. They communicated and, indeed, revealed complex laws of acculturation. On the one hand, the African cleric had nothing apart from the culture and the language in which he was born and that he did not have the time to interrogate and understand, when a magnificent and enlightened fate oriented him towards a new will to knowledge and power. On the other hand, a line, a horizon, and an absolute truth – incarnated by the missionary – reflected the only way to adult conscience and progress through new politics of human promotion. From the first day in a minor seminary, the young African knew he was a chosen one. Yet, throughout his long years of 'education', the religious system reminded him regularly, practically every day, that *multi sunt vocati, pauci sunt electi*, 'many are called but only few are elected'. Divine and political selection seem, in this colonial perspective, an exceptional privilege. How then could one be elected without trying to be a most perfect 'docile body'?

Three factors – space, time, and the constitution of a new individuality – contribute directly to the culmination of this African docile body.

First of all is the factor of space. I have noted already that the young seminarian has to leave his family. The physical and cultural distance is a positivity, along with the fact that during the colonial time, the seminary is far away from his archaeological locus. In fact, from Bishop Roelens at the end of the nineteenth century to Bernard Mels, in the 1960s, this separation is a condition *sine qua non*. Seminarians have to be protected from both the nocuous influence of their pagan milieu and the materialist culture that colonial civilization introduces. The truth is, however, that such an isolation is the best way for an emancipation from paganism and the essentializing of acculturated new beings, and it is conceived according to the Roman model as adapted by the Enlightenment. If in Europe the model as Foucault describes it (1979: 146) has a double role (a republican aspect promoting liberty) and a military one (actualizing the ideal schema of discipline), in the education of the African cleric it is the latter that is emphasized. The training is a permanent registration: the candidate goes from one confinement to another; and they are spatially all organized according to the same grid, that of a monastery, that is, a perfect transparency or panopticism. 'It reverses the principle of the dungeon; or rather of its three functions – to enclose, to deprive of light and to hide – it preserves only the first and eliminated the other two' (Foucault, 1979: 200). Generalizing and abstracting the real seminaries created in Central Africa from the end of the last century to the mid-1950s, we can concretely reconstruct a spatial model. On the North side is the residence of the 'father-professors' (with its own chapel, dining room and library); on the South, seminarian refectories and recreation rooms segregated according to scholastic levels (young, junior and senior groups); on the East, the dormitories and all other facilities (washing rooms, etc.); and, on the West, the classroom buildings and student library. In the centre of this square, the church stands upright, symbolic and the spiritual equivalent of Bentham's tower in Panopticon. It represents God's eye. It also reflects the sovereignty of the conversion that the space signifies. Enclosed onto itself, this square on an African space overimposes its own rationality on a pagan soil, thus affirming an ideal objective, which is also an obvious one since it incarnates the achievement of indigenous revelations and in its authority manifests the fulfilment of Christian politics, conscience and human progress.

Although enclosed onto itself, the seminary is nevertheless a space of visibility. As in the Panopticon, its organization almost naturally tends 'to induce in the inmate a state of conscious and permanent visibility that assures the automatic function of power. So to arrange things that the surveillance is permanent, even if it is discontinuous in its action; that the perfection of power should tend to render its actual exercise unnecessary; that this architectural apparatus should be a machine for creating and sustaining a power relation independent of the person who exercises it; in short, that the inmates should be caught up in a power situation of which they are themselves the bearers' (Foucault, 1979: 210). At anytime the White 'fathers' and 'professors' may be anywhere in the square observing, praying, or simply walking, or not be there at all – the ratio was then one priest to ten or twenty seminarians – the centrality of the church and its symbol in the middle of the square delivering both a cultural outline and the significance of the seminary space.

The second factor, time, would confirm such a perspective. In effect, we must now move from the objectivity of a colonized space to an everyday scheduling of docile bodies, and see how this experience belongs to the same network of conversion. This is a schematic description of an everyday schedule in a seminary: 5:30 a.m., wake-up time; 6:00, meditation in the Church led by a priest; 6:30, mass; 7:15, breakfast; 8:00, classes begin; 12:00 noon, *Angelus*; 12:15 p.m., lunch; 1:00, free time and/or sports; 2:00, classes; 4:00, manual work or sports; 5:00, study and spiritual direction; 7:00, dinner followed by free time; 8:00, Complines; 8:45, study; 10:00, bedtime. This austere training, which in its formal representation explicitly wishes to reproduce the old monastic division of time – eight by three – eight hours of sleep, eight of prayer, and eight of work and distraction – adapts itself to a post-Enlightenment picture: Wednesday and Saturday afternoons are free and completely devoted to sports. Indeed, Sunday, the day of the Lord, has a special schedule: wake-up time is at 6:30 a.m. instead of 5:30, and meditation at 7:00, followed by breakfast. There is a grand mass at 10:00, then lunch at 12:00 noon, the afternoon consecrated to sports, and at 5:00 p.m. the weekly regiment recommences: study, supper, bedtime. Through what might seem like a spiral, a line that does not lose its traces always describes a temporal project. In this representation, it is a timetable cleric who is being created, subjected to a disciplinary paradigm whose major principle is the rule of non-idleness exemplified by the monastic schedule. Importantly, one may note the implications of such a norm, notably the correlation of time, body and mental disposition as well as the articulation of time and specific obligations. The whole procedure corresponds well to what military specialists in the European eighteenth century used to call a *manoeuvre*.

Thus, after Michel Foucault, this 'disciplinary power appears to have the function not so much of deduction as of synthesis, not so much of exploitation of the product as of coercive link with the apparatus of production (Foucault, 1979: 153).

The third, and last factor – the constitution of new individualities – would establish another, and perhaps the most basic, foundation of Christian conversion. The young minor seminarian learns it from the first day and, in principle, the discipline will follow him throughout his life, if he becomes a priest. Each of his days is 'maneuvered'. First there is the permanent self-analysis represented by the *Confiteor* every morning and evening: 'I confess to God the Omnipotent, and to you my brothers and sisters that I have sinned in my thinking (*cogitatione*), in my speaking (*verbo*), in my acts (*opere*) and in what I have not done, thought and foreseen (*omissions*).' Second, three major moments will mark every day: the examination of conscience in the morning, before the meditation; the second examination just after the *Angelus* at noon, and the last before *Compline*. Third, each week, there is the ritual of Confession: the candidate analyses scrupulously his behaviour, thinking, acts, even his dreams of the week, and confesses his sins and lapses from Christian norms. Finally, at least every fortnight, the seminarian has an hour's conversation with a spiritual director. The conversation generally dwells on the perfection of priesthood. The White advisor listens and since he has known his advisee for years, evaluates him, and recommends readings and techniques for mastering weaknesses. When necessary, his opinion will be instrumental in knowing whether the candidate is fit for the priesthood. Finally, at least once every year, the seminarians go into a week-long retreat: classes are suspended, an external preacher is brought in, and each day is organized around prayers, meditations, and religious lectures.

These three factors – the domestication of a space, the rigid inscription of the individual in a strictly regulated schedule, and the constitution of new individualities – indicate and achieve in their formative power the ideal point of conversion. Of course, the seminary is just a model, perhaps the most significant and rigorous of the 'Enlightenment pact'. Other institutions operate according to the same basic premises and educate African nuns, catechists and lay Christians.

Yet, it is the seminary that convincingly illustrates a meticulous programme of an absolute conversion and spiritual normalization, which systematically wishes to erase the distinction between 'us' and 'them' and produce new individualities inscribed in both the election of Christianity and 'civilization'. Still more characteristic is the nature of this African Christian pact. If the 'idol' is signified by what is out there (a negative paradigm or sign, to refer to Frantz Fanon's *Peau noire, masques blancs*, articulating in the unconscious of the 'homo occidentalis' the Black, or better the colour black as symbol of evil, sin, misery, death and famine), it is opposed by the procedures of this new pact. Yet, the confession of faith does not seem mobilized in an individual adherence but is supposed to come almost naturally, thanks to institutional instances and programmes represented by what the pact represents in the colonial library of salvation.

Cheikh Hamidou Kane's *The Ambiguous Adventure* (1972) gives another picture of the constitution of a 'docile' body through a complex Islamic initiation process. The shattering exposé emerges from a conflictual cultural background: European civilization versus an African Islamic culture. An 8-year-old, Samba Diallo, discovers the rigours of Koranic education: for three years we can follow his integration into a spiritual norm. His master guide exemplifies the law in its harshest discipline: to educate is to assign the candidate to an irreducible economy in its absolute purity. Yet, against this education into a traditional 'manhood' that goes along with a call towards 'sainthood', there is now, efficient, the new school or, in other words, the new objective efficiency presiding over the land and the destiny of its people. A hierarchy of power demands thus a second rupture: Samba Diallo will have to invest himself in the knowledge that would account for the colonial power. A third rupture opens itself with his sojourn in France: he is studying philosophy, discovering new fields and objects of knowledge, action and desire, and how it is always possible to be right even when one is wrong. When he goes back to his native country, one has the impression that his education as initiation has led him to an ambiguous elsewhere: no longer really one of his people, the Diallobes, he cannot either be one of those exploring the promises incarnated by the new power. Only his own death can thus respond to that of Thierno, the exemplary master who, in his childhood, magnified a supra-natural vocation:

Samba Diallo sat down on the ground.

'How I wish that you might still be here, to oblige me to believe, and to tell me what! Your burning faggots on my body . . . . I remember and I understand. Your Friend, the One who has called you to Him does not offer Himself. He subdues Himself. At the price of pain. That I understand, again. That is perhaps why so many people, here and elsewhere, have fought and are dead, joyously . . . . Yes, perhaps at bottom that is it . . . . In dying amid the great clamour of battles waged in the name of your Friend, it is themselves whom all these fighters want to banish, so that they may be filled with Him. Perhaps, after all . . . '

Samba Diallo felt that someone was shaking him.

He raised his head.

'The shadows are falling. See, it is twilight. Let us pray,' said the fool, gravely.

Samba Diallo made no response.

'Let us pray, Oh, let us pray,' the fool implored.

'If we do not pray immediately, the hour will pass, and neither of the two will be content.'

'Who?'

'The teacher and his Friend. Let us pray, Oh, let us pray!'

He had seized Samba Diallo at the neck of his boubou, and was shaking him.

'Let us pray, speak, let us pray.'

(1972: 173)

The Power of Conversion

For people familiar with African Christianity, the conversion model in both its intention and realization would describe the African critique as generally violent and often, alas, excessive, not only in its evaluation of conversion policies but also of the missionary. To limit myself to the Francophone space, I refer to Ferdinand Oyono's and Mongo Beti's novels which insistently ridicule the missionary, mock his or her activity, and even doubt the sincerity of the whole project of conversion: *Une Vie de boy* (1956), *Le Vieux Nègre et la médaille*

(1956), *Chemins d'Europe* (1960), *Le Pauvre Christ de Bomba* (1956), *Le Roi miraculé* (1958), *Ville cruelle* (1954), etc. These novels depict the *oeuvre* of missionizing and conversion in such a bleak way that the Canadian scholar, Lucien Laverdière, in an appendix to his doctoral thesis presented at the University of Paris ('Les missionnaires et le Christianisme dans la littérature Camerounaise') opened a brief evaluation of missionary activity by a scandalous question: *chrétien ou crétin*? (see also Laverdière, 1987). Father Drumont, a character in Mongo Beti's *Le Pauvre Christ de Bomba*, might be considered as symbolic of the ambiguity of the conversion policy: he is an administrator directly sustaining the way of colonial power by his multiple enterprises (business, building initiatives, and involvement in social native affairs). He is also simultaneously submitted to other rigours, such as his vocation as a priest with a rigid schedule, regular rituals (quotidian mass and recitation of the breviary, for instance), and a steadfast commitment to his mission of generosity for, and conversion of, a pagan space. As Mongo Beti put it, Drumont the colonialist is also the *alter* of Jesus: 'and my father tells them [the children] that Jesus is the Reverend Father Superior [Drumont]; they are one. Since then, the children call the Reverend Father Superior "Jesus Christ"' (Beti, 11).

Most students of African affairs have considered the anti-Christian literature of the 1960s as a discourse of affectivity, a simple reversal, and a negativity of the missionary initiative. I would suggest that we re-read it from a radically different viewpoint. Generally written by angry former seminarians in the 1950s and 1960s, this literature also testifies to something else: the erased part of the Enlightened conception and actualization of the Roman model in missionary practices – that is, the republican aspect and all its implications of freedom and demands for dialogue and compromise between equals. In fact, to the military discipline of the *legio,* so well exemplified in the seminary and criticized by African writers, it was necessary to conceive a modernized context for the Roman *Senate*, and also oppose the open discussion of the *forum* to the normative arrangement of the seminary as a military *camp* for battles against the 'idol'.

One of the best expressions of this right to a re-examination of the Enlightenment pact is probably Fabien Eboussi-Boulaga's *Christianity*

Without Fetishes (1981). A Cameroonian, Eboussi-Boulaga is a
philosopher and the author of many philosophical and theological
books. The objective of this post-colonial critique of Christianity is,
beyond the fact that Christianity is now part of the African horizon,
to sketch a project of authenticity that would constitute itself as a
challenge and a response to three hypotheses. First, that 'in a framework
of generalized domination, the liberation of the faith will have the form
of power and self determination, rediscovered and rectified' (Eboussi
Boulaga, 1981: 218); second, that 'in reforming themselves, the African
churches will reach, from within, the alienated society of which they are
total parts' (222); and, finally, in order to transcend the negative legacy of
the colonial rivalry between Christian churches, 'communication among
the churches is necessary. This will suppose, in each, the courage to be
itself and the ability to receive and administer "fraternal correction"'
(224). These propositions for a new formality of Christian conversion
and practice are deduced from a critique of foundations of the missionary
power of eradication.

As we have already seen, in its sublime project, the seminary is
both a sign of cultural emancipation that confirms the candidate in
his acculturation and a paradigm actualizing a mission, the destruction
of paganism. The traditional African religious practice is paganism,
understood as unfaith, as the stamp of the *infidels*, and thus evil in its
own being. The missionary move was absolutely impeccable, logical
and perfect.

The logic is ineluctable. The obliteration or absence of the correct understanding of God as he is either entails the degradation of the human being or is its
nefarious consequence. Human beings who suffer the loss of their perception of
'values' lose as well a perception of the God who constitutes the basis of these
values, or rather, who prescribes them. The converse is equally true: the one
who, explicitly or implicitly, denies the true nature of God falls prey to passions
and vices.

It follows that paganism is not a neutral state, a lack to be made up. It is
a state of guilt, of rebellion against God, and of fall beneath the threshold
of humanity. Incorrectly to worship God is necessarily to have recourse to
substitutes and simulacra. Idolatry, fetishism, and animism are the necessary
forms and concrete shapes of error. We are not dealing here with intellectual
error merely; this is error lived, existential error, which causes the human

being to fall beneath the level of human 'nature'. Because it is against nature, paganism is inhuman. Inevitably it is accompanied by slavery, infanticide, cannibalism, polygamy, and all manner of other aberration and imperfection. This being the case, to Christianize will mean to humanize, to civilize the degraded human being. It will mean the taming of human beings, and their progressive rearing to a normal state by education, by tutelage as if of minors, until such time as they may attain to their majority and win emancipation.

(Eboussi-Boulaga, 1984: 19–20)

Hence the authority of conversion procedures and their meaning is both natural and religious. The natural claims its own necessity in the interplay of beings and history, in the name of progress; the religious refers back to the primacy of a true revelation. Consequently, conversion is an imperative, a *sine qua non* condition for inscribing oneself into a history. The newly elected, the chosen ones, moving from the darkness of idolatry and primitiveness to the light of Christianity and civilization are, for this obvious reason, indeed expected to be 'docile' and 'grateful' bodies: they have been saved from the terrors of genesis. They were living in a 'negative' time, the absence of history. The theological interpretation of the history of salvation doubles here the evolutionary postulations for civilizing primitives.

The pagan past has no value itself. The fullness of Christianity acknowledges its value by suppressing it. The continuation of a promise after the promise has been fulfilled is a contradiction. Leave a like scandal to Jews. Let proclamation and prophecy now fade and die: breach with one's past is an absolute imperative of conversion to Christianity. Christian time admits of no interruptions. Its advance is rectilinear: its strides from the age of Judaism to our own, passing by way of the primitive church, the Middle Ages, the Renaissance, and modernity. Conversion means integration into this current. The only history Christianity has consists in a radial diffusion, outward from a primitive focal point, being solely and exclusively the dissemination of completed forms and fully constituted truths whose identity admits of variations only in their degree of repetition and expression. The converts are half-breeds, adopted ones. Their temporal continuity and unity are shattered. They become a mass of confusion, unable to differentiate between the time of mystery – -the life of Jesus as commemorated in today's sacred festivals – and the history of the West, which they now will wish to sacralize and 'repeat' for their salvation's sake.

(Eboussi-Boulaga, 1981: 25–6)

The politics of evangelization promote a 'middle-class Christianity', which is the equivalent of the bourgeois norm of Westernization. Specific rules sustain them. Personalizing truths or, as Eboussi-Boulaga puts it, 'Christian truth must be personalized in order to become believable'. The seminary programme, for instance, uses an institutional authority that, in the practice of the everyday life of the seminarian, forces him to personalize and internalize Christian truth: it is his and he should become responsible for it. Then there is the simple fact of historicization that brings together both the colonizing and the Christian missions.

Christianity, we found, is historical not because its founder can be assigned a certain place in an objective chronology, but because it was, part and parcel, a response in history to a situation born of history, that is, of the shock of the collision of cultures and civilizations, a response to questions born of the advent of history.

(Eboussi-Boulaga, 1981: 194–5)

Rule three, aesthetics, or more exactly redemptive aesthetics facing the elementary fact that the human soul to be saved is also a human body that is 'born, ingests food, copulates and dies'. As a matter of fact, an 'aesthetic African Christian' would fulfill the Enlightenment paradigm of openly expressing the freedom of republicanism and the discipline of the legion, and in such a search would have to face the last rule, the question of universalization and the universality of Christianity.

Neither in fact nor by right could Christianity be said to be universal in the obvious or current sense of the term. Factually, the whole world is not Christian. Christianity is minoritarian today as it was yesterday. Long confined to the Mediterranean basin, it left there and sped only by dint of a European expansion, in the form of migrations and the colonization of indigenous peoples. Other forms of expansion have since replaced this, but it is given to no one to know the day or the hour in which the whole of humanity will stand under the Christian allegiance. If this were ever to be, we would still be dealing with the circle of a historical humanity, and not of all possible humanity.

Why not universal by right? In default of a universal extension, must we not still affirm a universality of *intention* of Christianity? No. Here, as well, we see that in its very constitution Christianity is tied to something less than universal. It is bound up with singular events, with the life and death of a particular person. Historicity affects with its particularity not only the immediate content of Christianity, but its very form as well. Therefore it cannot be reduced to the general, the original without complicated discursive detours. Because it occurs in history, it cannot pretend to be the foundation of what precedes it, except by pretending that it has always been. It must postulate its preexistence. It must postulate its own timeless transcendence. By the same token, 'revelation' as an event is no more essential, no more necessary and salutary a mediation than historical Christianity. Revelation manifests that which has always been: the eternal act of the redeeming love of God. This is what saves, and not its historical unveiling in one place and one person.

(Eboussi-Boulaga, 1981: 206–7)

These rules bring us back to the Enlightenment pact. It is a liberal project of thought and a political line of performance, well exploited by Eboussi-Boulaga who, as we shall see, exemplifies a trend that went from a theology of salvation to an African theology of inculturation.

Education

Conversion and education, in the name of politics, conscience, and progress, coincide in the same movement that aims at the rearticulation of dominant narratives: Christianity, Enlightenment, and colonial science witness a violence which posits itself as a condition for modernity. It is thus obvious that we could conceive this violence as paradigmatic of any modernizing process, and reflect this analysis in the scandal represented by the old paradox of Epimenides, the liar. Either you believe I am not lying and my affirmation is not legitimate, so you cannot believe me when I say that any conversion as well as any education is violence. Or, you believe I am lying and my affirmation is legitimate, so you still cannot believe what I advance when I tell you that conversion and education are violence.

From the other side of this conversion process, that is, from an *ad vallem* standpoint, or our present-day vantage point, we might observe the constraints and privileges of this violence. Let me suggest some of these by invoking the concept of development and a will to knowledge. The first would, from disciplinary grids such as those expounded by history, sociology and demography, evaluate politics of spatial and human transformations in the sense illustrated by a recent research of the French Institute of Population: *Politiques de développement et croissance démographique rapide en Afrique*, edited by Jean-Claude Chasteland, Jacques Véron, and Magali Barbieri. This research overview (1993) includes analyses of such issues as (a) the problematics of development in Africa, specifically policies of economic organizations and perspectives; dynamics of production, growth and their impact on social relations of production; and (b) sectorial studies of the correlation between development and demographic transformations, as well as modifications, arrangements and performances in educational spaces. Insofar as education is concerned, two sustained paradoxes are now highly visible. First, from the viewpoint of its global population and compared to, say, Asian countries, Africa is *under-scholarized*: one third of African countries have a primary scholarization rate inferior to 50 per cent of its population; 4 per cent have a secondary degree and this rate is inferior to 15 per cent. Women are remarkably absent from the education space. For example, in Sahelian countries, if both sexes are included, then one adult out of four is illiterate; and since 1980 the general economy of a formal education in Sub-Saharan Africa has been in a relative disintegration. Second, from the viewpoint of financial investment and employment structures, Africa seems *hyper-scholarized*. To put it simply, when one compares Africa to Western Europe from an identical rate of scholarization, the African financial effort is ten times superior to that of European countries (Chasteland *et al.*, 1993).

These paradoxes carry out in themselves a judgement on the process of conversion and development. If interrogated, they can designate causes for the partial failure of the conversion, namely, reasons such as political instability, inter-ethnic conflicts, poor creativity in the organization and innovation of production procedures, feeble local returns of invested capital, demographic pressures, and fragility of economic structures versus macro-economic international disequilibriums, etc.

They do not fundamentally question the major decision, that is, the will to a universal knowledge that up to now still justifies and establishes the conversion and development processes. Thus, contemporary critiques of the African crisis tend to demonstrate that they comment on modalities of conversion and development, and not on conversion in its profound meaning as a will to knowledge and will to truth that could transcend all differences.

Indeed, the evidence of socioeconomic factors can silence what conversion and education mean: etymologically, 'a turning around, an alteration' (*conversio, -onis*; *converto*); and 'bringing up' (*educatio, -onis*) from *educo* (*-are*) and *educo* (*-ducere*), 'to bring up, to draw out, to raise up a person, to rear a child'.

Anthony Appiah's *In My Father's House* (1992), a critical meditation in philosophy of culture, is an excellent illustration of an African will to truth facing the most significant themes of conversion, namely, those of progress and absolute knowledge.

'In my Father's house, there are many mansions,' say the Scriptures. Why does the title of Appiah's book seem to silence the implications of the complete biblical statement? In fact, the focus is on the father. The procedure allows original openings, new keys to both the biblical story and the history of a memory in its complex capacity for rewriting an *I-Thou* report. Here is a meeting between cultural individualities and, to use Levinas, one could add not 'in any sense in one or the other participant, nor in a neutral unity embracing both, but in the truest sense between them in the dimension accessible to them alone' (Levinas, 1994: 22). From other possible angles, as in the case of Colette's *In My Mother's House*, this philosophy of coexistence could also thematize itself in the human plenitude that a mother's mansion, a sister's room or a brother's quarters would manifest. Michel Foucault writes, somewhere in his history of madness during the Classical Age, that 'our memory is the most populous location of our present'. If it is, as we believe, sociality, which means the dialogical relation of the *I-Thou* as a *co-esse* or to be with, as being and presence, how should we then think of it as memory? Memory of whom? Memory of what? Which memory?

After reading Appiah's book we could suggest a test that might bring the ekstasis of an *I-Thou* relation into an empirical domain: (a) How would I rethink, through Appiah's remarkable case, the paradoxical statement of Jean-Paul Sartre: a freedom thematized as what is not? We could relate this question to the understanding of being as always being for someone or for something. Leibniz has, in one his letters of 1687 to Arnauld, an image that we could keep in mind as a metaphor of this apparently irrational definition of an I: solid bodies might seem to have coherent and well-united parts or elements simply because of the pressure of environing bodies. (b) How could we name and qualify this mode of being and becoming in a philosophy of culture, interrogate its experience and knowledge as a critical questioning of concepts such as race, identity and similitudes?

The privileges manifested in the fullness of a knowledge brought about by a conversion are, indeed, always secondary to any 'human incarnation' and 'ontological mystery', to use Gabriel Marcel's expressions (1956). In other words, before everything else, there is simply the world of experience and its problems and, beside it, the ontological plane and its meta-problems coming from the very experience of being there. In fact, as Levinas puts it, 'the incarnate I is not, in its consciousness of self, for itself only; . . . . Its being-toward-itself is immediately, a *being exposed to others* and, in this sense, it is itself obscurity' (1993: 25). Appiah theorizes correctly by eliciting this in the concrete case of an African thinker, Wolé Soyinka:

It is intended (and to a large extent this intention is achieved) that *Myth, Literature and the African World* should be a work that, like Soyinka's plays (and unlike, say, Achebe's novels) takes its African – its Yoruba – background utterly for granted. Soyinka is not arguing that modern African writers should be free to draw on African, and in his case, Yoruba, mythology; rather, he is simply showing us how this process can and does take place. He tells us in his preface, for example, that the literature of the 'secular social vision' reveals that the 'universal verities' of 'the new ideologue' can be 'elicited from the world-view and social structure of his own (African) people'. I have every sympathy with the way Soyinka tries to take the fact of Africa for granted. But this taking for granted is doubly paradoxical.

First, the readership for his dramatic texts and theoretical writings – *unlike* the audience for his performances – is largely not African. *Myth, Literature and the African World* is largely to be read by people who see Soyinka as a guide into what remains for them a literacy point of view (and this is, of course, a reflection of political realities) the Dark Continent. How can we ask people who are not African, do not know Africa, to take us for granted? And, more importantly, *why should we*? (Observe how odd it would be to praise Norman Mailer – to take a name entirely at random – for taking America for granted).

It is part of the curious problematic of the African intellectual that taking his culture for granted – as politics, as history, as culture and, more abstractly yet, as mind – is, absurdly, something that does require an effort. So that, inevitably – and this is the second layer of paradox – what Soyinka does is to take Africa for granted in reaction to a series of self-misunderstandings in Africa that are a product of colonial history and the European imagination, and this despite Soyinka's knowledge that it is Europe's fictions of Africa that we need to forget. In escaping Europe's Africa, the one fiction that Soyinka as theorist cannot escape is that Africans can only take their cultural traditions for granted by an effort of mind.

(Appiah, 1992: 78)

Too many aberrations are often advanced and asserted by a simple negation or, more generally, a misunderstanding of the paradoxes of being exposed. Rightly, Claude Lévi-Strauss sees this simplification as based in Western dualism, a sign and symbol of objectification. Emphasizing the connection between reflection and objectification of the Other, Lévi-Strauss notes that 'the absolute gap which was accepted as a matter of fact by the seventeenth century (French) philosophical dualism' (1979: 24) initiated a radical separation of humanity and animality, nature and culture, self and other, while granting to one all that is denied to the other, and thus creating a remarkable 'vicious circle'. A supposed limit, constantly pushed back, 'separates man from other men and allows men to claim – to the profit of every smaller minorities – the privilege of a humanism, corrupted at both taking self-interest as its principle and its notion' (Lévi-Strauss, 1976: 41). For Lévi-Strauss, Western culture wishes to master the entropy of everyday life by strengthening the differential, and thus promoting objectivization. On the other hand, a number of 'primitive' narratives would, generally, integrate the absence-difference and through well-conceived procedures manifest opportunities for 'wrong use' of words and concepts in order to make believable their 'right use'; they would explicitly favour displacements of tensions such as male/female, nature/culture, subject/object, so that meanings belong to and come from an everyday creativity.

In Africa's cultures, as Anthony Appiah remarks 'there are those who will not see themselves as Other. Despite the overwhelming reality of economic decline; despite unimaginable poverty; despite wars, malnutrition, disease, and political instability, African cultural productivity grows apace' (Appiah, 1992: 157). Or, to use a stronger and highly polemical statement by Lévi-Strauss criticizing Jean-Paul Sartre's 'Hell is Other People,' let us face this:

> The formula 'hell is other people' which has achieved such widespread fame, is not so much a philosophical proposition as an ethnographical statement about our civilization. For since childhood, we have been accustomed to fear impurity from without.
>
> When they assert, on the contrary, that 'hell is ourselves', the savage people give us a lesson in humility, which, it is to be hoped, we may still be capable of understanding. In the present century, when man is actively destroying countless living forms, after wiping out so many societies whose wealth and diversity had, from time immemorial, constituted the better part of his inheritance, it has probably never been more necessary to proclaim, as do the myths, that sound humanism does not begin with oneself, but puts the world before life, life before men, and respect for others before self-interest: and that no species, not even our own, can take the fact of having been on this earth for one or two million years – since, in any case, man's stay here will one day come to an end – as an excuse for appropriating the world as if it were a thing and behaving on it with neither decency nor discretion.
>
> (Lévi-Strauss, 1978: 507–8)

Decency means a critical position apropos the ill-founded ambitions of the I *vis-à-vis* the evidence of others' existence as well put by Sartre when he says: 'It must be understood that there is no such thing as man; there are people, wholly defined by their society and by the historical movement which carries them along' (Sartre, 1976: 36).

Appiah's testimony is about types of paradoxical expositions as events. It claims to bear witness to the subject as the one who remembers and thus brings to light the relative reality of an experience. Let us note briefly a manner of rendering the experience of *existing* as *being exposed.* Insofar as Appiah's general argument is concerned, we could briefly dwell on the notion of race as facticity.

Race – that is, an arbitrary grouping of humans by supposedly distinctive and universal physical characteristics – is, indeed, one of the most discredited notions in contemporary natural and social sciences. Yet, a major tool as a classificatory concept in the conversion process of non-Western people, *race* is still perceived in today's general culture as a pertinent category instead of what it is in actuality, an extremely dubious and unstable facticity. An article on this concept of race in the November 1994 issue of *Discover: The World of Science* (Diamond, 1994) could be used as exegesis to Appiah's questions on what *race* might be, conversely, that Appiah's project could be reinterpreted as a thematization of contributions contained in *Discover*. I could, polemically, refer to the 'science' of race *vis-à-vis In My Father's House* with such proclamations as: Race is a meaningless concept; the classifications of human populations initiated in 1795 by Blumenbach are not only unnecessary but completely false representations of what is out there; the recent debates on melanin in the United States are a waste of time, contributing directly to prejudice and bringing nothing to knowledge. But instead I will use four capsules from Jared Diamond's article on 'Basing Race on Body Chemistry'. Indeed, as he writes, it makes no sense to base race on appearance. The following are capsules for a possibly more rigorous classification of race – by resistance, digestion, fingerprints and genes.

Capsule #1 – Against the classical criteria of geography and physical characteristics, one could suggest another arbitrary yet perfectly reasonable division of races by the presence or absence of a gene. For example, take the sickle-cell gene; on this basis we will have in one race some North Europeans such as Norwegians, several African populations and in another race, Greeks, Dinkas from Africa, Yemenites and New Guineans.

Capsule #2 – Race by digestion: in this case, the notion of race would be defined in terms of the capacity to retain the power of digesting milk among adults, thanks to the enzyme lactose. On this basis Northern and Central Europeans will constitute the same race with Arabians and some West Africans such as the Fulani. In the lactose negative race, one will find most Africans, East Asians, American Indians, Southern Europeans and Australian First People.

Capsule #3 – The concept of race might also be theorized from an economy of fingerprints, in which case we will have in the same race most Europeans, Africans and East Asians, sharing some basic common features. In a second race, we'll have Mongolians and Australian first people. And finally, in a third race, South African Khoisan and some Central European populations.

Capsule #4 – Finally, in order to challenge the arbitrariness of traditional classifications of race, some biologists are using key genetic distinctions. Thus here, one could manipulate elements defining three main races: (a) the South African Khoisans, (b) African Blacks and (c) the rest of the world. (Diamond, 1994)

These capsules illustrate concretely the absurdity of racial tables from Blumenbach's and Arthur de Gobineau's pronoucements to contemporary fallacies of the *Bell Curve*: one is the arbitrary classification of 'races' and another the racism that they allow, and which, in turn, in an antithetic reaction, justify that its victims may mobilize 'race' against a 'racism'.

Shall we then plead for the 'conservation of races' as Lucius Outlaw suggests (1992)? His basic argument dwells on the transparency of 'race' as a sociohistorically given system of grouping human beings. Referring to Du Bois, Outlaw writes that

the unit of focus, for Du Bois, if one is to understand human history and attempt to structure the making of the future through organized effort, is the 'racial' group, the 'vast family' or related individuals. Individuals are necessary, but they are neither sufficient nor self-sufficing, the political philosophy of modern Enlightenment liberalism notwithstanding. Survival is tied to the well-being of the group; and the well-being of the group requires concerted action predicated on self-valorization without chauvinism. Further, the 'racial' life-world provides the resources and nurturing required for the development, even, of individual talent and accomplishment such that distinctive contributions can be made to human civilization. Thus, must the 'race' of African people – 'races' – be 'conserved'.

(Outlaw, 1992: 27)

Yet, after a careful examination of this issue, and taking into account the obvious, namely, that if it is a biological fact that humans differ in their distributions of genes, it is an empirical fact that biology cannot be used as a reliable means of classification. Outlaw concludes by a dramatic question mark:

In a very important sense Appiah is right: what is at the heart of the matter, what exists 'out there' in the world – communities of meaning, shading variously into each other in the rich structure of the social world – is the province not of biology but of hermeneutic understanding. But what are the socio-historical bases of 'communities of meaning'? How do communities come to be? How do they cohere? If, on some relevant occasions, we cannot use 'race' to define the persons constituting such a community, particularly when the members of the community *do* share physical as well as cultural and geographical characteristics, how ought we to describe the socio-historical world in *sociological* terms? Since there are various groups composed of persons who are more or less physiologically, culturally, and geographically distinct that seem appropriate candidates for being designated 'geographic races', how are they to be defined?

(Outlaw, 1992: 27)

By avoiding the trap of a physiology of facticities and instead choosing a hermeneutics of transcendence, Appiah departs from the banality of *a focus*, of *a place* – that a plane which is 'the order (of whatever kind) in accord with which elements are distributed in relationship of coexistence' – and orients his thinking towards the demands of a specific *space,* which 'occurs as the effect produced by the operations that orient it, situate it, temporalize it, and make it function in a polyvalent unit of conflictual programs or contractual proximities' (de Certeau, 1984: 117). Thus, he can elaborate on Africa in a philosophy of culture according to the best teachings of both an education and a *Weltauschauung*:

Often, in the ensuing struggles, I found myself remembering my father's parting words, years ago, when I was a student leaving home for Cambridge – I would not see him again for six months or more. I kissed him in farewell and, as I stood waiting by the bed for his final benediction, he peered at me over his newspaper, his glasses balanced on the tip of his nose, and pronounced: 'Do not disgrace the family name.' Then he returned to his reading.

(Appiah, 1992: 181)

The Time of Inheritance

Toward the late 1940s, specific signs in African Christianity organized contradictory tables. Statistics indicate the success of Christian missions. In Catholicism, for example, the quantitative augmentation of the membership from 1900 to 1985 went from 1 Catholic in 100 to 12.7 in 100, which represents more or less 63 million members in a population of approximately half a billion individuals – a startling development which, in the presence of 170 million African Muslims, might seem unimpressive. But the dynamism of Catholicism goes beyond the visible parameters of statistics when one pays attention to a number of factors. At least in Central Africa, this dynamism reflects itself in Christian values even if one might ask, repeating an old question, how Christian is this Africa? On the other hand, because they are historically and institutionally parts of what made possible the new nation states through colonization, Christian educational systems seem more integrated in the general sociopolitical atmosphere and more structured than Koranic schools. Yet, after analysing such a panorama in their evaluation of Christian missions focusing on Catholicism versus Islam and sects, Alain Brezault and Gérard Clavreuil conclude that 'as to the colonial period, one must note the failure of the (Christian) Church that believed possible the exorcization of Africa and the suppression of its cultural, political and social past' (1987: 81).

If such a conclusion is so clear, it might be that it refers to the well-defined paradigm of Christianity (as the future) and paganism (as the past) mapped out at the end of the nineteenth century and the beginning of the twentieth. In the 1940s, and most visibly in the 1950s, it was neatly observable that conversion meant willy-nilly cultural exchanges and both a process and experience of *métissage*. 'Paganism' was forcefully negated since it was conceived as the impurity to be transcended by Christianity. In fact, in its theology and politics, Christianity could not but ignore (when it was not perverting) what was its own alterity; and in so doing overemphasize its own rationality. Thus, throughout the nineteenth century, classifiers prevented many students of African affairs from seeing the obvious: the bipolarity between paganism and Christianity did not correspond to any concrete reality. To illustrate this, we might note three cases. The first is about paganism dubiously presented as a negative, closed and uniform field. Aylward Shorter's analysis of the concepts of God and the sun in the religious thought of East Africa (1977: 61–78), a historical case study, demonstrates a fabulous case of linguistic and cultural *métissage* between many ethnics during the last millennium BC:

> According to Ehret, the semantic linkage of sun and supreme being was a characteristic of the Rift Southern Cushitic languages which spread over western and central Kenya and into Northern and Central Tanzania during the last millennium BC. Through loan words and loan translations, it seems likely that religious ideas expressed in the Southern Cushitic languages influenced both the Southern Nilotic languages and the languages of the Bantu people about 2,000 years ago and 1,000 years ago respectively.
>
> (Shorter, 1977: 65–5)

I could refer to ten other examples challenging the missionary prescribed notion of paganism (see e.g. Heusch, 1971, 1972; T. Fourche and H. Morlighem, 1973). The second illustration concerns itself with a mythical representation of an African Christianity that erased the obscure visibility of Antonians in the Kingdom of Kongo, an eighteenth-century Christian heresy about which information is not lacking (e.g. Jadin, 1968; Thornton, 1983). The movement was created by two women, Appolonia Mafuta Fumaria and Béatrice Kimpa Vita, who dreamed of a political and religious renewal of the Kongo kingdom. They were both executed on 2 July 1706, as heretics. In fact, their sin was that they blurred the space distinguishing paganism from Christianity. Béatrice Kimpa Vita's case is exemplary: she was baptized a Catholic, yet she claimed to have been visited by two 'white children' and initiated into a traditional cult, the *marinda*. Moreover, she was 'married' to two men. Despite all this, she was said to be possessed by the spirit of St Anthony, pretended to die every Friday and resurrect the following day, and healed diseases in the name of Christ, the Virgin and St Anthony (Biaya, 1992). John Janzen has demonstrated that the Appolonia Mafuta Fumari/Béatrice Kimpa Vita event was in Kongo history just one moment, perhaps the first, in a long process of negotiations between traditional beliefs and Christianity. The third and last illustration is the case of 'syncretic' churches. Bishop Bengt Sundkler, in *Zulu Zion and Some Swazi Zionists* (1976), shows convincingly that there are 'religious mixtures' contradicting the purity of the colonial map: Archbishop Mdlalose, ordained in 1915 'by a group of "Apostolic" pastors'; Grace Tshabalala, 'a widow at Kwa Mashu in Durban', born in 1904 in a Christian family; 'apostolic women' such as Ma Nku and Ma Mbele who organized the Church as 'a women's lib, long before that term was invented'; and, finally, Job Chiliza, the leader of the African Gospel Church. All these 'prophets' incarnated what the colonial map could not integrate. The evidence forced Sundkler to suggest a classification of religious *métissages* which, indeed, destroys the purity of the first map: (a) *Churches*. Some of the groups described are churches, such as the African Methodist Church, the Bantu Methodist Church, etc.; (b) *Christian Sects*. Under a sect is here understood Jesus Christ plus something else, especially adult baptism or the Sabbath; (c) *Nativistic Movements*. While most of the Christian sects are literalistic and fundamentalistic in their interpretation of Scripture, the nativistic movements are also fundamentalistic, that is, they wish to restore aspects (at least) of the traditional African religion (Sundkler, 1976: 306).

Conversion and Its New Strategies

The whole costly map opposing purity to impurity of beliefs and values collapsed in the 1950s, and by the mid-1960s it designated both simplification and authoritarian ignorance. Traditional practices are now investigated in their own right in functionalist and post-functionalist anthropology. In missiology and religious studies, African beliefs are questioned in the density of a curious comparison: have they preserved an ancestral memory of a primitive revelation? It is also during this period that we see the extent of the reconversion of the map. In Anglophone countries, the legacy of the methodological transformations of functionalism intermingles with Pan-Africanist ideologies and begins to reflect in its objectives something like an African essence (e.g. Abraham, 1962; Middleton, 1967). In Francophone countries, the theme of *Négritude* had been playing the same ambiguous role since the 1930s. Jean-Paul Sartre's *Black Orpheus* (1948) makes the concept highly visible and *Négritude* becomes a good or a bad word depending on what it implies, the possible negation of an integral assimilation:

Europeans of an ancient divine right, already we are feeling our dignity crumble under the gaze of the Americans and the Soviets; already Europe was finding herself a mere geographical accident, almost an island which Asia pushes out to sea. At least we were hoping to retrieve a little of our grandeur in the domesticated eyes of the Africans. But there are no more domesticated eyes; these are eyes savage and free which gaze in judgment upon our country.

(Sartre, 1976: 9)

If Anglo-Saxon functionalist anthropology in the 1940s did not seem to understand the 'scientific' pertinence of Marcel Griaule's research and that of his school, let us note that the *International African Institute*, with its well-known feel for the game, arranged a dialogue that led to the historical landmark edited by Daryll Forde, *African Words* (1954). This project manifested a new intellectual configuration that also accounted for a strange little book published in 1956 by a group of Roman Catholic priests, *Des Prêtres noirs s'interrogent* (1956). An intellectual discontinuity then made possible a radical re-evaluation of past discourses on primitiveness and paganism. A new perspective detached itself from the ancient map and arranged a completely different epistemological space. Let us also remember the influence and impact of Herskovits, Lévi-Strauss and Radcliffe-Brown in anthropology. In African religious studies, there was the visibility of Father Tempels whose project met Marcel Griaule's interpretation of a dialogical anthropology and led, as we shall see, to the constitution of an ethno-philosophical school.

This discontinuity also meant a new intellectual climate, in which one could see points of coincidence between nationalist ideologies (e.g. Krumah's, Nyerere's or Senghor's), the practice of social sciences (e.g. Vansina's work on oral tradition, 1961), and the reconversion of religious studies (Theuws, 1951; Mulago, 1965). The novel search is subordinate to a political principle on the difference of historical traditions, and signifies the possibility of a dialogue between cultures. From this viewpoint, Christian practices of conversion now witness particular ways of structuring and articulating expressions of the same basic and universal revelation.

This mutation, which pluralizes the discursive practices of conversion also alters the technical grids for classifying African religious beliefs and understanding them in the midst of conflicting knowledges about religion, identities and differences. In 1968, D.B. Barret could suppose the existence of six thousand independent Christian Churches in Africa (1968, 1970), blurring the tension between paganism and Christianity on the ancient map. In 1988, a Zaïrean scholar, G.T.K.M. Buakasa, suggested the amazing figure of one thousand new churches organized in his country of 30 million inhabitants. Whatever the credibility of these figures might be, they expose the complete dislocation of the first conversion map and, at the same time, represent new politics of dialogue and exchanges between Christianity and 'paganism' or, more exactly, traditional religions.

It might seem paradoxical that such a process of pluralization, which at first sight seems to emphasize the highly limited singularity of particularized performances, could be seen as a sign of an authentic religious quest. Instead of generalizing, let me try to illustrate this point by rearticulating it in the depths of some very recent enterprises deploying arguments for both a political and religious liberation of 'marginalized' believers. The books concern the practice of Christianity and are signed by very different personalities: a US attorney (Steven Bachman), an American professor of theology in Cameroon (Thomas Christensen), two American university professors (Michael Dodson and Laura Nuzzi O'Shaughnessy), an African scholar (Jean-Marc Ela), an American missionary in Tanzania (Michael Kirwen), a Belgian Jesuit from Central Africa (Paul de Meester) and, finally, a South African academic (Charles Villa-Vicencio). They all claim that if there is such a thing as religious transcendence, its meaning should develop as an investment from and a response to the norms, rules and systems of concrete human beings and their existential experiences.

'Theology today is inductive and empirical in approach. It is the ever-changing struggle to give expression to man's response to God. It is always inadequate and provisional. Variety is to be welcomed because no one approach can even do justice to the transcendent reality of God' (Maurice Wiles, Regius Professor of Divinity, Oxford University). These books offer a new vision of Christianity and, at the same time, provide a radical new perspective whose roots go back to the 1960s. This religious practice which, to refer to Paul de Meester (1991: 54–5), has moved from a ministry strictly centred around transcendence to a new one, more concerned with concrete existential conditions of humans. Despite existing obvious divergences, which could leave one with the feeling that there is not a common thread uniting these various contributions, their references propose at least an identical background: a critical re-reading of the Bible made possible by what has been called 'theology of liberation'. The recent collapse of Soviet Union Marxism has, indeed, brought about questions on the pertinence and credibility of these intellectual and sociopolitical policies – since, at least in the United Sates during the Reagan administration, 'liberation theology' was perceived as a means of fostering an international Marxist agenda. Yet the problems addressed by these books – those of poverty, marginalization and exploitation, etc. – are not going to disappear. It is obvious that these types of studies will continue to foreground them, thus giving a voice to the voiceless.

Preach Liberty by Steve Bachman, a practising US attorney born in 1951 and raised in Indiana as a Lutheran, undertakes the task of reclaiming 'the Bible for the people'. It explicitly opposes 'the interpretations of right-wing television and radio preachers' for whom 'the Bible has become no more than a justification for the mistreatment of children, the subordination of women, and the undermining of prospects for peace between nations of the survival of the planet' (1990: 1). The rationale of the argument springs from a different quality reading, scrutinizing 'liberating figures' such as Moses, an inventor of 'boycott and general strike', King David, at the beginning of 'his career, as a Hebrew Robin Hood' and, indeed, Jesus as a hero 'executed by the authorities for political agitation' (1990: 1). The chapters thus have entries with themes that aim at a reconceptualization of carefully chosen biblical verses and passages, such as 'Egalitarianism', 'No Social Pretense', 'Peace', 'Public Decency', 'Respect for the Environment', 'Respect for Women', 'Respect for Minorities', 'Respect for Justice', 'Social Justice: against the exploitation of the Poor', 'Social Justice: affirmatively aiding the underprivileged', 'Social Justice: assuring fair practices', 'Righteousness over Ritual', etc. Bachman's project seems primarily didactic. It indicates ways of resisting racist and sexist endeavours that have abused and overturned the biblical messages. In itself, this intellectual resistance might be also the weakness of the project. In fact, how do we explain

symbolism. In fact, the *soré* functions, as commented by Christensen (1990: 135–52), as a referent with different levels of symbolic meanings: concrete, insofar as the tree, or simply its leaves, are considered the best means 'for making a new village, for cooling murder, or for reconciling two villages' (1990: 186); operational, particularly in ritual contexts in which, from the concrete to the abstract level, the *soré* establishes codes for interpreting (through analogies and similitudes) 'the ever-fresh creativity and freedom of life' (1990: 137); finally, a positional level which, according to Christensen, 'refer(s) [the *soré*] to the totality of cultural elements in Gbaya society and illustrate that its meanings may vary in different contexts' (1990: 137).

In analysing these levels after an introductory chapter on 'deep symbols we share on the run' (which conjunctures on the *Soré* tree as a new naming Jesus), Christensen begins by describing what Christianity brings versus what it discovers in the Gbaya settings, and how the meaning and processes of Gbaya meals rationally lead to the analysis of connected rituals, sacrifices, purification and cleanliness rites. This covers the first six chapters (Christensen 1990: 1–70), followed by four sociological chapters, respectively on growing up in Gbaya society; the Gbaya dance of *habi* or initiation; the rites of reconciliation; the case of Karnu who resisted French colonization and in African versions of his resistance is depicted as a 'prophet' and in European versions as a xenophobe. Christensen's last three chapters, more theological, are concerned with such topics as the symbolism of the *Soré* tree, the Gbaya Naming of Jesus, and theology as the way to missiology.

There is in Christensen's project a commitment to put together arguments for cultural coincidences, namely, that in the Gbaya tradition there are signs witnessing the Christian revelation. Thus, the author can discover in the Gbaya tree of life both a particular case and an image of the Gospel's message. In this intellectual process which re-actualizes the classical method of looking for *Evangelii praeparationes* – that is, searching for stepping stones of Christianity – what might be lost is the reality of conflicts between cultures and interpretations of founding events and symbols.

In Nicaragua's Other Revolution, Michael Dodson, a professor of political science at Texas Christian University, and Laura Nuzzi

O'Shaughnessy, an associate professor of government at St Lawrence University, face this issue of conflicts of interpretations, focusing successively on three themes: religion and democratic revolutions, the traditional Christian Church and the Prophetic Church; and religion and revolutionary struggle. The study as a whole situates itself at the intersection of Christianity and its 'capacity to shape political life', especially in relation to the challenge of development.

In the first part of the book, Dodson and O'Shaughnessy analyse the 'Nicaraguan revolution', and its antecedents, dwelling on 'the religious roots of North American politics', the 'patterns of political development in the Americas', their general project being to account for differences and specificities. They assert, for example, that 'the two halves of the Americas do appear to have a great deal in common in their historical development. . . . In practice, however, their colonial experiences were sufficiently different to lay the basis for a historical relationship plagued by misunderstanding' (1990: 51).

The second part offers an elaborate analysis of 'the nature of the Catholic Church and its historic impact on society and politics in Central America', unfolding two conceptions of the Church: a traditional one, which emphasizes the importance of the *Magisterium* and, since the Vatican II Council and the Medellin Conference, a different understanding of the Church as 'a historical community of believers, or the *people of God*'. The traditional view tended to give precedence to the institutional hierarchy as embodiment of the Church and the Faith. In its formulation, the second view had democratizing effects and meritably led to a greater participation and responsibility of the 'people of God' in the Church and an antithetical postulation favouring the disinherited and the poor. Even though the newer view 'did not imply a rejection of the *Magisterium* but rather an insistence that the hierarchy take account of, be accountable to, the entire community of the faithful' (1990: 242), it divided the Church into two factions: a traditional, hierarchical Church and a popular, grass-roots Church. The Sandinistas in Nicaragua accommodated this newer vision in their politics and aroused the ire of the institutional Church and of the rich.

The tension between the two views raises a simple question: what is the Church? Dodson and O'Shaughnessy chose to respond to it by simply presenting a case study. The third part of their book articulates powerfully the contradictions brought about, directly or indirectly, by this tension in Nicaraguan society. The confrontation is not only about a religious, orthodox geography opposing a new imagination and its references. What is at stake is the immense struggle concerning power and the possibility of alternatives by reference to the credibility of a dominant discourse and its normativity. The Sandinistas lost, as we know. However, the question about the nature of the Church remains and is of concern for a number of believers in many countries. Throughout the Third World, it appears to be linked to tasks of development and the promotion of the human dignity of the poor and the exploited. Dodson and O'Shaughnessy rightly note that the Medellin conference

called the churches to be servants of the people. This implied that the religious authority of the churches would be a function of their faithfulness in pursuing the integral development of the people rather than in preserving the continuity of their ancient and venerable institutions.

(1990: 241)

Jean-Marc Ela, a Cameroonian Catholic priest, articulates this new option from an African viewpoint in his *My Faith as an African* (1989). One would have expected to find the author – who holds a doctorate in theology from the University of Strasbourg and a doctorate in sociology from the University of Paris – in a university chair or teaching at a major seminary instead of in the northern Cameroon, an extremely impoverished area where he has been living and doing pastoral work for more than ten years among the Kirdis. It is a challenge he has chosen, a witness for the exploited:

I find myself in a northern region affected by a state of invisible slavery, as the older priest, Baba Simon, explained on the night of my arrival. My first impression was that the people of the high country among whom I would live for many years are not merely rejected and bereft of decision-making power; they are also totally defenseless and deprived. The mountain people are poor because they have been exploited and oppressed for generations, not because they do not work.

(Ela, 1989: 4)

What kind of Christianity should a black priest actualize among the poorest of his brothers? Ela deals directly with his convictions:

Faced with this situation [the exploitation of the peasants in the northern Cameroon], I had to free myself immediately from a certain number of constraints in order to get a fresh perspective on the problems of my mission. I did not feel called to become the manager of a form of decaying Christianity, bound up in its doctrine and discipline, so I decided to keep my distance from a model of a church designed elsewhere by people who do not know the conditions of the mountain people. I had to refuse the false security available to someone who moves into another's house. . . . In order to capture the meaning, I *had* to live in insecurity. That led to radical questions: 'What is the cutting edge of the gospel that can be most directly accessible and meaningful for these people? How shall we live our faith, and thus create around us a desire for the living God? Don't we have to convert ourselves before preaching conversion to others?' Everything impelled me to abandon the traditional Christian questions and patiently let another language of the gospel burst forth from the life of the people.

(Ela, 1989: 5)

My Faith as an African comments on this quest and the problems it implies. How does one revalorize polluted beliefs and revise and refound political fables about salvation on the authority of the Christian revolution? Ela, as Simon E. Smith puts it in the foreword to this English version, 'takes us by the hand into village Africa, helps us feel the painful reality behind the statistics of exploitation, and shares with us the pragmatic grounding of his conviction that very authentic inculturation of the Christian faith is conditioned on the liberation of the oppressed' (Ela, 1989). Ela's strengths reside in this sometimes inconoclastic ambition.

Part of the book, 'Reawakening the Wellsprings', is a spiritual kind of autobiography that first presents Ela's intinerary and unveils his signifi-cant discovery of the 'sacrament of community' – 'where people aspire to escape from misery and captivity, we must move from catechism to revelation' (1989: 8). He also reflects on the possible connections between African ancestors and Christian faith from the background of a reconstructed African symbolism. He wants to reformulate the issue on how to live in Christ – the role of sacrifice and the styles of

Christian celebrations, veneration of Saints and preaching the Gospel – in an African context. Next, he meditates on how to tell 'the story of God's Revelation' and inculturate Christianity in both the African memory and the present. This section concludes with programmatic pages on the 'future of local communities', in which Ela questions the power of the clergy and reconsiders the issue of leadership in Christian communities. Part two, 'Faith at the Grassroots', illustrates the author's advocacy for the poor by dwelling on health issues, the economic exploitation of the Kirdis, and liberation theology's demands from biblical and Christian perspectives. God is not neutral, asserts Ela, since 'the "locus" in which God is experienced lies in the promise of a liberation continually renewed' (Ela, 1989: 103); and, moreover, 'the presence of misery and oppression is a basic form of the "sin of the world" that contradicts the kingdom of justice inaugurated by Jesus of Nazareth' (1989: 109). In the last part of the book, Ela 'missiologizes', from an interpretation of the Gospel and the calvary of the poor, the spirit of African Catholicism in the 1980s and the new requirements for 'speaking about God'.

By now, one fact has been established: we no longer need to discuss the principle of the possibility or legitimacy of an African theology. The principle has been established. Appeals have come from the magisterium itself, inviting Africans to assume their own responsibilities for building a theology incarnated in the living thought of the men and women of our continent.

(Ela, 1989, 162)

The recitation of formulas is no longer important to us. What is important is that we try to extricate the contemporary meaning of the Word of God and of the plan of salvation, beginning with the historical understanding that Africans have of themselves and of the world.

(Ela, 1989: 166)

Ela's analysis is impressive, solidly grounded in the Scriptures, and even strictly under canonical control. He quotes profusely from the Bible and pontifical documents and might be radically in favour of reconverting the classical understanding of the Church. Nevertheless, although he affirms himself a faithful son of the Church, he does not hesitate to raise delicate questions about the pitfalls of Africanization and explicitly questions some official policies of African Catholicism, as in these two far-reaching statements, for instance:

A liturgy using indigenous music might cause Africans to forget that they are human beings under domination. Expressing their calvary through the rhythm of their own music give them the hope of celestial happiness – as happened through Negro spirituals in America. When Christianity was implanted in Africa, something important happened at the same time: while the converts were distracted by the Bible thrust into their hands, their land was stripped from them.

(Ela, 1989: 147)

The rhythm of drums and balaphons within our churches cannot shelter us Africans from the threats of the 'weapons of food' brought to bear on peasants crushed by the dictatorship of peanuts, cocoa, and cotton. The famine of the Sahel appears to be not so much a natural calamity or an outcome of climate as a result of a policy of oppression and domination over peasants and herdsmen.

(Ela, 1989: 147)

Ela's commitment to the cause of the poor is fascinating. The substance of the book – which carries forward the preoccupations of his preceding publications, such as *African Cry* (1986); *Voici le temps des héritiers* (1981); *L'Afrique des villages* (1982); *La Ville en Afrique noire* (1983) – reflects a number of major points also present in the more recent study by Michael Dodson and Laura Nuzzi O'Shaughnessy on Nicaragua. In brief, it is faith and faithfulness to the Church that make thinkable these intellectual enterprises. From a strictly agnostic position, one might wonder why this dependence on an institutional Church should be needed in order to conceive and commit oneself to a task of development. Is development unthinkable without Christianity? Can theories of development be based on something other than the connections of the Church and why should theology colonize sciences and techniques of development?

The ambiguity of theological projects cannot but lead us back to an essential question: how can we comprehend the credibility of Christianity in the Third World? The late Michel de Certeau notes in *The Practice of Everyday Life* (1984) that 'the credibility of a discourse is what first makes believers act in accord with it. It produces practitioners. To make people believe is to make them act. But by a curious circularity, the ability to make people act – to write and machine bodies – is precisely what makes people believe. Because the law is already applied with and on bodies, "incarnated" in physical practices, it can accredit itself and make people believe that it speaks in the name of the "real"' (de Certeau, 1984: 148). In this sense, a receptive reader of liberation theology understands that the Latino-American experience and scholarship of Michael Dodson and Laura Nuzzi O'Shaughnessy, as well as the knowledge and intellectual generosity of Jean-Marc Ela's *Faith of an African*, are, essentially, even in their signs of revolt and impatience against the Church, witnessing to it, to this institution which gives both meaning and hope to the contradictory expectations of the 'people of God'.

The Missionary and the Diviner by Michael C. Kirwen exemplifies the preceding analysis. To refer to Laurenti Magesa's introduction, the book 'tackles what is perhaps one of the most central concerns for African theology today. What, from a Christian perspective, is the worth of the pre-Christian divine self-manifestation in Africa?' (Kirwen, 1988: 7). It clearly inscribes itself in the problematics of the African theology of inculturation. Michael C. Kirwen, a Maryknoll missionary in Tanzania since 1963, relates a personal experience that may be reminiscent of the spiritual itinerary of Jean-Marc Ela. The only difference between the two, and it is major one, is that Kirwen is a White American missionizing in Africa and Ela is a Black African doing the same job among his people. Yet, their testimonies coincide perfectly and the exploration they testify to in the name of Christianity seems similar, as Kirwen writes:

Over the more than twenty years that I have lived in Africa as a missionary, I have been deeply affected and changed by my African friends. I have not been 'converted' from my Christianity, but I have come to understand and live my religion differently and better through what I learned from them. Many of my African friends actually converted to Christianity; I would be ashamed if this had not also meant that they appreciated more fully their own African beliefs, so that they became better persons. (Kirwen, 15)

The book is a pedagogical tool: an introduction to a present-day prac-tice of missionizing in Africa. Kirwen converses with a diviner/witch doctor on such subjects as the idea of God, the source of evil, divination, remembrance or resurrection, etc. The dialogues are contexualized and favour an explicitly pluralist epistemology. They claim to follow 'the conversational style . . . [of] a Luo diviner from Nyambogo Village in North Mara, Tanzania' (Kirwen, 1988: XXV). But the whole thing is a montage: 'the diviner featured in the book is a composite figure', but 'the settings and scenes in the book are descriptions of actual places and events' and 'moreover, the conversations reported . . . are based on actual discussions; they are not contrived' (Kirwen, 1988: XXIV). On the other hand, let us note that the author insists on the peculiarity of his dialogical method:

(The) words, judgments, and observations (of the diviner) were drawn from live research sessions, which I – together with my students and African informants – conducted with a variety of African religious leaders over a ten-year period from 1974 to 1984.

The commentaries that I have appended to each chapter seek to delineate the important issues and dilemmas arising out of the conversations that are relevant to the Christians of the Western world. This kind of reflection represents a type of reverse mission in which traditional African theology challenges, judges, and enriches Western Christian theology.

(Kirwen, 1988: 24–5)

The book has been praised in Tanzania. 'Well-researched . . . recommended reading to any serious-minded pastoral agent, and to transcultural theologians', states Joseph T. Agbasiere from the Gaba Pastoral Institute. 'Kirwen has skillfully combined a deep knowledge of Christian theology, his many years of productive pastoral work in Tanzania, and a systematic and tireless search for empirical explanations to the complex co-existence between Christianity and African indigenous religions', adds B.A. Rwezaura of the University of Dar es Salaam.

One would tend to trust these specialists, despite the fact that the method used by Kirwen draws its strength from concordist techniques that seem to confuse the *documents* of revelation, the *vouloir dire* or message of gods given to two radically different traditions, and the *vouloir entendre,* or the perceived meaning that establishes the beliefs of Kirwen and his African interlocutors. The *montage*, at any rate, has produced an essay which is, in reality, fiction. It could have been moulded as well into a novel, and its credibility and force would not have been transformed. In fact, both the essay and the potential novel would be situated at the point where social and religious African beliefs and practices intersect with the poetic imagination and theological techniques of Michael Kirwen.

Paul de Meester's *Université et conscience chrétienne* (1991), modestly subtitled 'Pages from a Professor's Notebook', also testifies to a theology of inculturation in an original way. The book consists of quasi-autobiographical essays that develop as meditations on a variety of topics, such as the African university, education, ideologies, the study of classics, a trip to South Africa, the Virgin Mary and death, etc. All are under the umbrella of a challenging entry: the goodness of human beings and the suffering of the people. Paul de Meester, presently the Chairman of the Department of Classics at the University of Lubumbashi in Zaïre, is a Belgian Jesuit who has been living in Africa for more than thirty years, serving as pastoral agent and university professor. His book is simultaneously an endless production of an identity (African, Belgian, Jesuit and Christian) and a reflection on cultural, social, spiritual and textual corruptions, and the avatars of an intellectual activity in Mobutu's country. Autobiographical meditations can, as proved here, illuminate the heterogeneity of procedures and scandalous networks that can progressively deprive a human milieu of its motivations and hopes. Modest, unpretentious, de Meester's book perhaps mainly signifies a longing for a purity that is challenged every day by the mediocrity of some people and the bad faith of others. Here is a significant, and one of the strongest, pronouncements from the essays:

The needs of the poor have priority over those of the rich; the freedom of the weak has priority over the liberty of the powerful; the integration in the society of marginalized people has priority over the preservation of the order that excludes them.

(de Meester, 1991: 55)

Challenge and longing for purity are expressions that could also be used apropos of *Trapped in Apartheid* (1988) by Charles Villa-Vicencio, an associate professor of religious studies at the University of Cape Town, South Africa. Archbishop Desmond M. Tutu considers the book 'a devastating indictment of the so-called English-speaking anti-apartheid churches', and Allan A. Boesak's backing of the book is straightforward: 'This is more than just a very good book. It is a call to conversion.'

Trapped in Apartheid has two parts. The first part is a sociohistorical and theological study of English-speaking churches in South Africa; the second, a sociological and theological analysis that focuses on two themes: religion as domination and rebellion; and a liberating ecclesiology. The thesis (which, paradoxically, might also be seen as the conclusion) goes as follows:

> Concerned to preserve its place and influence in society, the dominant church has rationalized the demands of the gospel, heeding the demands of the rich and powerful rather than the cries of the poor and oppressed. Theologically compelled to show charity and given to dealing kindly with those who suffer most, the English-speaking churches have nevertheless refused to contradict the dominant social order or reject the legitimacy of the state; thus they find themselves trapped in apartheid.
>
> (Villa-Vicencio, 1988: 6)

In the first part, the author convincingly attempts to associate sociohistorical evidence of the churches' practices with the political and economic constraints that controlled them. Chapters 2 ('Imperialists and Missionaries') and 3 ('Gold, Politics, and the Churches'), for instance, address well the scandal of 'missionaries (who) were simply not able to distinguish between the message of the gospel and the cultural baggage of imperialism' (1988: 56). They problematized the contradictions of churches which, on the one hand, in the name of theology, condemn apartheid, and, on the other hand, did not 'attempt to consider an alternative economic or political program' (1988: 79). From this background, the two chapters of the second part forcefully argue for a conversion. They are both politically committed and 'prophetic'. The first brings together Karl Marx's critique of religion as a 'compensatory factor' and Max Weber's theory of religion as an option for a 'social renewal'. The hypothesis redescribes a classical proposition: theology cannot be dissociated from its social context and, thus, since 'ecclesial structures which are shared with the dominant classes, are also dominated by these classes, it follows that ideas and programs of action representative of the poor are invariably found in the margins and on the edges of church structures' (1988: 190). The second chapter, one of the most central in Villa-Vicencio's study, elaborates a liberating ecclesiology as a theological imperative, coming from a close reading of basic Christian texts. With competence, Villa-Vicencio rethinks and reformulates the 'mystery of God', 'the mission of Jesus', 'the power of the spirit', 'the worship of the Church'. He then concludes by invoking the 'memory of Jesus' ('who identified himself with sinners, publicans, prostitutes and rebels – marginalized people') and celebrating 'a Christ whose presence continues to be made known in those whom Matthew 25:31–46 defines as the least important people of society' (1988: 211).

'"Too little, too late" is not an inaccurate description of the role of churches in South Africa,' states the American theologian, Charles E. Curran, in *Transition* (53: 153). These studies in theology are indicative of a new era. We have come a long way from the theologies of conversion and salvation (whose objectives until the 1940s were still to destroy everything pagan in order to implement Christianity) to this new epoch. Cultural differences and voices that were distorted or silenced can now be seen or heard confronting the Bible. More importantly, it is the nature of the Church itself that is a question mark in such a climate of inheritance. One could think of Jung's curious statement: 'Christianity had come to stay (in Germany) because it fits in with the existing archetypal pattern. In the course of the centuries, however, it turned into something its founder might well have wondered at had he lived to see it; and the Christianity of Negroes and other dark-skinned converts is certainly an occasion for historical reflections' (Jung, 1980: 14).

III

The Practice of Misunderstanding

> Genealogy does not resemble the evolution of a
> species and does not map the destiny of a people.
> On the contrary, to follow the complex course of
> descent is to maintain passing events in their proper
> dispersion; it is to identify the accidents, the minute
> deviations – or conversely, the complete reversals
> – the errors, the false appraisals, and the faulty
> calculations which gave birth to those things that
> continue to exist and have value for us; it is to
> discover that truth or being does not lie at the
> root of what we know and what we are, but the
> exteriority of accidents.
>
> Michel Foucault

The 1950s and 1960s contest a past, and in anthropology, theology and
missiology there is a contrastive policy *vis-à-vis* the colonial policy and
its norms. Tempels' African disciples – Alexis Kagame and Vincent
Mulago, for example – illustrate well this reconversion of a symbolic
capital by rediscovering and arranging a silent treasure they claim to
translate.

Relativism and Retrodiction: Christian Ethnotheology

The whole project of ethnotheology is about the roots of a spiritual and
cultural knowledge and the control of its production. Whatever name
one chooses to label it (*Indigenism*, *Stepping Stones,* or *Incarnation
Approach*, etc., Kä Mana, 1992; Shorter, 1975), the main thing is
to clarify its aims, particularly from the general space that made it
possible. Strictly speaking, ethnotheology can be seen as a subfield

uncomfortably situated between theology and anthropology, opposed to reductionism and claiming to speak in the name of the vitality of local cultures. In this double movement, it faces its major paradox. As a resistance project, it takes place in the very space that it questions: Western anthropology, missiology and theology – that is, discourses already witnessing to specific cultural exotic geographies. Mulago's project, for example, is an 'Africanism', in which a cultural nationalism simultaneously challenges the politics of anthropology and their representations and legitimizes itself and its motives as a discourse from *inside*. It is also a *theology*, in which the same nationalism competes with, and wishes to transcend, missionary models and policies for the control and responsibility of acclimating Christianity in African cultures.

Theoretically, Mulago's project, as in *Un Visage africain du Christianisme* (1965), *La Religion traditionnelle des Bantu et leur vision du monde* (1973), or *Simbolismo religioso africano* (1979), can be summed up as follows: in the name of the truths of a locality or place, it questions the pertinence of colonial 'scientific' and 'religious' dominant discourses; insists on their shortcomings by reminding their practitioners that there is always a radical deviation between a lived experience (e.g. succession of seasons) or an experienced fact (e.g. death), and its possible multiple levels of interpretation presented as history, epic or simply narrative. Yet the project itself has recourse to the same controversial logical empiricism it wants to relativize. In fact, the invocation of the truths of the place against those of the interpretive space implies that there is somehow (almost necessarily) better reflections of the locality in the insider's discourse; and this hypothesis then becomes an ideological framework and a means for negotiating a right to the authentic speech in the field of discourses about the native place.

There the paradox is clear. The emergence of the ethnotheological project is grounded in a 'scientific' tradition that is external to the African 'place'. This is a 'space' of practice that has organized models and disciplines (e.g. Orientalism, Africanism), which 'suggest the re-edification of a zone of cultural difference through the ideologically motivated representation of otherness' (Herzfeld, 1987: 64). These spaces of discourses, faith and knowledges, comment upon the framework of practices, their theories as well as the economy of their geographies. They might claim to offer more or less good pictures of studied places, but not perfect, comprehensive and definitive renderings. Paul Veyne, in his evaluation of the practice of history, writes that 'the history of science will be that of the relations between the biography of a scientist, the techniques of his time, and the categories and problems limiting his field of vision at that time' (Veyne, 1984: 94). Moreover, the organization of normative discourses and their structuration are never divorced from the tensions functioning in the real 'place', which make them possible as intellectual or cultural signs, particularly from the influence of objective material conditions, the interaction between human freedom and chance, and the plurality of temporal lines and experiences.

That Kagame or Mulago may or may not be sound and credible students of functionalism or structuralism (in anthropology) and of missiology (in theology) seems a false problem. This fact was used in some missionary and anthropological circles in the 1960s to discredit a project which, as we have seen, comes from, and is intimately linked to, the very experience of both a rethinking of the Enlightenment and the promotion of an African nationalism. As a voice and a theorist of an alterity project, Kagame or Mulago should thus be evaluated on the basis of their discourse that claims to signify a negotiation between two main tasks: the first, on how to adapt critically the rules of the game in theology and ethnography to the 'native's' viewpoints and interests without falling in the empiricist's fallacy about a perfect coincidence of the *doxa* and the *episteme*; the second, on what the best strategies are for technically reconciling such competing theses as outsiders' models and insiders' paradigms and expectations.

Interestingly enough, we can compare this African Catholic task of adaptation and inculturation to another, the Islamic deconstruction of a traditional mission of conquering the world. The nineteenth century experienced intolerant politics of certainties carried on by missionaries, politicians and prophets. Al-Hjj Umar (1794–1864) forcefully applied his understanding of the *Jihâd* in West Africa, from Fûta Djallon to Fûta Toro, to establish a new 'great nation in its fidelity to the purity of Islamic doctrine'. In East Africa, in 1881, Muhammad Ahmad ibn

'Abd Allah made himself Mahdi or God's representative, people's guide, and in 1885 organized a theocratic power in Khartoum with the explicit aim of purifying the country according to the Islamic law. They reflected well their Christian counterparts, a Lavigerie or a Roelens, and their ambition to destroy paganism in the antithetical materiality of new kingdoms. To this divinely inspired mission, Islamist reformists in West Africa opposed, since the 1930s, the possibility of a different vocation. Against the classical style and its combatively intolerant policy, the faithful graduated from Al-Azhar in Caïro, Ben Badis in Tunisia, Qarawiyyin in Fez, and from within the community, as a clairvoyance coming out of the Koran, proposed a call to modernity: how can we reorganize Islamic schools in today's context? How and why should Islam be an African challenge and a response to modern cultures, and thus really present in the city, and not be perceived only as a far-away religious reference, accepted or tolerated for civility reasons, and reserved to a marginal group of practitioners? Since the 1920s and the 1930s, reformist institutions have been working in this sense. In 1937, Amadou Hampate Ba, a young reformist thinker, was invited to speak in the Dakar *Fraternité Musulmane* on the contemporary significance of the Faith (Ba, 1980). Since the 1960s, Mamadou Dia, a politician and theologian, has been exploring the Islamic heritage in its transmission through generations, balancing the tension between modernism and conservatism in terms of interpretive exegeses (1975), and invoking a socioanthropology of Islam that would respect and could fulfill both the Prophet's *parole* and the wellness of African cultures (1979, 1980). This reformist movement in Islam seems to face a predicament similar to that which confuses Christian theologians like Kagame or Mulago: how do we maintain a sacred revelation in its decisiveness while simultaneously confronting the modernity expressed by contemporary human and social sciences, and incarnating this complex mixture in concrete African cultures?

The task not only indicates a commitment to a projet but defines also the ambition of an intellectual and spiritual endeavour searching for the truth (Mulago, 1959) and expounding an allegorical metaphor about a society, that is, in Musil's expression, 'a state of mind in which everything takes on more meaning than it honestly ought to have' (see Veyne, 1984: 119). This is a very ordinary ambition. What is interesting in Mulago's intellectual project, for example, resides in the double or triple dimension (African, Africanist and Catholic theologian) that accounts for the ambiguity of his discourse and its possible contradictions. It traces its origins back to local spaces of interpretation (and thus to esoteric cadres of knowledge in precapitalist societies), yet its arguments and rationality organize themselves as a renewed economy within the space reified by missionary and anthropological knowledges. It claims to unveil the uncontaminated fundamentals and proprieties of regional localities, yet it is not in their own specificities, nor in the experience of their traditions and the intentional acts of past explicit actors, but rather from their possible grasp, understanding and sublimation by Christianity. In its paradoxical aim, the project leads to what we can perceive as a relativistic approach. In fact, it comments on the failure of 'traditional intellectuals', and transcends ancient canons using the authority of new forms of consciousnesses, and then negates its own move by sorting out and spatializing the shortcomings of this negation. As noted by Zygmund Bauman, 'the relativist attitude is . . . a kind of "negation of negation"; first one tries to criticize historical form of consciousness in the light of an a-historical standard of truth, and then one concludes rightly or wrongly, that the endeavor is futile and, consequently, the "emic" (rather that "etic") approach, the approach from "indigenous categories", is the only way in which various forms of knowledge could be judged' (Bauman, 1978: 103). Zygmund Bauman commented on K. Mannheim's work:

Now each society has a group of people who specialize in answering, for the society, all sorts of questions related to the interpretation of the ways of life in which the society is engaged – 'to provide an interpretation of the world for that society'. Mannheim calls this group the 'intelligentsia'. In a stable society, the intelligentsia is stable, with well-defined and rule-governed status. In a caste society, the intelligentsia is itself a caste. The new intelligentsia, however, is as unstable and as un-caste-like as our modern society. Again we learn that 'decisive fact of modern times is that 'in place of a closed and thoroughly organized stratum of intellectuals, a free intelligentsia has arisen.' (1978: 102)

To clarify the issue, let us contextualize the intellectual discontinuity represented here by situating it in its own history. Students of African theology insist on three main trends: (a) salvation theology, (b) adaptation theology, and (c) incarnation or inculturation theology (Tshibangu, 1987; Kä Mana, 1992). The first, *salvation theology*, traditional and classical, is an inextricable part of the very fabric of historical Christianity and assures itself on a major dogmatic argument: *Extra Ecclesiam Nulla Salus* (there is no salvation whatsoever outside of its historical experience). Accordingly, paganism had to be the negative side of Christianity and its practices transformed by Christian revelation as actualized by the religious and cultural experience of Christendom. The fusion of Christianity and Western civilization inscribes itself in a theory of history and thus reflects on both their genesis and destiny as providential. As such, they indicate the sole way to normal human evolution and religious fulfilment. Depending on circumstances, pagan experiences are reduced to a *tabula rasa* or to tables of devilish aberrations. It follows that, as an activity, missionizing parallels colonization in the programme of civilizing and promoting non-Western cultures. The German Münster School of missiology, well-known for its foundational arguments, implies two interwoven operations to Christianize: a negative one, capturing differences and destroying them at the advantage of universal similitudes; and a positive one, generating a new culture, a perfect image, of the Christian West by implanting the Church faithfully in all its demands in terms of doctrine, structures, rituals and traditions.

Following Benedict XV's *Maximum Illud* (1919), one observes a new trend in African Catholicism. The papal encyclical posits itself as an *incipit*, the beginning of a new philosophy of converting. If, in an orthodox manner, it still emphasizes the incorruptibility of Christianity in its message and subsequently the absolute necessity for its meticulous transmission to pagans, it now pays attention to what could be known as *stepping stones* of Christianity. It had become clear that it was possible to pinpoint, describe and integrate indigenous values in the new Christian culture and, more importantly, to associate natives fully to the implementation of the Church, contrary to *salvation theology* which, out of Europe, saw nothing good. This *adaptation theology* – as, for instance, thematized by Pierre Charles

(1939) in the 1920s and 1930s – found some of its best expressions in *Bantu Philosophy* by Placide Tempels and, on the Protestant side, on *Bantu Prophets in South Africa* (1948) by Bengt Sundkler, and *The Primal Vision: Christian Presence and African Religion* (1963) by J.V. Taylor. With this new angle, Christianity stretches one of its basic paradigms by extending intrinsic values to all cultures expecting a Christian redemption. A new intellectual arrangement lends itself to such comprehension and accommodates old Patristic maxims, as, for example, Tertullianus' *anima naturaliter christiana* (any soul is naturally Christian); Cyprianus's statement on prayer, *publica est nobis et communis oratio* (our prayer is collective and general). In the same movement, the new perspective revises traditional policies for conversion, renovating ancient stipulations by Saint Gregory in his letter to Augustine: In order to convert the Anglo-Saxons, Gregory advised using real customs, ceremonies, and places of pagan sacrifices and only progressively transforming them into Christian loci for the celebration of the true God. Another major reference is the 1659 official 'Instruction' of the *Sacra Congregatio de Propaganda Fide*, which demands respect for indigenous traditions. Finally, a surreptitious element gradually unfolded in this new configuration: the hypothesis of a universal primitive revelation discreetly worked out by the Vienna School of Anthropology under the direction of P.W. Schmidt (1933–49) made possible some varying theses on adjacencies and equivalencies of religious systems, the fundamentally identical meaning of a primal religious light, and the universality in time and space of the idea of God and that of salvation.

Before such a theological acceleration, which in Catholicism ulti-mately led to the 1970s propositions for theologies of incarnation, one noted two complementary occurrences: an inversion of arguments that used to decline the logical interdependence of colonization and Christianization; and, absolutely provocative, the emergence of a new theological space. In the name of the same eternal truths that justified a political and cultural alienation as a *sine qua non* condition of conversion to Christianity, this space now suggested the concept of difference in the multiplicity of its concrete variations as loci of God's revelation. In 1951, when Pius XII's *Evangeli Praecones*

(1951) stabilized a policy already expressed by Pius XI in *Rerum Ecclesiae* (1926), the adaptation approach theologians quasi unanimously looked for ways of reconciling local stepping stones with the *Traditio Christiana*. In short, with these very original motivations, they were now competing with anthropologists, exploring African traditional institutions, customs and myths and, in their own practice, reconceiving sacred art, liturgical vestments, and ritual music as well as the architecture and style of churches. This was the period during which Kagame's and Mulago's research blossomed. They accommodated the historicity of Christianity with the freshness of pagan networks now reorganized in a new rationality, qualifying itself as *praeparatio evangelica* (preparing its own fulfilment in the Christian gospel). In the good intentions of the enterprise, one could already see the potential for another critical step: why posit the local religious experience in a subservient relation to the Western experience of Christianity? Inculturation theology, in the 1970s, interrogated the native locus as a sign and symbol of the Christian revelation itself against Mulago's thesis of adaptation.

Understood from this historical background, the intelligentsia represented by Kagame and Mulago could only face their mission as a reversal of colonial practice. With a spirit of consequence, it chose to rewrite history and to reconceptualize cultural and religious beginnings.

In both moments of negation, as illustrated by Kagame and Mulago, as well as by most ethnotheological disciples of Placide Tempels, retrodiction seems to be the main technique that establishes both the new right to speech (and the power of spatializing indigenous localities) and the intellectual efficiency of its interpretation). Retrodiction – from Latin *retro* (on the back side, behind, in time back) and *dicere* (to speak) – denotes the idea of speaking (and thus synthesizing) from an illusory, invented moment back in time. In the process, the present invests its values in the past with its questions and hypotheses, and rediscovers in the invented, reorganized spaces, laws, paradigms, or the truth of its suppositions. Indeed, the new creation is often in contradiction with the colonial adapted Enlightenment paradigms and its library.

The foundation of 'retrodiction' can thus be seen; it is not the supposed
constancy with which effect follows cause, nor is it the foundation of induction,
the regularity of natural phenomena. Rather, it is something very empirical;
there are customs, conventions, types in history. Here is a recumbent Roman;
why did he recline? If men behaved capriciously and were only caprices, the
number of possible answers would be indefinite and it would be impossible
to 'retrodict' the right one. But men have manners and more or less conform
to them; in that way the number of possible causes to which one can trace
backward is limited. Things might not be so, men might ignore every custom
and live only by strokes of genius and strokes of madness, history might be
made only of hapax legomena. Then 'retrodiction' would become impossible,
but the irregularity of laws would exist no less and the epistemological edifice
would not thereby be modified by one iota.

(Veyne, 1984: 152)

Thus, the colonial library, in its content as well as in its significance,
generalizes a conceptual rule, a historical paradigm, and a political
project. An imaginary relation, worked by travellers' narratives since
the beginning of European expansion overseas at the end of the fifteenth
century, finally stabilizes itself with the scramble for Africa in the
nineteenth century and claims to make explicit and scientific the links
that Europe can have with all its others. The normative human being
is incarnated by the European as ecstatic transcendence. It follows that
the colonial library will articulate and illustrate two manifestations: on
the one hand, a judgment establishing the recognition of European
sovereignty not by positing it against its own historicity, but as
unveiled by a difference situated somewhere beyond or besides it.
On the other hand, such a desire of historical triumph (which should
be reduced to the banality of the Lacanian 'desire of recognition', that
is, the terror of facing one's nothingness) could and did demand a
mission already elaborated in the very history of the Natural Law
that theologically and philosophically established the right to colonize
all *terras nullius*. Thus, logically, the library cannot but document a
political responsibility. Indeed, the library presents the 'universality'
actualized by the European cultural and political saga as the only project
for all other cultural 'singularities'; and thus colonization institutes itself
as an imperative service contributing to the promotion of the greater
glory of humankind.

In the same way, colonial Christianity knew what it negated. Through retrodiction it classified procedures and significances of local celebrations of divine beings, the cult of ancestors, and numerous rituals of birth, initiation, death, etc. Directly or indirectly, the library thus constituted allowed concrete policies for conversion and assimilation. In the colonializing and missionizing practices, the self-evidence of the enterprise could only suscitate interrogations about more efficient methods of fulfilling the promise of the Gospels. The questioning came, indeed, from within the programme itself. Hulstaert (1980) and Tempels (1944) are just two names to which we might refer, with Kagame, Mulago and their disciples as their successors. The debate that unites and at the same time separates them is about values and techniques of retrodiction and useful interpretation. So, after Veyne, we can say that:

Historical experience is composed of all that a historian can learn in his life, his reading and those with whom he associates. So it is not astonishing that there are no two historians or two clinicians with the same experience, and that endless quarrels are not rare at the sick man's beside. This is not to forget the naive who think they are working wonders by using techniques in tandem, labeled sociology, religious phenomenology, and so on, as if the sciences in question were deduced from heaven, as if they were not inductive, as if they were not history under a scarcely more general aspect, as if they were not, in a word, the experiences of others that the historian will certainly use for his own profit if he knows how not to let himself be put off by falsely strange labels. That is why the naive who do not forbid themselves access to that experience, under the pretext that sociology is not history, are in fact the really clever ones, and those who make fun of them are only half clever. Historical experience is the familiar knowledge of all the generalities and regularities of history, in whatever wrapping it is fashionable to present them.

(Veyne, 1984: 156)

Historical experience and retrodiction may be seen in some recent books on African philosophy and their wonderful theoretical wrappings. The real issue is intriguing: how can we inscribe a past and the difference of its traditions in both the validity and the respectability of a philosophical discourse?

The books under review address the same problem – the foundation and meaning of African philosophy – and all of them were designed to be contributions to an ongoing debate on what African philosophy is or should be. Their common message could be summed up in a perfect existentialist argument: African philosophy is what it is not and it is not what it is. Let us use an analogy. In his analysis of bad and sincere faith, Sartre notes about a homosexual that he 'struggles with all his strength against the crushing view that his mistakes (sic) constitute for him a *destiny*. He does not wish to let himself be considered as a thing. He has an obscure but strong feeling that a homosexual is not a homosexual as this table is a table.' Is he wrong? (Sartre, 1966: 107–8). The homosexual plays at being what he/she is not in order to be what she or he is, exactly as more and more African philosophers seem to state: 'I am not a philosopher' in the sense of 'I am not what I am', which implies another proposition, 'I am what I am not'.

That is the issue and it has been with us for a number of years. Back in the 1940s, some European scholars, such as Tempels and Griaule, opposed the idea that was accepted for a long time: there is no such thing as African philosophy. Their African disciples rapidly ran into the demands of the discipline. Fortunately, it is now 'out of the closet' that a new generation of philosophers is struggling on how to unite contextual authenticity to the perspectives of a multi-secular thinking practice, that is, philosophy.

The purpose of A. Ndaw's *La Pensée africaine* (1983), a byproduct of his doctoral dissertation at La Sorbonne, is, as he tells us, 'déchiffrer l'expérience humaine concrète telle qu'elle est vécue dans l'Afrique traditionnelle' (1983: 46) [to decipher the concrete human experience as it is lived in traditional Africa]. In pursuance of this objective, the author insists on three stages for a rigorous practice of philosophy: first, philosophical *reprise* of symbolic language; second, hermeneutics as means for a good understanding of symbolic meaning and, finally, philosophizing as a bet on the significance of the symbolic and reflexive world in Ricoeur's sense: 'je parie que mon pari me sera rendu en puissance de réflexion dans l'élément du discours rationnel.' The book strictly addresses only the first stage in a grandiose challenge. An affirmation, says Ndaw, of an Africanity rejecting the Western philosophical tradition is not the best way towards an authentic philosophy; on the other hand, there is the necessity for an African context as a frame for philosophizing. As Ndaw puts it, 'La question qui se pose est de savoir comment en entrant dans la mouvance de la modernité, la pensée Africaine traditionnelle peut apporter sa conceptualité propre' (1983: 42) [the real question would thus be how African traditional thought can bring about its own conceptuality now that we are entering into modernity]. The discussion falls into two main parts. The first (chapter 1) concerns a general description of forms of knowledge (*savoirs*) and their definition – that is, mythical thought, divination, and the values embodied in relationships between initiation and knowledge (*connaissance*), thought and mysticism, ethics and spirituality. The second part provides a more in-depth analysis of these various *savoirs*. It successively focuses on the knowledge of the world (chapter 2), the knowledge of the human being (chapter 3), the knowledge of society (chapter 4), the knowledge of God (chapter 5). In two concluding chapters, Ndaw first reviews the question of a 'Negro-African ontology' as hypothesized by Tempels and Kagame, and then comments on methodological problems in African philosophy, emphasizing the usefulness of joining with anthropology, linguistics and psychology as auxiliary disciplines.

A rapid look at Ndaw's book may lead the reader to label it 'ethnophilosophy'. The author himself allows this possibility when he plainly – but in a provocative way – states that his enterprise stems from the 'ethnophilosophical' tradition (1983: 41). He is right, yet his work is ethnophilosophical with a major difference. The subtitle of the book – A Search for a Foundation of the Negro-African Thought – is a sign of both its modesty and ambition. In contrast to most of his predecessors, Ndaw deals with the major question of a *reprise* of the symbolic language. Why is the *savoir* of myths hidden? How do we read it and on which basis do we interpret a conception of the human in divination? What are the functions of speech and language? Where do we inscribe the discontinuity between signifier and signified, conscious and unconscious? A parallel but discreet re-reading of philosophers and anthropologists leads Ndaw to agree with Claude Lévi-Strauss on the importance of symbols (1983: 122), to hint at a collective philosophical configuration which is not quite explicit (1983: 205 and 234) and to ask triumphantly: 'Il y a une pluralité de sens dans la notion de force. Il reste à se demander si le concept de force peut jouer le même rôle que le concept d'être' (1983: 248) [there is a plurality of meaning in the notion of force. Yet should we not ask whether the concept of force could play the same role as that of being]. The question offered, Ndaw chooses to contribute to the foundation of a *philosophie de l'être*. While the overall effort is really stimulating, certain weaknesses should be noted. The book does not live up to its 1983 publication date in terms of anthropological references (cfr. bibliography 272–81). Second, the return of the notion of animism and its celebration (226–8) is a bit perturbing. Third, the manipulation of such concepts as *métaphysique sous-jacente, savoir, connaissance* does not always seem convincing, and one admires how L.S. Senghor has succeeded in correcting such flaws in his preface to the book. Finally, Ndaw's argumentation is sometimes quite irritating by its use of authority references. 'Bastide, Cazeneuve, Griaule have demonstrated that . . .' 'Lévi-Strauss, Bastide, Leenhardt, Zahan have proved that' (e.g. 84 and 121) are just two types of axes frequently used by Ndaw when he faces difficult problems. These criticisms notwithstanding, this is a good book. It remains close to its subject, it is well written and organized, and Ndaw's French is an intellectual pleasure to which one surrenders with admiration.

Assane Sylla's *La Philosophie morale des Wolofs* (1978) offers a controversial example of what ethnophilosophy can do in terms of retrodiction. It is an interpretive survey of Wolof's *Weltanschauung* that sums up dreams of lost intellectual palaces and paradises. It draws its information from various sources (history, anthropology, linguistics, etc.) in order to describe 'l'unité intégrative de la pensée Wolof, découvrir les caractéristiques essentielles, l'orientation ou les préoccupations majeures de cette pensée' (1978: 18), that is 'to apprehend the integrative unity of Wolof thought, to discover its essential characteristics, as well as its orientation and major preoccupations.' Sylla does not break new ground in his analysis, but rather attempts, through a sophisticated reading of a culture (i.e. religion, art, language, education, political institutions, etc.) a comprehensive synthesis of Wolof thought. His major methodological key is Gusdorf's grid of human evolution, which he challenges.

The French philosopher distinguished three steps: (1) the instinctual,

(2) the passage from instinct to myth during which humans establish the basis of a culture, and (3) the critical age that permits the replacement of mythical thinking by philosophy. Relying on a selective but highly subtle body of interpretations of both the Western tradition (e.g. Greek philosophers, J.J. Rousseau, R. Le Senne) and the Wolof experience as documented by Maurice Delafosse, Georges Hardy and others, Sylla insists on the complementarity of phase two (the mythical) and three (the philosophical) and, in a quite brilliant manner, elaborates on the still ongoing combination in the West between 'les mythes romanesques' and 'l'élucidation de la condition humaine'. Thus, he can analogically assess a 'Wolof philosophy' that through the centuries has been determined by six principal factors: the permanent contact of a human milieu with the outside world since the tenth century; the existence in the culture of 'techniques suffisantes de survie'; the fact of a strong social cohesion which, as in the case of Damels (Cayor region) or Bourba (Djolof), goes back to the fourth century; the reality of a complex language and system of education; and, finally, the experience of difficult sociopolitical historical mutations.

How does one summarize the Wolof philosophy? The author answers:

Philosophie de l'homme, la pensée wolof repose sur des options précises et convergentes: prendre conscience de la dignité de l'homme, du respect qu'on lui doit, le connaître, l'éduquer en conséquence, guérir l'homme par l'homme, l'attacher à la société sans l'asservir, le conduire à des niveaux de perfection morale de plus en plus élevés, le rendre propre et suffisamment apte à gravir les degrés de la spiritualité qui conduisent au tout puissant Dieu qui lui tend les bras.

(1978: 200)

Nevertheless, I do not see why we should not call this a *Weltanschauung*, and Sylla's book could have been entitled *Introduction à la culture Wolof* or *Morale et culture des Wolofs*. At any rate, it is a passionate, perhaps too passionate, description of Wolof past and modernity.

Amady Aly Dieng's *Contribution à l'étude des problèmes philosophiques en Afrique noire* (1983) is also a passionate survey of the ongoing debate on African philosophy and its demands. According to the author, 'le débat sur les problèmes philosophiques est en train de s'élargir pour prendre des dimensions socio-politiques' (1983: 9) [a debate which is now enlarging itself to the point of including socio-political dimensions]. A Marxist and an admirer of Sheik Anta Diop, Dieng centres his discussion around the themes of historical origins of philosophy, Krumah's views and contribution, and the contradictions of African interpretations of Marxism. The overly detailed presentation of the history of the concept of African philosophy is a curious mixture in which one wanders from a poor description of the genesis of the concept to a complacent critique of Sheik Anta Diop and a gratuitous celebration of Marxism–Leninism. The tone is often one of intellectual guerrilla warfare, as illustrated by the following statement from the conclusion: 'les marxistes révolutionnaires doivent se liguer pour chasser cette faune qui empêche le matérialisme de vivre et de se développer' (1983: 172) ['revolutionary Marxists must unite in order to expel the fauna preventing the life and development of materialism']. Hastily written, full of typographical errors, and poorly organized, this is, without question, an unsuccessful book.

Hegel, Marx, Engels et les problèmes de l'Afrique noire (1978), by the same author, is more solid. It is a miscellany of texts that Dieng used for his teaching at the University of Dakar in 1975. The volume is a concise interpretation of Marxist perspectives that a number of Africanists could take into account. Its purpose is double: to describe the Marxist thinking about Africa and delineate the missions of African Marxists. It is divided into two parts. The first comprises three chapters: (1) Marxism and problems of Black Africa, (2) Hegel and Black Africa, (3) Marx and Black Africa. Part two includes seven chapters: (4) The nineteenth century, Marx and Africa, (5) Civilizations and historical materialism, (6) *Négritude* and civilization, (7) Philosophy and Africanisms, (8) Missions of the new generation of philosophers, (9) Mathematics and *Négritude*, (10) Social classes in Senegal.

Although somewhat flawed by an excessive pro-marxist bias, this collection ranks among the most interesting studies of this type by an African scholar. Dieng has consulted a vast array of literature and strongly marshals his evidence. For example, Hegel is an 'Européocentriste forcené' (1973: 46). Marx did not really challenge

Hegel's perspectives about Africa, but rather, in a historical manner, established 'une relation entre le développement de l'esprit et le développement de la production des échanges' (1973: 52) ['somehow reconciled historically the development of spirit with that of the production of exchanges'], thanks to which it becomes possible to think of Africa's destiny within the general framework of European history. The catch is, however, on the one hand, Dieng's investment in a critical Marxism which, according to him, is the sole condition of maturity for African social sciences and philosophy and, on the other hand, his discreet celebration of Sheik Anta Diop throughout the book.

If someone with no knowledge of African ideologies asked me for a brief introduction to the present-day debates, I would probably recommend Dieng's book, particularly his amazing short chapter on 'Négritude and Mathematics' (1973: 131–44). It reflects well our ideological contradictions and vividly illustrates the tensions between universalism and particularism, intellectual demands and myths of otherness. This book is excessive, nervous and rapid, yet one would agree that it is an obsessive pleading for a critical reflection in Africa and, at the same time, a desperate inscription on mythology as well as on the history of the theatrical power of reason.

Pathé Diagne's *L'Europhilosophie face à la pensée africaine* (1981) will disappoint readers who expect a systematic study. The longest part of the book (pp. 13–98) is a detailed report of the 1978 Cotonou meeting of the Inter-African Association of Philosophy. Diagne opposes ethnophilosophy to Euro-philosophy. The latter, according to him, is characterized by its willingness to depend on the Western tradition and institutions. Euro-philosophers, writes Diagne, are 'perroquets savants' and their discipline has no future.

L'Europhilosophie est piégée par l'académisme universitaire. Elle est condamnée à la spéculation abstraite à défaut de se préciser un domaine et un objet propre et original.

(1981: 33)

[Europhilosophy is a trap of university academism. It is condemned to abstract speculation since it lacks and cannot specify its own original object.]

Sarcastic, Diagne rejects both the neocentrist Euro-philosophy, as represented by Franz Crahay, and the critical Marxist Euro-philosophy symbolized by Paulin Hountondji and other African disciples of Althusser. They are wrong, states Diagne, in the same way Tempels and his disciples were wrong, because they 'déportent la problématique du fait africain ou négro-africain aussi loin sinon encore plus loin de ses axes que l'ethnophilosophie elle-même' (1981: 83) [the are wrong for transferring the problematic of the African or the Negro-African factum as far away, and even further than the practitioners of ethnophilosophy]. They are also wrong, adds Diagne, because in their linking of the genesis of African philosophy to alphabetic revolution in Africa, they are presenting a political thesis: African philosophy is conceived as the consequence of colonization that brought about alphabetic writing and thus let us celebrate colonialism, thanks to which African philosophizing has become possible.

One does not understand why Diagne uses disguised or direct insults in order to make his points. On the other hand, it seems to me that his apparently well-evidenced generalizations are not philosophically obvious. The concepts of Africa, Negro-African, for example, are not transparent, particularly when the author claims to extend them as far back as the pharaonic periods. In the same vein, to postulate – from the pharaonic Egypt to Edward Blyden, Ogotemmeli, Anta Diop, Chinua Achebe, Senghor, etc. – the continuous epistemological history of a Negro-African cultural context is surely a nice hypothesis, but it is untested and probably untestable.

Diagne is more serious in his propositions for an African philo-sophical *praxis*. With a few neat strokes, he indicates the theoretical conditions for philosophizing: a *dëgg* (argumentation) in which a *texxale* (critical reflection) should be promoted distinguishing valid and non-valid propositions (*woor ag sanxal*) in order to construct a *xelaat* (epistemology).

So far there has been nothing quite like this in the confrontation between philosophy and African *Weltanschauungen*. The very fact that in his innovative 'book two' – strangely entitled *Epistemology and Neo-pharaonic Problematics* (1981: 129–219) – Diagne's constant use of Wolof categories is a tour de force, may make the translation of texts by Plato, Althusser, Tempels, Crahay, Kagame, Mulago, Diop, Césaire, Senghor, Ndaw, Towa and Hountondji seem a simple curiosity. This takes on a radical meaning when, in his conclusion (1981: 213–19), Diagne puts aside French as mediation and synthesizes his philosophical theses directly in Wolof.

The issues expressed and called upon by these books represent a new intellectual configuration. We are in the post 1960s period. The independence myths as absolute resources and virtues have lost their glamour but not the subtle logic of a right to otherness. If the social and human sciences, subdued by new epistemologies (i.e. *structuralism* and then *post-structuralism*), were raising their methodologies to new levels of relativism and knocking down registers of such master concepts as history, humanism, the subject, the self, etc. – they were also reactualizing the mission of philosophy and its practices in an extremely exacting fashion. In fact, enshrouding the *here lies something* in its own right (a thing, an event, an idea) immediately invites a rigorous thinking at the heart of the *something*, its existence, appropriation, finitude and how to conceptualize and qualify this exposed finite-thing in its own always possible infinite exposure. Interestingly, it is a preoccupation and an anxiety about this issue that we can observe, during this period, in some of the most stimulating African practices of philosophy. Briefly, three features dominate: a suspension and bracketing of anti-colonial discursive practices as a preliminary condition for an opening towards alterity; a radical suspicion of the Tempelsian notion of an implicit and subterranean ontology of vital force expounded and generalized by Kagame and Mulago; a reformulation of the philosophical task – indeed, the theological, also – as perpetual recommencement and search for the supplement to what is supposedly *there* in the *some-thing*.

The articulation of these philosophical, as well as theological, practices no longer goes through the antiracist racism signified by *Négritude* or other essences. Even when doubling the famous paradigm of *Négritude* – reason is Greek and emotion Negro – it proceeds to a reversed essentialism by postulating a distribution of creativity and reducing, as did the 1985 Kinshasa symposium, Europeans to speculative rationalism, Americans to pragmatism, and Africans to a spiritualist realism. New trends (in their practices), annul even obligations towards

the false transparency of confused notions, such as race, tradition, or
philosophy understood as *Weltanschauung*. In philosophy as well as
in theology, the work presents itself now as a question, a comment,
and an approach to a solution. This work is an explicit, systematic,
critical and autocritical reflection on a particular in its temporal and
spatial incommensurability facing, in the juridical sense, what in method
and theory is given as disciplinary exigencies. As examples, we may
cite the following three: the popular *Foi chrétienne, crise africaine et
reconstruction de l'Afrique* (1992) by Kä Mana, a Zaïrean minister
serving as the pastor of the protestant international parish in Dakar,
Senegal, analyses contemporary Negro-African theological movements
and, from a new reading of the Bible and a diagnosis of today's
ethical mutations, suggests a theology for an African reconstruction. A
highly similar enterprise, *Eglises d'Afrique: propositions pour l'avenir*
(1984) by Efoé-Julien Pénoukou, a theologian from Benin teaching
at the Catholic Institute in Abidjan, elaborates on theoretical conditions for reconceiving and promoting Christianity and its mission as
faithfulness to its evangelic genesis and service to concrete human
beings. Finally, we should note the masterful theological manifesto
of Bishop Tshibangu, *La Théologie africaine* (1987), which dwells
on theology as a discipline, its practices in Africa, and disputes on
the meaning of the adjective 'African' that would qualify the practice.
Significantly, the author introduces this treatise by presenting excerpts
from a letter he received in 1965 from the renowned French theologian,
Henri de Lubac:

It is through works of theology and nothing more [des travaux de 'théologie tout
court'] conducted without caring for producing African more than European,
or French, or Belgian, that . . . as I wish for, a theology will constitute itself,
and in which one will discern afterwards African trends, qualities, intellectual
manners. This will come almost by itself, thanks to good workers like you. Thus
in the unity of Faith, we shall have an organized, pluralist concord of theologies
and a more harmonious apprehension of revelation.

(Tshibangu, 1987: 5)

De Lubac's intervention specifies a scholastics' principle – 'action
comes before thought' – and, simultaneously, insists on a preliminary:

theology as a discipline is, for its practitioners, an absolute scientific project despite its relative actualizations, and this dimension should impose itself as an inescapable principle.

These three illustrations are submitted to an ascetic reflection, in which thinking is nothing but the perception that it has of itself when it thinks about something (theology, Africa, the Gospel, or otherness), describes, or represents it. Gone are now anticolonialist, ritualistic recriminations; gone also, at least in these cases, are the facile and beautiful generalizations on African religions, whose main merit resided in their antiprimitivist stances; gone, finally, are the imprudent prescriptions romanticizing African cultures through retrodiction.

The rigour of this new aptitude reveals itself magnificently in the philosophical practice. In the brief presentation of some recent books, I have already painted various shades and nuances that could be perceived from, say, Tempels to Pathé-Diagne. In my opinion, the clearest and strongest milestone in the field remains Paulin Hountondji's *African Philosophy, Myth and Reality* (1983).

There is no doubt that J.E. Wiredu's *Philosophy and African Culture* (1980) would represent a compromise of great lucidity between the easy generosity of ethnophilosophy saturating the operas of its retrodicted readings and, on the other side, the excessively pedagogical vigilance of Paulin Hountondji's lesson of philosophy. Polemical, well reasoned, and conscious of its own discursive elegance and philosophical orthodoxy, Hountondji's essay often exceeds its own critique by transmuting a bit too easily and too often illegitimate practices of philosophy into philosophical monstrosities. The book is divided into two main parts, totalling eight chapters, all of which have been previously published in French or African philosophical journals. The first part comprises four theoretical articles dealing with the significance and the status of philosophy in Africa: 'An alienated literature' (1969), 'History of a myth' (1974), 'African philosophy, myth and reality' (1973), and 'Philosophy and its revolution' (1973). The second part, entitled 'Analyses', presents four case studies: 'An African philosopher in the eighteenth century: Anton-Wilhelm Amo' (1970), 'The end of "Nkrumaism" and the (re)birth of Nkrumah' (1973), 'The idea of philosophy in Nkrumah's consciencism' (1973), and 'True and false pluralism' (1973). The central argument of the essay is that up to now African philosophy has been a myth based on a confusion: 'the confusion between the popular (ideological) use and the strict (theoretical) use of the word "philosophy"' (1983: 47). Initiated by Tempels' *Bantu Philosophy*, the myth would have been continued and expanded by Vincent Mulago, Alexis Kagame and all the African disciples of Placide Tempels. 'Each and every African philosopher,' writes Hountondji, 'now feels duty-bound to reconstruct the thought of this forefathers, the collective *Weltanschauung* of his people. To do so, he feels obliged to make himself an ethnological expert on African custom' (1983: 52). According to Hountondji, this is both wrong and philosophically unhealthy. He thinks that even though some of the African philosophers claim to distinguish intuitive from critical philosophy (e.g. Kagame), and material from formal philosophy (e.g. Mulago), these distinctions seem to be just theoretical assumptions preceding concrete analyses. Thus, the philosophical undertakings are simply ideological in 'trying to define, to codify a supposedly given, ready constituted thought.'

On the other hand, Hountondji believes that African philosophy, if it exists, should be understood in a very precise sense as 'a set of texts, specifically the set of texts written by Africans and described as philosophical by their authors themselves.' From this viewpoint, Hountondji argues that Mulago, Kagame, and others are certainly philosophers insofar as they claim that their own texts are philosophical, but they are wrong when they pretend to restore an African traditional philosophy. He writes, 'we have produced a radically new definition of African philosophy, the criterion being the geographical origin of the authors rather than an alleged specificity of content. The effect of this is to broaden the narrow horizon which has hitherto been imposed on African philosophy and to treat it, as now conceived, as a methodical inquiry with the same universal aims as those of any other philosophy in the world' (1983: 66).

Hountondji's critique is directed principally towards an anthropological tradition. It displays the superiority of a critical and autocritical conception of philosophy. A disciple of Canguilhen and Althusser, Hountondji looks at African philosophical practices from a very specialized viewpoint. The confusion between the vulgar and the strict understanding of philosophy that he emphasizes is a good point that the Belgian philosopher Franz Crahay had already drawn attention to in a notorious article (1965). Hountondji's conception of philosophy clearly implies the controversial thesis that, up to now, Africa has not been philosophizing and that in her past there is nothing that might reasonably be called philosophical. On the other hand, it is important to note that for Hountondji, philosophy must be understood as metaphilosophy, that is, as 'a philosophical reflection on discourse which (is itself) overtly and consciously philosophical.' According to this choice, one may say, for example, that the pre-Socratics are not philosophers and one could even doubt the philosophical character of most of Kant's or Gabriel Marcel's works.

Hountondji's book, as already noted, is polemical. Moreover, its epistemological foundation is very French. His thesis makes tremendous sense when referring to Althusser's doctrine as to what philosophy is and to Canguilhem's advocacy of the universal promotion of science. The range of problems prompted by this book might fill a far larger volume than the book itself, but the book is worthwhile. As a radical alternative to Placide Tempels' philosophical school, it was, and still is, a challenging and valuable contribution to the debate on African philosophy. At the same time, this brilliant and stimulating text witnesses to the distinctive spirit of the Ecole Normale Supérieure of the Rue d'Ulm in Paris, where Hountondji was educated, and as such represents one of the best illustrations of *métissage*, a topic on which we shall focus in the last chapter.

Strictly speaking, all these narratives by knowledgeable intellectuals are part of a history of philosophy in the making. They stimulate ongoing research about African experiences, provide vivid sketches of the field, its techniques of retrodiction, integration and exclusion, and thus inscribe themselves as moments in the history of the African practice of philosophy. Paradoxically, through their ambivalence, diversities, promises or original drives towards a rigorous meditation on *some-thing*, they offer the plausibility of the subject they comment upon. The question of an African philosophy is now clear. It no longer has anything to do with the fallacy of an implicit philosophy but concerns the conscious and critical activity of philosophizing in Africa. It does not define itself outside of the discipline but within the constraints of a *texxale* even when, in the name of a possibly new *xelaat*, African philosophers object to the fascination of the discipline, its nightmares and, obviously, its multisecular mythologies too.

Pedagogical Experiment: Joseph Guffens (1895–1973)

At least in Catholicism, the liberation of difference illustrated by ethnotheology and philosophy has a history. It should be illuminated by lessons and experiments that in the 1930s took seriously the ambiguous teachings from the Vatican for an adaptation of Christianity. *Maximum Illud* by Benedict XV, issued on November 30, 1919, exemplifies this order. One of its major tenets is, indeed, the education of a body of native clerics. The argument is strategic: Christianity will become African if it is taught by Africans to Africans. The project had already been partially actualized in East Central Africa by Bishop Roelens. This innovation, if it is one, resides in the Roman pontiff's official commitment. In 1922, Father Ledokowski, General of Jesuits, enforced the pontifical wish by ordering his Central African Jesuits to open up immediately a minor seminary at Lemfu. This motion, at this particular moment, has more than a simple symbolic value for the politics of conversion. I have elsewhere (1988) and in some of the chapters here noted the epistemological mutation that takes place in human and social sciences during this period. Missiology and its practices belong to the domain of social sciences, as does anthropology and its offshoot, applied anthropology, that during this very period begins to constitute itself as a field. Without questioning the veracity of the colonial library, these disciplines begin to exercise an immanent critique, distinguishing illusions and preconceptions from experience and reason. But, let us note that earlier on, generally in the second part of the nineteenth century, protestant missionary churches underwent the efficacy of adaptation programmes, including in dogmatic standards (e.g. Raison-Jourde, 1991; Salvaing, 1994; Zorn, 1993).

Joseph Guffens, a Belgian Jesuit in Kikwit, Belgian Congo, remembers that in the mid-1930s he was approached by a young boy who told him that he wanted to become 'a religious brother', but not in the Order of the 'Christian Brothers' who then were in charge of a local school. The youth wished to be a teacher and a brother, but not a priest. Later on, Guffens would comment on this encounter, saying that this was 'a sign' of what became his vocation: the institution of a local congregation of Catholic brothers, the *Kifrère*, specialized in teaching their own people. The new congregation was canonically constituted on 2 September 1937, at Kinzambi and at that time had some fifteen candidates. Some thirty years later, recollecting this beginning, Guffens, then retired and living in Brussels, Belgium, could not forget the reactions of his fellow Jesuit priests: 'We need (normal) teachers, they (some Jesuits) take away the (native) children for the seminary, and now comes the *Kifrère*. How many will be left to become teachers?' (Kiangu, 1992: 45).

Three main issues should be dissociated. The first, in Guffens' memory, is what seems to be a fact for him: a new intellectual hierarchy that goes without discussion (the seminary, the *Kifrère*, and the school for lay teachers) and its impact on the conversion of the African space. The second is an implicit debate about priorities that comes from the reaction of other Jesuits to the institution of the *Kifrère*: what should be its agenda? Indeed, when one keeps in mind the basics of the Belgian policy, it is the level of teachers' education that should come first, since it would ultimately upgrade the whole country in a progressive cultural conversion. The implications of this ordering are important and they bring about a third problem: the real significance of the conversion. This is, in fact, very clearly recognized or negated in the mission and the significance of the teacher in the implicit primacy. It signifies something else. The master in primary schools makes a major difference since, in the long term, he does work on the focus for the transformation of both the symbolic and the imaginary of an entire population. The children he faces every day have a perception of the real and the symbolic marked by the tradition of their parents and equally the capacity of a new world. In the Lacanian sense, the Christian master is the adult in power, *the Master*, who, despite the fact that 'the imaginary is there, (yet) completely inaccessible to us' (Lacan, 1988: 219), can influence it. On an everyday basis, he determines how, from the child's experience of a tension between two sets of symbolic and real paradigms (the ancient, incarnated by the family), and the new (actualized by the school), to 'select' the sense in which to specialize and diversify the imaginary of one's identity as well as the symbolic dimensions in a culture and human vocation. In this process, the priest is – in terms of influence and the everyday life of the child – at the extreme order of the teacher: a white 'prince' saying mass on Sundays, richly vested and speaking in an incomprehensible language. When the priest meets the child, it is once a week in the obscured anonymity of a confessional where the penitent cannot always distinguish Father A from Father B.

Why the *Kifrère*, this strange locus promoting a new mentality and a form of desire completely different from those of the priestly and lay Christian? Throughout the years, Guffens faced the question and tried to respond. This is a synthesis of the most important problems (Kiangu, 1992: 49–54). (1) Why the congregation? He thinks that on the one hand 'classical religious institutions are not any longer sufficient because of their rules conceived in and for older times'; and, on the other hand, 'lay people have their families, interests and mentalities even when they are practicing Catholics.' (2) Why should this congregation specialize in teaching and not in contemplation nor in blue collar professions? Guffens notes an urgency in the 1930s: the usefulness of 'a cadre of Christian teachers', and he adds that the climate then was not ready for contemplatives, nor blue collar or religious people. (3) Why a non-clerical congregation? The response seems political: 'The modern teacher should be educated as a professional and such an education demands time. A double education (of a teacher–cleric) would be longer at this moment of the history of Congo where the work of the priest *as such* or that of the teacher *in its own right* are *very* urgent, *very* important.' (4) Yet, one might insist, why establish a new congregation when the candidates can join existing orders or the seminary? Guffens distinguishes two types of arguments: the first, strictly spiritual, is simply, why not?, since, as he puts it, 'the Spirit blows as it wishes'; the second, more empirical, is also a question: 'How do we respond to young people who explicitly want to become brothers, not in the Society of Jesus, nor in the Order of Brothers of Charity?'

When the *Kifrère* was canonically established in 1937 by Rome,

Joseph Guffens was 42 years old, a mature man. The idea had come to him two or three years earlier following a conversation with a boy to whom he had promised to consider the possibility of such an enterprise. Later, an older Guffens would admit that, indeed, 'without doubt, I had entertained the idea of educating brothers some day, but it is that boy who set off the mechanism' (Kiangu, 1992: 45). That conversation or accident triggered a silent project. What Guffens understood was his own desire to conceive and organize a simple institution which, in its originality, would translate into a project he had already envisioned. His decision to create the *Kifrère*, in its arguments, is remarkable insofar as it brings together an empathetic understanding of a cultural milieu and its needs for transformation and, on the other hand, a causal explanation and justification established from a religious perspective. A well-educated Jesuit, Joseph Guffens knew what he was doing. From this viewpoint, one may begin to perceive the patience and fidelity of an old man who, humiliated and sent back to his country of origin, remained faithful, until his death in 1973, to the ultimate goal of a vocation he had invented for Africans: the appropriation of both a capacity of textual interpretation in Christianity and its transfer to the practice of a well-determined teaching profession.

A will to truth and power marks the *Kifrère*. However, one might note two things. First, it is not fundamentally different from that invested in other local congregations for 'natives' in which, to use Michel de Certeau's expression, 'ecclesial election is turned into a Western privilege' (1988: 217); nor does it radically distinguish itself from thousands of second- and third-rate institutions educating future lay teachers. The difference, and this is the second point, resides in a pedagogical philosophy and a political vision: on the one hand, one finds the promotion of an elite made to incarnate, simply, the values of a Christian conversion by internalizing the colonial hierarchy. In Joseph Guffens' dream, on the other hand, it is possible to see the promotion of a charisma and the constitution of a group that can potentially function with competence and, when necessary, challenge the inconsistencies of the general economy of the Church's and the colony's paradigmatic distinctions. 'Why,' asked Guffens rhetorically, 'a well educated and capable brother should be (seen) as more inferior to the priest than the

MD, the engineer, the lawyer, the merchant, the industrialist, or the army officer? The priest has a power that the lay person, practising or not, does not have. But does the priest have the professional knowledge and power of the doctor, judge, engineer?' (Kiangu, 1992: 53).

The Rules of Election

The genius of Joseph Guffens was to conceive a new cadre in which the priestly could coincide with the professional, each losing some of its particular characteristics, the secular dimension for the professional and the priestly dimension for the sacerdotal. Under watchful and expert eyes, a new desire – that is, a *manque-à-être*, became possible and unveiled itself in the quotidian. As Lacan noted, 'desire, a function central to all human experience, is the desire for nothing nameable. And at the same time this desire lies at the very variety of animation' (1988: 233). Indeed, as we know, the emancipation of desire brings with it a promise of fulfilment and very specific caveats concerning forbidden *jouissances*.

The general context in which Joseph Guffens' action takes place is simultaneously very simple and somehow complex. In fact, before 1940, three main systems of education existed in the Belgian Congo: an official system under the control of the Catholic Church and regulated by a 1906 convention between the Holy See and the Congo Free State; a second system, qualified as free system but recognized and subsidized by the colonial government; and, finally, a non-subsidized free system of schools generally organized and staffed by Protestant churches. As a concrete example, Guffens' *Kifrère* (as well as the seminaries) would fit into category two, whereas all other schools (e.g. primary and secondary directed by the Catholic clergy) were defined as official and thus functioned under the umbrella of category one. Briefly, the only way to get an education was to convert to Christianity, preferably to Catholicism.

The education programme for 'natives' (Liesenborhs, 1940; Litt, 1970) is comprised of three cycles that are theoretical insofar as the scarcity of schools and the rules of selection reduce the whole complex project to the first cycle for the majority of the Belgian Congo population. There is first the primary cycle, divided into two sections: the elementary lasting two years, the second section lasting four years. In 1940, if almost all significant geographical centres had the first section of the primary cycle, only seven complete primary cycles existed for the whole country and were all based in the principal cities. The second cycle, known as the 'post-primary', is a three- or four-year programme, and its designation means what its strange expression qualifies: the 'summit' education, which had three main orientations. The first was a professional one, training boys in specialized workings (carpenters, joiners, blacksmiths, etc.); and for girls there were fifteen schools that, from today's perspective, would qualify very generously as teaching home economics. The second orientation, *l'Ecole moyenne*, used to prepare candidates for 'inferior positions of clerk in the (colonial) administration and the private sector' (Liesenborghs, 1940); and, finally, the teachers' schools or *l'Ecole normale*. In 1938, there were thirty-two such schools, which produced students who taught in primary schools and served as role models in their lives, concretely symbolizing a cultural and spiritual conversion for the whole indigenous population. To these three main structures of the official educational system one should add the particular case of the nineteen minor seminaries, which then existed. Non-subsidized by the colonial government and completely autonomous from the political power, they delivered the best education to the few elected who were being prepared for the major seminaries and priesthood. Before 1940, the third (the last and highest) cycle included two very different types of education: on the one hand, two four-year programmes (one in Léopoldville and another in Kisantu) educated medical doctor assistants (*Assistants médicaux*) and, on the other hand, the four major seminaries which prepared candidates to priesthood in six or seven years of training.

Karl Marx suggested that instead of asking, 'who should be emancipated?' the question should be, 'what kind of emancipation is involved?' (1967: 7). The reference was to the Jewish question and its similarity to the African context is striking. The emancipation project was rigidly formulated in this colonial, highly elaborated grid of acculturation for a few chosen ones. Through this investment, it was expected that well-calculated policies of acting on society at large should transform a culture and its people. There is more than simple social engineering manifesting itself in such programmes. One might think that through the complicated and very serious educational games inaugurated by the civilizing father, a cultural infantilization imposes itself and, in the best cases, produces new instinctual impulses in the being of the acculturated. Correctly coached, despite the trauma implied by the process of such a transformation, any normal child in good psychological health would be, in principle, capable of going beyond the traumatic experience and somehow justify Freud's remarkable phrase: 'No experience could have a pathogenic effect unless it appeared intolerable to the subject's ego and gave rise to efforts at defense' (Freud VIII: 276).

The emancipation promised by education means two complementary things: a discrete policy for forgetting that the African past seems determined in the objective of acquiring the character of rationality and universality incarnated by the school and the Christian religion. In the specific case of any child going through such a system, indeed the project is obvious: he may suspect that in the long run he will only be an auxiliary in the new social order that would not discourage him from achieving the goals imposed upon him. Should he not do so, what would be the alternative? Thus, the educational system efficiently produces a local elite that accepts the incarnation of the new values of both civilization and Christianity, which represent – in the Hegelian sense – the fundamental principle of both reality and history, that is, the true and absolute. Indeed, the poor African is alienated, but it is education that, in the first place, cuts him off from his customs and past, thus marking the actuality of a colonial consciousness in its most beautiful reproduction. As a matter of fact, one can now begin to understand the originality of Joseph Guffens' prophetism. He knew of the rationale of the colonial integrative system, particularly the cultural stability and orderliness it was supposed to reproduce by promoting two characters: the 'native' teacher, on the one hand, the 'indigenous' cleric, on the other. Yet he opened up the possibility of new questions by defining the efficiency of a new type of witness of professional competence, not completely dependent upon the simplistic interpretation of a natural law as the colonial authority still postulated.

Unfortunately, if such a commitment was original, it was not really revolutionary. Since the beginning of the century, throughout the continent, protestant missions had been more daring in promoting local talents. Their evangelical zeal was matched only by a sophisticated entrepreneurial audacity in their ways of connecting the cultural frontiers they were facing to their own self-imposed mission (e.g. Raison-Jourde, 1991; Salvaing, 1994; Zorn, 1993). Even in Catholicism, Guffens was not the only one who explored new avenues toward indigenous maturity. In the 1920s, other fellow Jesuits of Guffens had already challenged the hierarchical and racial division of the colonial and missionary ideology. In 1926, at Louvain, Pierre Charles was preaching of the day an indigenous clergy would succeed a White clergy (Charles, 1939: 92–9). During the same period, with the financial backing of Louvain University, Jesuits in the Congo began to think about and experiment with ways of creating an indigenous medical and agricultural elite, elaborating plans that ultimately would lead to the foundation of the Lovanium University in 1954 (see Litt, 1970). All these significant initiatives meant the possibility of moving from an education of values – that is, the promotion of consciousness submitted to a simple illustration of colonial and Christian values to the bringing out of a new type of consciousness: acculturated but capable of functioning in the civil society as well as in the Church on the basis of merits, competence and cultural integration.

In any event, Jesuits in Central Africa, although imaginative, were not politically subversive. They were working in the sense for a 'Christian' Enlightenment, vulgarizing a spirit, affirming its necessity, and working against odds. More accurately, they were intellectually sensitive to the 'signs' of their time. However, as already mentioned, the explicitation of the new logic for interpreting 'native' cultures will come from elsewhere: *Bantu Philosophy*, published in 1944 by the Franciscan, Placide Tempels, who was living in the southeast of the country. In his ambition, contrary to what has been said – mainly by people who have not read him carefully – Tempels did not oppose the colonial project. On the contrary, chapter 7 of his book, entitled 'Bantu Philosophy and

We, the Civilisators', expounds concrete modalities for making both the colonization and Christianization of Bantu people successful.

The break with the older mentality was not made at a brisk pace. The elitist organization of the colonial third cycle of education had sent more or less well-educated minds back to public and ordinary life, most of them bitterly frustrated by the rejection. Quite normally, they joined the ranks of 'évolués' produced by the *écoles normales* and *écoles moyennes*. In the 1940s, the super-exploitative experience of the 'war effort' on the masses touched this new elite that was capable of reflecting on the governance practices of the colonial power. In the same fashion and despite the existing censorship, this elite, produced by the system in order to actualize values, knew the major crisis that Western civilization was then experiencing. They had been directly or indirectly exposed to issues concerning the critiques of reason and the celebration of intuition (Bergson), the importance of the unconsciousness (Freud), the critique of capitalism (Marx), the rethinking of history (Bloch), and, indeed, heterodox interpretations of African civilizations by Edward Blyden, Leo Frobenius and William DuBois. There was also *Négritude's* dubious essentialism about the radical alterity of the Negro and its philosophical amplification made by Jean-Paul Sartre in *Black Orpheus* (1948). The entire colonial ideology, 'the inestimable treasure' that had been nourishing the elite's mind and behaviour was questioned. Tempels' type of 'philosophizing' became exemplary. Did it not somehow keep up with a search for authenticity? In the polemical book *Des Prêtres noirs s'interrogent* (1957), Tempels' voice and the concept of *Négritude* made a new representation audible and were accepted as the best way of conceiving African culture and its potentialities.

At that specific moment, a number of questions had already become very urgent. Was the intelligentsia still educated for values? Was it not shifting towards a competitive status with colonials, and thus witnessing to unforeseen consequences of acculturation or even something worse? Jean-Louis Litt, who asks the questions (1970: 181), makes them more explicit by noting two things: one should discern the original culture of the new elite, more precisely, the proportion of those who come from partially or totally acculturated families; and, furthermore, one should study the influence that the local cultures could still exert on this acculturated elite (1970: 181) in order to evaluate correctly its ideological restlessness.

Briefly, the *evolué*, this new product, seems to antagonize the premisses of the whole colonizing project. As Martinkus Zemp puts it: 'The White finds himself in an impossible predicament: he wants black people to stay with other Blacks, he came to Africa to bring to them Civilization, Religion, to educate and "humanize" them. That is the *raison d'être* of colonization, this colonization that deep in himself the White does not want to see achieved since it will imply the integration of Blacks into the white society. In effect, the theoretical position of the White is one thing, his inmost conviction another. From its very premisses, colonization was condemned to fail' (in Salvaing, 1994: 28). What should we do with such a vigorous and imprudent pronouncement? I would suggest that we conclude the issue of retrodiction in its intellectual representations; and then, abandoning preconceived theories and implicit constructions, we redirect the question of the being of the *evolué* by gripping two concrete existential cases: Jean Ishaku, teacher, pastor, and martyr and Alexis Kagame, priest and scholar (1912–1981).

As we have seen, by the 1950s retrodiction was already a paradigm. Let me synthesize this apparent closure. In West Africa, Sheik Anta Diop had applied retrodiction in his research (1954). In Central Africa, Alexis Kagame, following the steps of Tempels, had localized a 'Bantu Rwandaise' philosophy (1954), and Mulago, with his doctoral thesis in 1955, on the concept of vital union in the East Congo, imposed it on theology. The US based Belgian historian, Jan Vansina, who began his career in the Congo, gave his scientific support to the retrodiction process with his *De la tradition orale: essai de méthode historique* (1961). The reversal thus seems radical. Africans can read, interpret and reorganize traces of their own past in order to sum up the spirit of their own history or constitute the signs and modes of a religious revelation. The scientific norms of missiology have now been completely returned. At the same time, the political paradigms of the right to colonize were being questioned by nationalisms. But why should we separate the two currents? The best symbol of their proximity might still be Placide Tempels, the Belgian Franciscan. A new version of his ambiguous

Bantu Philosophy was published in 1949 by *Présence Africaine*, the Parisian 'cultural review of the Negro world', militant in the cause of both African autonomy and Black difference.

Jean Ishaku, Teacher and Martyr (1930–1964)

In the following brief story of an intellectual and religious *métis*, I present, first, excerpts from Lamar Williamson's biography (1992) of Ishaku and my own commentaries afterwards.

INCIDENT IN LUSAMBO

I knew a man in Africa.

His name was Ishaku Jean (the French form of John, pronounced [like the s in pleasure] followed by *on* without the *n*). He came from Lusambo, a sleepy riverboat port on the Sankuru and former capital of the Kasai Province in the colonial days of the Belgian Congo, now the Republic of Zaïre.

I first met Ishaku in September 1957. He was one of four students in the first-year class of the Theological School operated by the American Presbyterian Congo Mission at Kakinda, a mission station just five kilometers from the Shaba border near the railroad linking Lubumbushi (Elisabethville) to Ilebo (Port Franqui) in the Kasai. I arrived to teach in this school the year Ishaku entered it. Instruction was in French, enrollment was limited to graduates of the Normal School, and at the time it was the highest level of training offered to Protestant ministers in the Congo.

When Ishaku and I met, we both sensed that our work together was important, for we were nearing the end of the colonial era in Africa.

Neither of us suspected how soon that end would come in the Congo.

On Independence Day, June 30, 1960, Ishaku and his family were in Kaniama, a town some thirty or forty kilometers southeast of Kakinda in Shaba. He had spent six months of internship there as assistant pastor under the supervision of a missionary professor in the Theological School. In those days of excitement, irrational hopes and impossible dreams, Ishaku proved to be a stabilizing influence. Firmly committed to independence, he had rare insight into the responsibilities it would bring. He did his pastoral work thoroughly and well, with a sort of unflappable quietness that contrasted sharply with his environment.

During July, Ishaku and I both packed up and moved according to previously arranged schedules: he with his family to complete his theological courses at Bolenge near Mbandaka (Coquihatville) on the Zaire (Congo) river, and I with my family to return to the United States for our first home assignment. We all missed the trains we had planned to take because early in July the National Army, unpaid by the new government, had revolted. In the ensuing chaos trains ran erratically or not at all. Whites fled in panic, a smouldering ethnic war burst into the open in the Kasai, and both Shaba and the East Kasai seceded from the new-born nation.

Despite all this, Ishaku and part of his family managed to reach Bolenge, where he graduated from Theological School in June, 1961. I heard that he turned down offers of lucrative government jobs and a prestigious post with the Presbyterian Church in order to return to his own church, the Brethren, at Lusambo.

When, with my family, I returned to Zaire in the fall of 1962 to teach at the United Theological School near Kananga (Luluabourg), Ishaku was immersed in his work with schools and churches in the region around Lusambo. He wrote occasionally and sometimes, when he was in Kananga on school business, he would ride a bicycle the five kilometres out to Ndesha to visit with his friends, both students and professors, in the Theological School. His warm open face, his deeply concerned reports about his work, and his sincere friendship made these visits special treats for us all.

By 1964, disillusionment about independence ran deep. The Shaba and East Kasai secessions had been put down by United Nations intervention, but the populace was impoverished and discontented with the weak, unstable government of Cyrille Adoula in Kinshasa (Leopoldville). In these circumstances the revolutionary movement of a man named Mulele gained national prominence.

Beginning in December 1963, violence erupted in Mulele's home region of Bandundu (Kwilu). This effort to overthrow the government of Prime Minister Adoula quickly found strong support among disaffected political leaders elsewhere in the country. Although Mulele's personal following was largely limited to two tribes in Bandundu, revolutionaries throughout the country were called Mulelists or, from June, 1964 onward, 'Simbas'. The latter term belongs properly to partisans in the Popular Army of Liberation, backed by the Eastern bloc and China in particular, who used the Swahili word for lion, *simba*, as their password.

In May, rebel forces won stunning victories over the National Army in the eastern areas of Kivu and northern Shaba. Like scattered sparks, revolutionary forces erupted in the Maniema, Upper Zaire, and throughout the north and east of the nation as well as in the west-central region of Bandundu (Kwilu Province). By the end of June, they controlled more than half of the land area of the entire country and several of the regional capitals. The Adoula government resigned on Independence Day, June 30, 1964. President Kasavubu called upon Moise Tshombe, the exiled leader of the Shaba secession, to rally his Katanga gendarmes and mercenaries to save the nation.

While Tshombe organized his government and marshaled his military resources, the rebel strength continued to grow. By the end of July, Simbas were pushing west and south from Kindu in the Maniema in a drive on Kananga in the Kasai, hoping to cut the rail line, capture the strong military installations there and link up with Mulelists in the Bandundu Region. Lusambo, some two hundred kilometers northeast of Kananga, was an important stage in this advance. It fell to the rebels early in August 1964, as the National Army withdrew without firing a shot.

The Simbas secured and looted the town of Lusambo and then, in a few days, crossed the Sankuru and moved on Dimbelenge and Kananga. On August 21 at a bend in the road fifty-two kilometers south of Lusambo, near a place called Musungu Mwana, they ran headlong into a column of Tshombe's Katangan troops now integrated into the National Army. The encounter was a total surprise to both forces, and each opened fire on the other. The army troops stood their ground, but when the Simbas discovered that they were not impervious to bullets, as both they and the National Army had believed, they fled in panic. By the time troops moved up in force on September 1, the Simbas, like the National Army before them, had abandoned Lusambo without a fight.

During those uncertain days in August, the American Presbyterian Congo Mission was in annual session at Kananga. We were aware of our imminent danger, and our wives and children had suitcases packed for evacuation if the Simbas continued to advance past Dimbelenge. We also knew that missionary colleagues of the Westcott Mission were still in Lusambo, and when last we heard, Ishaku Jean and his family were still with them. We dispatched pilots Don Watt and Garland Goodrum to make daily reconnaissance flights over Lusambo, first to try to bring the missionaries out and then, after the Simbas had moved in, just to keep an eye on the rebels and to watch for any signals we might get from the missionaries (Williamson, 1992: 11–14).

These questions have haunted me for years. I tried to get such answers as I could in September 1964 from those who shared the ordeal with Ishaku. I encouraged one of Ishaku's fellow students, Pastor Kabeya Paul, to write a biography. My wife and I maintained a cordial friendship with Ishaku's wife and children until we left the Congo in 1966. Back to lead a missionary family retreat and a Theological School seminar in 1969, I made my first trip to Lusambo to visit Ishaku's grave. I interviewed all the eyewitnesses of his death that I could find, and many of his close friends. In 1973, my family and I returned to Zaire for a year to teach in the National University at Kisangani.

There were several reasons for doing so, but Ishaku was for me one of the most important. During that year I interviewed others who had known him, and I completed the first draft of this manuscript. His memory was still warm and strong in 1986 when

I taught for four months at Ndesha, West Kasai, in the theological school whose first years Ishaku and I had shared. I told his story one Sunday in the chapel where his memorial service was held in 1964, preaching on John 15:13, 'No one has greater love than this, to lay down one's life for one's friend.'

Faithful onto Death

The insurgents' concern about aircraft from Kananga was well founded. On several occasions since their occupation of Lusambo a National Army T-6 (single engine, two place training) had flown reconnaissance missions over Lusambo and fired on the town. Later an A-26 light bomber would attack the city. Don Watt had also flown the Presbyterian Cessna 185 over Dibatai once on Wednesday, shortly after the rebel occupation, in an effort to discover if the missionaries were still there. After that first inconclusive reconnaissance flight, the Presbyterians had stayed away from Dibatai for fear of reprisals on the Downses and Miss Flett – until Sunday. The Presbyterian Mission was in its annual meeting in Kananga, following with keen concern the advance of the Mulelist force. Rumors in the city were rife, and many Europeans were on the verge of panic. Leaders of the Mission decided on Sunday to make another reconnaissance flight to calm unfounded fears and to ascertain the actual situation. The whole Mission needed to make responsible decisions about the work of the Mission and the safety of its personnel. All were anxious about colleagues of the Westcott Mission in Dibatai. Garland Goodrum piloted the Cessna this time, with William C. (Bill) Washburn riding beside him. On the seat behind them were James H.E. (Jim) Wilson of the Westcott (Brethren) Mission and the Belgian consul who had only recently arrived in Zaire. Washburn had been born at Mutoto and knew the region well. He was in charge of the Presbyterian system of subsidized schools through which Ishaku had obtained subsidies for the Brethren schools also. Washburn describes the flight: We flew the road to Lusambo, with a side detour over Dimbelenge where everything was normal. In the years of turmoil in the '60s we had discovered a number of ways to size up a situation from the air. The most obvious and easiest to see from a plane was the *tshiombe* (manioc root) drying on the racks in the village. We would fly a thousand feet high, out of danger. If we could see the white *tshiombe* on the racks, all was quiet in the village and people were going about their daily activities. If there was no *tshiombe* it was obvious that the people had fled to the forest taking what they could. Everything was calm all the way. About ten kilometers from Lusambo we saw the first signs of panic. Sure enough, when we arrived at the ferry crossing, we saw the rebels crossing the Sankuru in force. We flew high over the city and made a low pass over Dibatai station, dropping a note. We came back flying at about two hundred feet altitude along the river bank headed downstream. Jim Wilson saw Norman Downs step out on the porch briefly and go back inside the house. About that time I saw a group of rebels running from the main road toward the station.

One of them, who was already at the river bank, pointed his rifle at the plane and fired. I saw the puff of smoke. I told Garland, 'Let's get the hell out of here. They're shooting!' We left. Later we learned that shortly afterward Ishaku was killed. Our flight had provoked the final incident. From the air the situation appeared dangerous. From the ground, the danger was palpable and, for Ishaku, mortal. These differing degrees of danger can be felt in the accounts of the two eyewitnesses closest to it.

Downs' Diary
Sunday, August 16.
Later in the afternoon, another visit from the plane brought the usual angry crowd of armed Mulelists. They demanded from Ishaku the keys of the Moyes' house, the only one they had not so far searched. Ishaku had only the key to part of the house, but they soon broke into the remainder of the rooms. I felt a little anxious, and walked out a little from our house.

There was a terrific yell, and one of them came out of the house flourishing a Belgian flag. The car drove off, and shortly returned with a number of high-ranking Mulelists, one of whom called himself the Major. He sent for me, and I was hustled along to where

Ishaku already was. Flora followed to see what was happening. They lectured us on the enormity of being associates of the Americans, on having a Belgian flag – there was also a Union Jack – and asking when the Congo became independent. If I was a Christian, so was he, the Major. Was he not baptized? We were evildoers. I tried to tell him that I was new to Lusambo, but he said the little paper on which I had jotted down the brief periods which we had spent at Lusambo was all lies. They made us, that is, Ishaku and myself, kneel down, and knocked us about with their rifles, and struck us with a truncheon. They then told Flora to say goodbye to me and to go away. No sooner she reached the house than they shot Ishaku and killed him instantly. They then told me to go. I went to tell Flora what had happened, and to say a word of comfort to Tshiela and the children. We could not stay long, and went back to the house. A little later the 'Major' came to the house with all the rest of the group, armed, and asked me what I was now thinking. When I said I was very sad at what had happened, he said a second time that a man who could regret the death of a 'traitor' deserved to die also. So once again Flora was bidden to say a long farewell, and once again they were restrained from firing. We were told to go into the house and wait until someone came. After a while, one of the group came and said they required 50,000 francs, which I handed over. Then we heard the car being driven away, and we were left alone.

Tshiela also remembered the appearance of the Presbyterian Mission plane over Dibatai as the occasion that precipitated Ishaku's death. Her account, however, lays greater stress on the matter of the house key, and on Ishaku's sense of responsibility for the safety of the man he had invited to come and help him.

The airplane circled the mission once; while it was making its second circle, the pickup of the rebels arrived. I stopped in front of Mr. Moyes' house. They found there an old man who had run away across the river but had come back. They asked him, 'Are you the sentry?'

They said, 'Where are the keys to the house?'

He said, 'I don't know anything about the keys.'

They grabbed this old man and took him to Mr. Downs and told him, 'Get they keys to this house and come with us.'

He (Downs) said, 'I don't have the key; go ask Pastor Ishaku.'

They came hurrying toward us and Ishaku said, 'Look. Something's up now.'

I came out of the house and looked and I saw the Mulelists coming quickly with guns – two people. Now when they arrived, they said to him, 'Come quick with the keys, come!'

And he (Ishaku) said to him, 'All right, I only have one key to that house, to the kitchen door. He left the other with his houseboy to put his clothes and things inside because he used to buy clothing in Kinshasa and bring things here to sell.'

They grabbed him and rushed him away.

I followed them, and a Mulelist said, 'Woman, if you follow us, I'll hit you with my gun.'

Ishaku said, 'Naomi, go back to the house and look after the children.' So I went back to the house and they took him up to Mr. Moyes' place.

Well, they didn't open the door with the key. The broke out a window pane with a gun butt and entered the house. They went upstairs and there they found some shells (cartridges of shotgun shells) wrapped up in a light handkerchief, and a Belgian flag. They took these things and threw them down on the ground and said to him: 'Look, you are a pastor. Why did you allow this white man to keep these shells to fight against us? And this Belgian flag which shows he does not accept our independence?'

He (Ishaku) said, 'No, I didn't know he had these things in the house. It's not my house; how was I to know what things might be in it?'

At this point of my interview with Tshiela on August 25, 1969, the tape recorder ran out of tape. Hasty but copious notes provide the substance of the following account of Ishaku's death. They sat Ishaku down in a chair on the veranda. Two of the Mulelists went to get the commandant and two stayed to guard him. At about 2:30 pm, Tshiela left her house, found Ishaku on the veranda, and asked him what had happened. About then a large number of Simbas came back in a truck, a VW, a car stolen from the priests, and a pickup. The Simbas had a taboo about women. Tshiela and her older sister, whose husband was a river boat captain, went to the guest house to hide. Mrs. Downs told Tshiela that maybe the Mulelists would let Ishaku go. Tshiela said, 'No, this is it.' Then they stood Ishaku up and went to get Mr. Downs. They roughed up both of them, made them kneel, get up, turn around. Then they told Mr. Downs to get up and go home. They told Ishaku that if he'd let them kill the white man, they'd let him go. They beat him with their rifle butts. They spoke Lingala, Swahili and Otetela. They accused Ishaku of harboring this man who refused Congo her independence. Ishaku said he didn't know what Moyes had in his house. But he refused to tell them to kill Mr. Downs, refused to buy his life at the cost of another person. They beat him severely about the head and back. He had Mr. Moyes' keys on his fingers – or rather in his pocket. One of the Mulelists fired at two meters' distance. The ball caught Ishaku in his left shoulder near the neck and knocked him down. One of them ran a bayonet through his head above the left eye, and another person fired a second shot through his forehead. Then the Mulelists left. They took a lot of sheets and cushions and other things from Mr. Moyes' house. The women and Mr. Downs and all the others came to Ishaku's body crying. Pastor Makelela warned them not to cry. The Simbas threatened them for crying. Tshiela begged the Simbas to let them bury Ishaku and cried to them about the five children. A rebel said that if Ishaku had answered their question, he would not have died. They allowed the women to keep food for the five children, also to bury Ishaku. When they lifted his body to move him to the veranda, his breath came out like a sigh.

(Williamson, 1992: 101–3)

Williamson, recalling a past that is not really one, in 1991 is writing about an encounter with a student that took place some thirty-four years earlier, in 1957. He was then the professor, theologian and initiator, and Jean one of the few chosen to study under him. Between the two dates, 'something' happened, an accident in the etymological sense of the word, latin: *accidens* (from *accido*, 'to fall upon' or 'down upon a thing', 'to reach it by falling'). This 'something', a death as a matter of fact, is not in itself the accident, since it symbolizes much more than the casual event that the word signifies. In actuality, it is the *sign* that makes Williamson's recollection an event: the former professor and initiator remembers now a *man*, instead of the student who, in the late 1950s, was one of the four registered at the Theological School of Kakinda mission. Williamson gives a premonitory value to their meeting: 'We both sensed that our work together was important.' The equality implied here might be seen as a first step in the process of archetyping Jean in this short *biography* that seems to belong to the *hagiographic* genre.

Let us be prudent and define our concepts. A biography is a written account of another person's life; a hagiography the writing and critical presentation or study of the life of a saint.

Williamson's narrative begins by a statement: 'I knew a man in Africa.' In the end, the same narrative expands into a comparison that allows us to qualify it as hagiographic: 'One thing is sure: I knew a man in Africa. He reminds me of a Man from Galilee.' Clearly, the story is about a model that reminds of another one, the original, a wonderchild, a remarkable example, an exceptional man, a saint – 'that is, a person of real virtue, holiness and benevolence' – in brief, an 'archetype' that is, to use Jung's language, 'an image belonging to the whole human race and not merely to the individual' (1980: 161).

The context in which Jean finishes his education is one of violence: the 1960s Belgian Congo crisis or the collapse of a State and its apparatuses. Hell might be a possible figuration. First, the Presbyterian spaces at Kakinda, then the Bolenge and Lusambo areas are presented as matrixes for Jean's activities. In fact, we have passed straightforwardly from educational years into his professional life without a break. The rupture from his family, his progression into manhood, and his marriage belong to a different register. Williamson depicts a strong character far away from initiatory trials and ordeals. The postulant pastor has transformed himself almost without problems into a mature and responsible adult amid ruins and disorder.

Depending on the political orientation of the analyst, the rebel forces or *Simbas* are usually presented as bands of bandits, rebellious and superstitious peasants, or as patriots who, after the death of Lumumba, fought for the 'second' independence. Benoît Verhaegen, a Belgian political scientist who studied extensively the rebellions of the 1960s Congo, emphasizes the second image (1966, 1969), which contrasts with the picture coming from Williamson's description. Yet, this picture should not be dismissed. Far from nerve centres controlled more or less rigorously by revolutionary leaders – in Kwilu for instance – the discipline of *Simbas* was not exemplary, and more significantly, no better than that of the National Army.

Simba is a theriomorphic symbol. That the fighters of the second independence would have chosen a lion as a comprehensive sign of their will is telling and also paradoxical. In fact, above all animals the lion indicates well a will to conquest and self-protection. Yet, such a symbol, in the particular case of the second independence partisans, was perfectly curious, the lion being an official Belgian emblem.

Zaïrean Presbyterianism is part of an international evangelical missionizing.

The *Livingstone Inland Mission* was the first to organize activities in the Lower Zaïre in 1878, followed, in 1879, by the London-based *Baptist Missionary Society*, also in Lower Zaïre, and, in 1891, by the *American Presbyterian Congo Mission*, in Kasai where its first post was Lwebo.

The Belgian Congo became independent on 30 June 1960, a promise made by King Baudouin some months before in January 1959, after riots in Leopoldville, the capital of the colony. Two factors could account for this rapid decision: the decolonization of neighbouring English and French countries (French Equatorial Africa, Uganda, Sudan), and the conviction of the Belgian Congo that the independence will be simply nominal. In fact, the country did not have an indigenous corps of civil servants that could immediately take over the responsibility of the new nation. If the rate of general literacy of the 15 million inhabitants was the highest in colonized Africa, the most educated people were teachers and ministers like Ishaku.

The independence ceremony was supposed to be a purely formal ritual. King Baudouin recited the civilizing saga of his family and his country; Mr Kasa-Vubu, newly elected head of State, responded accordingly by commenting on the colonial power, its legitimacy, and the succession symbolized by the independence ritual.

Unexpectedly, Lumumba, the new premier, destabilized the politeness of the context, challenging the official interpretation of a peaceful exchange of power and equating colonization and exploitation. A hazardous demand thus brought to light and focus what the masters of the ceremony had wished to avoid.

To Kasa-Vubu, entangled in his father's complex with the Belgian power and playing the good and grateful child, Lumumba was publically opposing the right to dissidence and revolt. In crossing the threshold of established rules of the game and insulting the Belgian king and his officials, Lumumba was bringing himself into relation with the trial that his own gestures had already initiated in questioning the existing order and its mythologies. In this public revolt, a venerable hierarchy of power was desacralized. The army mutinied. Lumumba reacted by dismissing all the Belgian officers and replacing them with Africans. The mutiny expanded. Without consulting Lumumba's government, Belgium invaded the newly independent country. Within a fortnight, two important provinces, Katanga and Kasai, seceded. Arrested in September by Joseph Mobutu, his former secretary attaché who was then in charge of reorganizing the new National Army, Lumumba was murdered in January 1961 in Elisabethville with the complicity of Moise Tshombe, governor of the secessionist Katanga.

A political chaos unfolded as Belgian advisors, with the help of white mercenaries, protected the administration of Tshombe and the copper-mining societies. In the southwest, Albert Kalonji presided over the fate of an autonomous South Kasai, dreaming of reconstituting the ancient Luba Kingdom. First in the east, then in the central region of Kwilu, Lumumba's partisans were opposing the central government of Kinshasa, which was then backed by American covert operations. The United Nations intervened with peace-keeping troops saving the unity of the country. Cyrille Adoula, a moderate socialist, became premier.

In 1963, UN forces put an end to the Katangan secession. President Kasa-Vubu named Tshombe as premier, thus fulfilling the Belgo-American programme of 'Katangalizing' the Congo. But in the east, as well as in important pockets in Northern Katanga and the Kwilu, Lumumbists were generating nationalist groups which for at least five years successfully harassed the undisciplined National Army of the now colonel Mobutu. Thanks to American aid, the services of an international corps of mercenaries, and a systematic politics of deception, Mobutu progressively pacified the country. Says S.N. Sangmpan, a Zaïrean political scientist:

'Thus, by 1962, the masses and Lumumbist forces were engaged in political struggle; having a common enemy, they combined their efforts in a series of popular rebellions. Starting in Kwilu Province in 1963 under the leadership of Lumumbist Pierre Mulele and in the northeast, these rebellions spread rapidly throughout the country; and by 1964 rebels controlled almost three-quarters of it. On 30 June 1964, in the face of spreading popular rebellions, the Adoula government resigned. Tshombe, the former leader of the Katanga secession, became prime minister. The major task facing his government was the eradication of popular rebellions, which was partially achieved by using mercenaries and the support of Western countries. A major blow to the rebel forces came in November 1964, when Belgian paratroops supported by the United States intervened in Stanleyville (Kisangani) and ended the rebellions in the northeast. With the end of the rebellions, a power struggle erupted among the pro-Western forces. To control state power, the Binza Group, via General Mobutu, ended the five-year competitive rule by means of a coup d'état on 24 November 1965.'

                                        (Sangmpan, 1994; 1566)

Let us say that things seem to work very well in this report, particularly in Down's diary that completes it. The general situation is a political chaos and we can measure its gravity by following the progressive dissociation of two orders. On the one hand, there is 'the Presbyterian Mission' and its regular programme and dynamics; on the other, a dislocating order in which the colonial transcendence is questioned in the name of a newly found liberty. From the rationality of the Presbyterian norm inscribed in the more comprehensive and sovereign mission of both Christianizing and converting, the questioning invites a repositioning of the mission. The Mulelist partisans, even in their excessive demands, have assigned a role to their refusal of the whole colonial culture, a radical transformation of the entire political space. In reality, what Down's diary reveals is something simpler: two subcultures, the Presbyterian and the Mulelist, the first reduced to a 'Western' mode and the second, conquering, representing itself in nationalist vestments. But there is something else: 'poor' partners in the colonial conquest, not really involved in the Belgian organization of colonial power and its concrete articulations, the Presbyterians – most of them non-Belgians – could not logically fear any political mutation unless it was basically 'anti-white'.

Thus, the Mulelists had only this way of justifying their action: ignore the 'mission' and its genesis which, by the way, was initiated by two Americans, a Black, the Reverend Sheppard, and a White, the Reverend Lapsley, and reconceive a nationalist political principle in terms of the tension between Whites and Blacks. A racial hiatus became the major criterion, separating camps and even intentions, thus accounting for calculations of self-interest.

Ishaku is thus caught between two objective worlds: his faith and everyday life regulate a representation apparently contrary to the nationalist terms of Mulelists. Although his identification with such a representation might be pointing in the direction of the essentials of any credible nationalism (as a critique and reconceptualization of human finitude and its relation to time and space), Ishaku unveils, or more exactly witnesses, the paradoxical: a dynamic fusion of cultures in which the unthought, in its absolute strangeness, meets the upsurge of a new, modern African subject, capable of reformulating the profoundest creation of Christianity.

Of course, this is not all. It is not even the essentials of what could be decoded to explain a death. Yet we cannot begin to understand its significance if we avoid the evidence of Ishaku's milieu as a symbol transcending many things and thus freed from the constraints of facile cultural and racial essentialisms. There might not be apparent deep thinking in the disarray of this small Presbyterian community facing incomprehensible violence. What is obvious, however, is an attitude of freedom *vis-à-vis* the utopia of a unitary community of nationalistic passion. Ishaku and his fellow Presbyterians actualize a realm in which the particular and the universal dialogically reproduce each other without absorbing each other in the anguish of each gesture of freedom. Here one remembers Heidegger: 'Existence' in its singularity is 'freedom', and 'thinking' as that which comes from the abyss of this freedom and which commits itself as 'sacrifice', that is as 'the sacrifice of the essence of the human being'. It is an abyss of freedom that Down's diary comments upon: what has been truly lived and thought in this small group of Christians is what is expended in the death of Ishaku, in the brutal passing of a witness.

Jean Ishaku is a *martyr* here, 'a person who is put to death on behalf of his beliefs and principles.'

But let us distinguish at least two things. There is, first of all, a political difference between the Simbas and Ishaku. If we refer to Benoît Verhaegen's masterful studies on rebellions, the Simbas' ideology was a socialist one and in its best expression necessarily led to a radical denial of Ishaku's political philosophy, which places itself under the patronage of God. Secondly, we could here transcribe what seems to be a political crisis into what is really a cultural crisis about the *métissité* brought about by colonization and Christianity *vis-à-vis* traditional values and romantic nationalism. These distinctions do not and cannot exhaust the precariousness of death and its essential instability. What we face here is a testimony about martyrdom, the meaning of choice, the mystery of a last convulsion.

Any death, particularly a violent one, has its conditions of possibility. Falling upon itself, death always marks a *here* on the topography of existence, coinciding with what announced it in a closure. In Ishaku's case, the framework is presented by James Williamson and the basic information gathered by Jean Flett for Ishaku's colleague, Norman Downs, to be used in the memorial service at Kananga and verified by Ishaku's widow, Tshiela Naomi:

1930 Born in April 1930, at Bakwa Mbule, Ishaku Jean was entrusted to the care of missionaries at the age of four months.

1937 Raised by Miss Jean Flett, he confessed the Lord Jesus as his own Saviour at the age of 7 years.

1946 At 16, he was baptized and received as a member of the Assembly.

Alexis Kagame Priest and Scholar (1912–1981)

The image that inevitably comes to mind when I seek to evoke Alexis Kagame is that of grandeur. Indeed, Alexis Kagame was and will remain a giant. He was and remains great.

Great he was, certainly in physical size, and when approaching him for the first time, one was immediately struck by his uncommonly tall and calmly robust stature. He seemed to be made of rock, and his strong face that age was somewhat weighing down on towards the end of his life, flaunted, almost violently, an invincible power, scarcely lessened by the extreme kindness of his eyes. He was a man of lineage and seemed to affirm this line of descent even in his body. But instead of the slenderness of the Lords of Mugambanzi, nature had made him a gift – beyond the height of his family members – of the massiveness required by tradition for the masters of the world.

Great he was, as well, in an eminent fashion, in his own exemplary life that not only closely followed the history of his country, in both its success and its misfortune but, by its fecundity, left a profound mark on the destiny of the human and social sciences in Africa. In particular, Kagame's *oeuvre* is monumental and complex before us. Subtle exegeses, such as Janheinz Jahn and Dominique Nothomb, revived his categories and hypotheses in order to describe African cultures and make them known. African philosophy (just as African history, linguistics and anthropology) seeks its starting point or attempts a particular reorientation according to what is represented in, or contrasted to, other concepts in Alexis Kagame's works.

Great he was, finally, in the aristocratic elegance with which he assumed, all throughout his life, his vocation and made his devotion

to Africa into a reality. Both were done with self-abnegation and
disinterestedness, calmly sustained, in a constant struggle against
illusions of all kinds. Both, even when they seemed to appear in the
form of a premeditated coolness or a scornful distance, and when they
seemed to disappear behind a style or an apparent *mise-en-scène,* always
signified the generosity that his mask of propriety, the extraordinary
sovereignty of his intelligence over his emotions, and a natural seal of
distinction protected from all indiscretions.

That was Alexis Kagame: close and warm to every partner in conversation, but always distant, critical, and masked – extremely vulnerable,
but impassive and frozen in a burning coolness. Two insistent memories
helped me to understand him. The first dates back to 1960 when he was
living in Butare, which, I believe, was still called Astrida at the time.
As a young Benedictine novice living in Gihindamuyaga, I had obtained
the authorization to visit Butare during that unspeakable period when
the Hutus and the Tutsis, the two major ethnic groups in Rwanda, were
clashing with one another; I needed his experience in order to survive
the crisis that Rwanda was experiencing. Friendly and yet often full
of polite moments of reticence, he eluded all my questions, and from
this discussion, I only recall a certain kind of advice that he offered at
the moment I was leaving him: 'We are,' he said to me, 'the servants
and victims of Destiny; the most important thing for us is to at least
try to remain the masters of our dreams.' Ten years later we resumed
our dialogue in Dar-es-Salaam where, at the invitation of UNESCO,
we were working on developing linguistic projections. I had left the
Gihindamuyaga Benedictines many years earlier. His taste for discreet
contours had remained the same but, physically ill, he was also going
through a grave psychological crisis. During the ten days of the seminar,
I became intimately acquainted with his thoughts. He criticized me for
having left Rwanda, for having abandoned a cause, and one evening
after another he brought back to life the gravity of the fratricidal conflict
between the Tutsis and the Hutus. The victims of this folly haunted him:
he invoked their innocence and, if possible, would have returned them
to life; above all – oh, just how much! – he would have annihilated the
supposedly intelligent sarcasm of the politicians and Africanist scholars
of every kind, for whom the institutionalization of hate in this nation

had become an object of desire and a pretext for science. The 1990s repeated the 1960s. What should be added to his wish? That I could trade my vocation as a Benedictine in the service of a tormented people for a peaceful career as a university professor seemed absurd to him. But only then did I understand what life might mean to this man who had voluntarily chosen to immure himself within his country, and for whom the authenticity of one's vocation was more affirmed by the experience of everyday martyrdom and the ongoing practice of faith than by the exercise of reason and rationality for the purpose of guiding one's existence.

Alexis Kagame was born in Kiyana, Rwanda, probably on the 15 May 1912, in the commune of Muganbazi, to a Tutsi family from the upper nobility. While still quite young he served as a page at the court of the Mwami before entering the primary school at Ruhengeri. At the opening of the school year in 1928, he enrolled at the junior seminary of Kabgayi and made his decision to become a Catholic priest. Without question, the strange and artificial atmosphere of social harmony strengthened his vocation. The Belgian trusteeship in Rwanda, seconded by the all-powerful Catholic Church and, in agreement with the clearest principles of 'Indirect Rule', patiently reinvented and extended the networks and codes of the traditional sociopolitical structures of the kingdom. The Mwami reigned officially as a 'constitutional' monarch but was dependent on the authority of the trusteeship; and Pierre Bitahurwina, the father of Alexis Kagame, was a powerful prince, influential in the court as well as with the European civil and religious authorities who kept the country under a form of 'Regency'. His son, the young Alexis, remarkably gifted and intelligent, was made for power. In this climate of ambiguity in which the sword and the cross of the 'white masters' reciprocally supported one another in order to transform the kingdom, a Catholic vocation, to which Alexis sincerely aspired, seemed to promise a very respectable position in society. That is not to diminish the significance of Alexis' vocation, but rather to indicate the social context in which, due to a number of intrigues and plans in which Alexis had no part, he chose his path and placed his dreams on a firm foundation. His sincerity was real and he remained faithful to it for his entire life. If I had to begin my life again – he confided to me in 1973, at a time when the apparatus of power under which he had been raised no longer existed and he had no illusions regarding his own political weakness – if I had to begin my life again, he said to me, I would still become a priest.

In October 1933 he entered the major seminary where he took up the study of philosophy and theology. In the course of those long years of preparation for priesthood his interest in the history and traditions of his country was awakened. What a strange seminarian! Instead of devoting his sparetime to childishness which, at that time, was the habitual form of distraction in these institutions of religious education, Alexis Kagame studied his own culture, attempting to interpret the effort of mind and the patience of reason for which philosophy, recently discovered by him, gave him the rules of 'explication'. Ordained as a Catholic priest on 25 July 1941, Alexis Kagame became an official member of the 'Indigenous Clergy of Rwanda'. This paradoxical title that he would wear with pride and use until the end of his life was, in fact, a sign of separation. As a priest, and because he was a priest, by order of his white superiors, he had to cut himself off entirely from his family and his people. As Bishop Bigirumwami, Dean of the Catholic Bishops of Central Africa recalled in 1978, he could not even spend a single night with his own family. He had become someone from another caste, but this group was not to be confused with the missionary factions that had come from Europe and were governed by other norms. Father Alexis Kagame, of the 'Indigenous Clergy' or of the 'Autochtonous Clergy' wore these signs of exclusion with such dignity and illustrated them to such a degree that many people, who were scarcely informed about religious matters during the period of colonization, believed that they referred to a learned association of African clerics.

After his ordination, Father Kagame divided his time between his ecclesiastical duties and his scientific research, but these two poles were not designed to prevent a discreet interest in the affairs of state. When his superiors sent him to Rome in 1952 for his university qualifications, Father Kagame was a formidable politician whom they were hoping to appease through a period of study in exile. He was also a proven researcher whose worthiness and originality were beginning to be recognized. By virtue of a number of his published works of beautiful craftsmanship, Father Kagame was elected as corresponding member of the Royal Belgian Academy of Colonial Sciences from 1950 onward.

After receiving his doctorate in philosophy in 1955 at the Gregorian University of Rome, with a thesis on *La Philosophie bantu-rwandaise de l'être,* Father Kagame took a year's leave and travelled in different Western European countries. In fact, the Colonial and ecclestical authorities wanted him to be far away from Rwanda where the political situation was delicate. The colonial trustees, as well as the religious institution, seemed to fear his presence in the country. He submitted and remained in Europe, devoting, as he would write in 1972 to R.P. Alfons J. Smet, 'a year to his research in Bantu linguistics either at specialized libraries, or together with African students, with a view to gathering the materials necessary for writing a *Philosophie bantu comparée,* whose original monograph had been his thesis.' In that same period, Father Kagame had already published two principal kinds of work: on the one hand, an important poetic *oeuvre* about, among other things, the history of the world and Christianity, written completely in verse, published in Kinyarwanda, and of which only two rather small parts have been translated into French, *La Divine Pastorale* (1) and *La Naissance de l'univers* (2). In a remarkably ambiguous compliment, Jadot admired these works of scrupulous intelligence and rigorous patience for their range and artfully complex organization, while expressing surprise that a 'Negro' had been capable of bringing them to a successful conclusion.

Reconstructed in chronological order, thanks to D.E. Herdeck and J. Jahn, they are principally the following works: *Inganji Karinga,* a historical rewriting of the pre-colonial Rwanda (3); *Icara nkumane irungu,* a volume of poems about misery and famine in the aftermath of the second world war (4); *Umwaduko w'Abazungu muli Afrika yo hagati,* a historical analysis of colonialism and of the arrival of Europeans in Africa (5); *Iyo wiliwe nta Rungu,* an anthology of Rwandan poems from the eighteenth to the mid-twentieth century (6); *Indyohesha-birayi,* a poem about pigs (7); *Isoko y`a´ámajambere,* a long didactic historical poem on evolution and progress published in three volumes (8); *Imigami y'imigenurano,* an anthology of 1730 Rwandan proverbs (9); finally, *umulirimbyi wa nyili-ibiremwa,* a masterwork that presents the history of Christianity in eighteen books published in two volumes (10) and among which the French versions, edited by Kagame himself (11), are a translation of the first three of the eighteen books published in Kinyarwanda.

Opposite this *oeuvre* in Kinyarwanda, there is another volume in French composed of specialized works on African history and philology, whose dimensions are equally impressive, including *Le Rwanda 1900–1950* (12); *Bref Aperçu sur la poésie dynastique du Rwanda* (13); *La Poésie dynastique au Rwanda* (14); *Le Code des institutions politiques du Rwanda précolonial* (15); *Les Organisations socio-familiales de l'ancien Rwanda* (16).

Father Kagame returned to Rwanda in 1956, the year when his doctoral thesis was published in a well-bound octavo volume of 448 pages by the Royal Academy of Colonial Sciences in Brussels. He was successively, professor of philosophy and African culture at the *Groupe Scolaire* of Butare, the junior seminary of Kansi, the major seminary of Nyakibanda, the National Pedagogical Institute, and at the University of Butare. This was a period of twenty-five fruitful years of teaching during which he tried to communicate and share his passion for African culture. In 1973, during my tenure as Dean of Humanities at the National University of Zaïre, I invited Father Kagame for a brief visit as a visiting professor at the Lubumbashi campus. Within a few weeks, I saw him convert entire annual classes of students to a 'nationalist' view of African history and philology. I told him that I feared that such a perspective, by generously glossing over the epistemological preconditions of the murder of the Father, ran the risk of further perverting the discipline of the social sciences in Africa, already so encumbered by a priori ideological assumptions of 'colonial science'. His response was surprising to me in its simplicity: 'obsession is also a path to the truth'.

Father Kagame was obsessed by the need to lay a rigorous foundation for the study of African culture. His thesis in philosophy had made him a master and a guide and the critiques and reservations that it occasioned offer evidence of its impact. In 1976, he provided a complement to his thesis: *La Philosophie bantu comparée* (17), a monumental enterprise that in a stubborn manner would assume responsibility for the outcome and promise of his method and path.

In history, it is to his beloved Rwanda that he devoted his most patient work. In 1958, he had published a brief *Histoire du Rwanda* (18), followed by four important works: *La Notion de 'Génération' appliquée à la généalogie dynastique et à l'histoire du Rwanda des Xᵉ et XIᵉ siècles à nos jours* (19), *L'Histoire des armées bovines dans l'ancien Rwanda* (20), *Les Milices du Rwanda précolonial* (21), *Un Abrégé de l'ethno-histoire du Rwanda* (22). To these works of history one must add three excellent studies in the field of philology: *La Langue du Rwanda et Burundi expliquée aux autochtones* (23), *L'Introduction à la conjugaison du verbe rwandais* (24), and *L'Introduction aux grands genres lyriques de l'ancien Rwanda* (25). But it is a little known fact that Father Kagame, faithful to his essential vocation as a priest, also devoted his expertise to the translation and editing of an excellent version of the Holy Scriptures which, for those fortunate enough to read and appreciate it, is the best in both its fidelity to the genius of Kinyarwanda language and to biblical inspiration – texts that are examples of an outmoded classicism, his opponents say, which is at least a recognition of the author's demand for aesthetic rigour. A graduate student, Nturo Icumu, confirmed this for me some twenty-five years ago when I had foolishly convinced him to write a thesis on biblical philology, asking him to study the linguistic differences between the Gospel according to John in the Septuagint as, the version in the Vulgate, and that of Kagame. In order to appreciate the latter better, he had to look at one or two intermediary versions used in the dioceses of Rwanda. Kagame, he told me several times, when compared with the Septuagint as and the Vulgate, gives evidence of remarkable creativity, yet rigorously abides by the message of the text, and his language is, of all the Kinyarwandan texts, incomparably beautiful and precise.

The diversity of his talents, the fecundity of his mind, and his patience in the act of creation are all facts that strike us when we contemplate the vast *oeuvre* that Alexis Kagame has left behind. Those in his lifetime to whom he offered his intimacy, or his friendship, are aware of the considerable amount of unfinished work and complex archives that survive in the wake of his death: research notes – provisional syntheses accumulated during more than forty years; results of inquiries conducted among his family members or traditionalists reputed for their learning; index card files of responses to multiple investigations conducted across the entire geographic space of the Bantu languages; plans and drafts of works begun or drawn up in the form of summaries; and, alas, thousands of hours of classical Rwandan text recordings, many of which are encoded, with Kagame seemingly alone in knowing the keys to these works. His death is thus, literally, an irreparable loss for African studies. Several people had foreseen this catastrophe and for years encouraged him to surround himself with competent assistants and make public those texts whose decoding was familiar only to him. There is a mystery in Kagame's constant refusal in the face of all these encouragements. It is true that some of these appeals, to be frank, were lacking in elegance, and this might, at least partially, explain his reticence. Thus, for example, a number of scholars criticized him for the time he devoted to 'religious futilities'. He resisted them, conducting his life and research as if an eternity lay before him. One day I said to him that he should at least be concerned about the fate of his archives after his death. Disarmingly, he responded only with a smile.

This man of science was also a man of welcome. Researchers of every age and country who visited him always found him available, ready to share what he knew, to advise, and to guide. School children and students found in him a master whose kindness and attentive grandfatherly consideration they loved. But it is with the common people and peasants of his country that Alexis Kagame was the most admirable. This scholar, overburdened with work and engagements, would drop everything to embrace their words and, with all the generosity of his patience, would listen for hours before modestly offering an opinion. Yet his extreme kindness was neither a form of timidity nor of weakness. Instead, it was a gift of the heart and understanding which, in certain circumstances, particularly when one attacked the milieu that he thought was the authentic expression of African culture, could be transformed into dreadfully violent fits of anger. When this happened, Alexis Kagame would abandon the art of parenthesis and detour to express his keen indignation, for example, to those young Westerners working abroad, in lieu of military service, whose brief stay in Africa succeeds in transfiguring into Africanists and in confirming their intellectual certainties. Some of these fits of anger gave rise to polemical texts whose excesses, we all regret, add nothing to the grandeur of Alexis Kagame. By bearing down on his opponents – all respectable scholars who simply had the courage to oppose him on unfamiliar territory, Alexis Kagame unwisely and unnecessarily cast a measure of suspicion on some of his works. These works never required any polemic parts to be recognized or to survive, as they had their own qualities and weaknesses. But this was one of the man's traits: his passion for Africa came before everything and, even in those disconcerting excesses, he was once again affirming the price of his love.

In spite of his righteous fits of anger, Alexis Kagame was a man who was free of hate. More than once I saw him celebrating the victories and successes of those who had been fighting him mercilessly, and when the good of Africa was at stake, his gestures of forgiveness were of an infinite graciousness. Thus, for example, he had a sincere affection for the current generation of African philosophers who worshipped the virtues of hypercriticism. Along with Placide Tempels, he was at the centre of attention and the target of African critical philosophy and knew that he would remain so for a long time still. He truly suffered from this and did not understand why one could not use his contribution to philosophy in a less negative way. I heard him hold forth a number of times on the question of his bitterness and say, by way of conclusion: 'I'm growing old, I am growing old, I do not understand what the young ones want from me.' But once, in Lubumbashi in 1973, he abandoned his usual commentary: 'They are, perhaps, right, these younger philosophers. . . . They force me to reconsider my position. . . . In any case, what they say is more important than my own sensitivities, even if I can't accept their critique. . . . They promise a history in which I am likely to represent a mere insignificant moment.' I made it clear to him that I was quite surprised. His response took me aback: 'But, my dear fellow, I'm a priest. . . . And it is quite natural that I am trying to live as a Christian and according to the spirit of the beatitudes.' Today, I still wonder what connection I should make between the two: philosophy and the beatitudes.

Yes, of course, this scholar was first and foremost a priest in the most classic, but also the most ordinary, sense of the term: a man devoted to the demands of the sacred, to the privilege of the gift and the privilege of sacrifice, a simple priest, a member of the 'Indigenous Clergy of Rwanda'. All his greatness lies in this, in the humility he would manifest, thanks to his science, to the virtues of intelligence, kindness, patience, and even his terrible fits of anger. How many times did I hear, 'What a bishop he would have made!' His spirit of independence, his commitment to secular learning, his passion for the City, would seem to be some of the reasons that made him shun ecclesiastical honours. This man who, by virtue of his origins, titles, knowledge and experience might have aspired to all the power within his reach, accepted his condition as a priest, simply and happily, submitting, as best as he could, to the whims of his superiors as well as to the accidents that fate imposed on him. As a priest, he lived through the ordeal of hate which, for many years, had been tearing his country apart. As a priest, he endured the contempt of some and the incomprehension of others for his own culture and research; he bowed as an obedient son and remained silent before the dogmatism of Roman Christianity that expected total and unconditional submission from him. It is in the wake of Vatican II that he spoke out, not as a rebel, but rather to offer his contribution to a collective self-examination. He had suffered greatly, and for him the signs of bitterness that one would find in *Le Colonialisme face à la Doctrine missionaire à l'heure de Vatican II* (26) or in the last pages of *La Philosophie bantu comparée* (27) simply meant that the admission of possible errors committed during the evangilization of Africa would once more give Christianity a future on this continent. Possible errors, he would tell me, – but, after all, to whom did he not reveal his thinking about this major scandal – how, in the name of Catholicity, the missionaries had imposed a foreign name, *Mungu,* as the appellation of God who, in Rwanda, was known for centuries by the name of *Imana.* As a priest, he had to accept this sacrilege that, from his knowledge of the Rwandan tradition, he knew was an extreme affront to the divinity and to his kin. But out of fidelity to his vocation and to Rome, he did submit. God alone knows how he suffered until the day when the Church of his country reinstated the name of *Imana,* after rejecting the *Mungu* of the missionaries.

With his death, Africa has lost not only a learned man but perhaps, and even more, a servant of *Imana,* and if *Imana* has a meaning, Alexis Kagame was, I presume, its luminous sign among us. May he remain so!

The Question

Christianity very visibly witnesses to acculturation. One could begin a possible analysis by going back to the concept of acculturation itself. In fact, when two cultures meet, three operations may take place: (a) the dominant culture completely absorbs the weaker; (b) the latter may adopt and integrate elements of the former in its own structures; (c) or, more generally, a transculturation takes place, actualizing a new mixed cultural order, that is, an *espace métissé.* Anthropological studies have shown not only the universality of the phenomenon of transculturation but also its cultural complexity and ramifications, which are generally profound and decisive in the reconfiguration of the dominated culture. Indeed, the most visible restructuration affects the economic space and impacts the reconceptualization of both the political space and its historical imagination, more so than the pundits of official national histories would accept.

The effects of 'transculturation', that is on the one hand a radical mutation from the past and, on the other hand the constitution of an *espace métissé*, take place under a paradoxical paradigm that seems to have marked all Christian evangelizations since the beginning of the sixteenth century: the exploitation of goods meant by God for all humankind (and thus politics of enslavement or, at best of colonization in the etymological sense of the word) and the proclamation of a Gospel of universal brotherhood and equality' (e.g. Mendieta, 1870).

The question of the acknowledgment and constitution of this new space, at least in Central Africa, has been studied by colonial and post-colonial historians and generally accounted for by a dichotomic paradigm: a modernity has been incarnated in the conquering colonization and Christianization versus the world of tradition qualified as essentially characterized by ethnicity, more exactly by a 'primordialist ethnicity' qualifying the indigenous experience of the tradition as 'the essentially different'. As a matter of fact, this theoretical paradigm operated universally, reducing all non-Western cultures and historicities to the fundamental otherness exemplified by the concepts of primitiveness and ethnicity (Devalle, 1992: 228).

Primitiveness depends on civilization in a strange relation of necessity. Even though the tension that unites the two concepts has a long history – and one could go as far back as to the time of Herodotus' *Histories* in the fifth century BC – their radical questioning is very recent. It takes place paradoxically during the triumphalist period of African colonization, when some European thinkers began to ponder on what they believed to be the decadence of Western civilization. As concrete examples, one might refer to Oswald Spengler's *Der Untergang des Abendlandes* (1918) that popularized the very expression of 'decadence of the West'; Paul Valéry's less known essays on *La Crise de l'esprit* (1919), which explores the same predicament from an identical a priori positing a linear development and understanding of normative civilizations; Sigmund Freud's *Das Unbehangen in der Kultur* (1929), which radically makes possible a relativist comparison between savage pulsions and civilizing demands; and, finally, the 1936 archicelebrated text by Edmund Husserl on *The Crisis of European Sciences and Transcendental Phenomenology*.

The dynamics of this highly technical criticism reflect back to the Enlightenment dream: a rational and absolute mastering of nature, of all empiricities and individualities in order to inscribe them, each in its own right, in a logical, scientific and historical development. Condorcet put it very well: 'We should study human society as we study communities of beavers' (Banditer, 1988: 185). During the same period in the 1920s, from the same Enlightenment principles, the colonial practice in tropical Africa tends to actualize the project of rational conversion. In this specific case, the movement implies some preliminary postulates: first, the necessary integration of the primitive space into the European historicity and, second, the narrativization of the primitive space and its potentialities from the Enlightenment grids. The first postulate simply affirms Europe and her history as a universal model; the second, in its concrete practices – travellers' and anthropologists' narrations, Christian inscriptions on African bodies and cultures, and colonial ascriptions and programmes of taking-off – signify the very mission of conversion. In their confusion and contradictions apropos the paradigmatic value of the Western experience, the critical inquiries of Spengler, Valéry, Freud and Husserl already clearly reflect the scepticism and pessimism that some years later responded to aberrations and barbarisms, such as Nazism or apartheid issued from or formed from the Enlightenment postulations on rationality, science and historical development (see e.g. Jay, 1972). Nevertheless, they are the road companions of one of the most systematic historical experiences of social engineering that invented and organized a transcultural *espace métissé* in order to duplicate the history of the West according to the Enlightenment prescriptions.

The conversion process that led to the constitution of the new space can be negatively understood. It is basically a negation. First, negation of the otherness and particularly of non-Western spaces. Differences are thus summoned as signs that can be erased or, even better, rearranged according to elementary rules of design. Does a garden not always proceed from the colonization – that is the cultivation and mastery – of an unattended space? Second, as magnificently illustrated by Hegel, negation of the very possibility of imagining that there are other times apprehended, conceptualized, and lived up according to specific physical environments and psycho-intellectual configurations; that there is a plurality of historicities and, thus, that the dynamics of History are always relative to something else and, at best, witness conflicting negotiations from within and from without a culture. As a paradox, one might note that if the Hegelian theological history makes sense, it is because it predicates its reality and becoming as a fatality into which all historicities vanish. Indeed, from this perspective, nineteenth-century Africa does not and cannot exist, unless she is to be subsumed in and by this unique Hegelian effort. Finally, an absolute negation stipulates that no respectable consciousness could arise and function outside of a cadre that has conjugated, in a totalizing manner, Greek rationality, Judeo-Christian ethics, and scientific procedures and practices.

All Christian instructions for missionizing in Africa, as well as all applied anthropology prescriptions for the constitution of colonial nation states, comment on these major negations and result in the projection of an idealized type of space, time and consciousness that, *de facto*, devalue the so-called traditional spaces as ethnic and ahistorical in the name of an imperative conversion. Now might be the moment to address the isomorphic intention that I have established in linking colonialism and Christianity, and colonialism and anthropology. In the first case, it is obvious that important divergences and sometimes conflicting choices existed between the policies of colonial powers and those of Christian missions. Cardinal de Lavigerie, for instance, developed his own programme for the occupation and transformation of Black Africa. Against the principles of geographical demarcations and colony building stipulated by the Conference of Berlin, he entertained the idea of organizing Christian kingdoms throughout the continent with the 'army' of his white fathers. The Italian Comboniani missionaries in the Sudan and neighbouring areas followed Roman directives instead of faithfully espousing British imperial programmes. In the Congo, during the first decade of the century, Protestant missionaries defied the politics of King Leopold II and dramatically succeeded in questioning its morality at the international level. Later on, Freemasons and other open-minded agents of the Belgian colonial administration challenged the meaning of missionary Christianity. In a remarkably Voltairian fashion, they mocked its validity and, in the day-to-day administration of the colony referring to Enlightenment projects, opposed Christianity's legitimacy and tried to block its spread among the natives. On the other side, one might evoke the romantic figures of the Western missionary indicting the exploitation of natives and more generally criticizing colonial practices (e.g. Kiangu, 1992). These tensions between colonialism and Christianity are real and should not be underestimated as they were in the 1950s literature for African liberation (Laverdière, 1987). Yet they should not be overestimated either, to the point of negating the isomorphic intention of both colonialism and missionary Christianity. In fact, objectively, colonialism and missionary Christianity belong to the same cultural conquest. Despite specific and real situations of conflict, they actualized themselves in a context of mutual interdependence, referring to the same signs, symbols and justifications. Evolving from the same epistemological terrain, they are, in the language of Antonio Gramsci (1973), interacting processes of dominance and complementary modes of conversion – that is, systems for the reproduction of a cultural a priori already given elsewhere as paradigm.

As to the deviation and linkages between colonialism and anthropology, the issue has been sufficiently analysed (e.g. Asad, 1975; Copans, 1974 and 1975; Devalle, 1983; Leclerc, 1972). Claude Lévi-Strauss' structuralism, by reworking the very opposition primitive versus civilized, nature versus culture, and replacing it at the heart of all human societies invalidated the hegemonic and ambiguous ambitions of both colonialism and the old anthropology. Their power of inclusiveness was masterful (Leclerc, 1972). One has simply to go through some texts by Malinowski (1938), Evans-Pritchard (1946), and Lucy Mair (1936) in order to capture the common privileges of both anthropology and colonialism (Devalle, 1983). They account for such definite presuppositions as (a) the necessary universality of the Western programmes postulating, as Malinowski believed, that between Europe and African one does not deal with two cultures in contact but with one culture dominating another, and thus the obligation of the African to convert to civilization since he is the one to be educated and transformed into a consumer of imported goods; (b) the construction of Africa as an object of anthropological knowledge with new operative concepts such as 'ethnicity', 'tribe', 'lineages', 'age-set', etc., conceived as arguments illustrating the difference between ahistorical and historical societies; (c) the scientific and ethical missions of the anthropologist who is to remain objective in his observations and studies and, at the same time, to conceive of himself/herself as a faithful interpreter of the native moving from a relatively simple condition of existence to a more complex one, that incarnated by a civilized Christian, a European citizen.

Thus the imperative conversion projected itself as a promise of the African future and this began manifesting itself in the gradual arrangement of a new *espace métissé* implemented by the conjunction of colonialism, anthropology and Christianity. The promise deploys itself as both a new culture and social order moulded from the evidence of Western experience. Commenting on this process and using Chateaubriand's *Le Génie du Christianisme* as a symbol, Laënnec Hurbon (1993) depicted the new imagination as characterized by three main entities: the liberating light of a religion of the letter; submission and order; and a grid promoting antithetical new customs meant to destroy the whole pagan tradition. This process of transplanting a promise into a creative imagination in actuality fuses Christianity and colonialism. Cultural interrogation on the real identity of Christianity is transformed into an interrogation on Western civilization and vice versa. In the conversion to Christianity, colonization is justified and the *genius of a civilization* affirmed; in the implementation of colonialism, a civilization extends itself and witnesses to the exemplarity of the *genius of Christianity*. Both movements problematize all non-Western cultures and, in the same effort, consecrate the West as an absolute achievement in the Hegelian schema. All cultures which, willy nilly, participate in history can thus be evaluated and designated not in their original otherness but according to such classifiers as technical performance (Morgan), historical evolution (Tylor) or even the craniological 'capacity' of their members (Blummebach).

The *espace métissé* is the product of these two complementary movements, which inscribe on a supposedly linear scale becoming all the steps of human development, and then metaphorize them chronologically on the basis of a biological scale: infancy, adulthood, seniority, decadence, death. The prescription brings together all the qualifications of an infant in the ill-defined status of the primitive – that is, of a not-yet-socialized being (or more exactly of a being facing a cultural a priori and its rules for self-reproduction). This being cannot freely and consciously adhere to Descartes' statement according to which the predicament of all adults is that they have been children and socialized in a historical a priori. No wonder that the primitive or, to use Hurbon's expression, the 'imaginary barbarian', is a mixed locus. He actualizes the savage origins of History and, simultaneously, still signifies the silent side of the most civilized West in its supposed negative pulsions. He accounts for the innocence and purity of absolute beginnings and, at the same time, incarnates in an exemplary manner the original sin – the black void that marks the transition from nature to culture. In brief, even when, or because, situated outside of margins of history, he is a remarkable negation, the absolute evil and, curiously, can also be understood as a stepping stone of yesterday and today for the absolute celebration of the history of the spirit magnified by Hegel.

In any case, this 'imaginary barbarian' became Christian. The poverty, withdrawal, and misery of some of his people no longer formulates the simple tension between *us* and *them,* but rather a new set of social relations of production brought about by the conversion. Independent from the violence to convert incarnated by the process itself, three factors contributed to the constitution of the new culture issued forth by the rupture. First, the existence in indigenous contexts of myths and stories about the superiority of the white invaders, sometimes doubled, as in the case of the Congolese basin, by ancient symbolisms of colours opposing the black to the white in terms of evil versus good. There is, secondly, and more important, the fact that contrary to what the conquest narratives claim, Christianity was advancing in a fertile terrain. Local beliefs about life and death, destiny and history conveyed ideas about a transcendent divinity and superior spirits. Moreover, throughout the continent mythological charters had been transmitting for centuries narratives on the creation of the earth, the original sin, universal flood etc., all of them perfectly reconcilable with biblical lessons. Other lines of coincidence, particularly such ritual practices as circumcision, regular prayers to God(s), celebration, and veneration of ancestors, should also be added. In brief, the indigenous traditions seemed like a sort of old alliance waiting for its conversion and transmutation into a new one. Finally, one could note a widespread dissatisfaction with the older political regimes. The white invaders appeared objectively as if announcing a new era which, in Central Africa, would abruptly end incursions of the last slave traders.

The new space created by this radical discontinuity in Central African traditions did not lead, as expected by the colonizers, to the institution of a perfect Western model. Indeed, the reproduction on an experimental model of new processes of production and, subsequently, the creation of different social relations of production could not, for obvious reasons, perfectly re-enact the source mode of production. The repression of real histories backfired in passive and ambiguous responses from African populaces. Also, in the name of ancient group identities, the relationships between the novel organization of power and its political discourses did not integrate completely the soul of previous local models. Thus, a new sub *espace métissé* organized itself.

In the case of West Africa, it is interesting to note that the so-called traditional block of traditions, as analysed by Jean-Loup Amselle, was, in actuality, a monument of intermixing cultures to the point that all their own geneses were always already plural. Thus, the new *espace métissé* was allowed by at least three factors that made a complete reproduction of the Western model difficult. First, the reformation of the indigenous past in what it signified as violence for rewriting a genesis created a spirit of resistance among the indigenous people. In order to protect their memory, they moved their most signifying practices from an open to a hidden social space, often restructuring in newly organized esoteric lines what were before the popular narratives and rituals of the colonial experience. The confusion initiated by the competition between Christian churches could not but accentuate such a move. In fact, the question was, who can be trusted? The response seems to have been, let us wait, protect ourselves, and see. Soon, from the margins of the most liberal Protestant churches, counter-cultural and syncretic churches organized, marrying local habits and inspirations to biblical sources (e.g. MacGaffey; Sundkler, 1976). Second, another factor that made a complete conversion problematic: the barrier of languages. There were more than five hundred different languages in Central Africa. Colonial policies encouraged missionaries to describe indigenous languages in a systematic manner and, generally, promoted their work for standardizing certain idioms. Nevertheless, the existing multitude of languages reflected itself as a barrier for the penetration of both the colonial rationality and the Christian message. Concretely, it accounted for the unequal progression of the conversion process and made possible new cultural forms of misunderstanding created by the Christian impatient politics of translation. Here I will invoke a magnificent case related by Kwasi Wiredu in his 'Formulating Modern Thought in African Languages: Some Theoretical Considerations':

In 1911, Italian Catholic priests put before a group of Acholi elders the question 'Who created you?'; and because the Luo Language does not have an independent concept of *create* or *creation*, the question was rendered to mean 'Who moulded you?' But this was still meaningless, because human beings are born of their mothers. The elders told the visitors they did not know. But we are told that this reply was unsatisfactory, and the missionaries insisted that a satisfactory answer must be given. One of the elders remembered that, although a person may be born normally, when he is afflicted with tuberculosis of the spine, then he loses his normal figure, he gets 'moulded'. So he said, 'Rubanga is the one who moulds people.' This is the name of the hostile spirit which the Acholi believe causes the hunch or hump on the back. And instead of exorcising these hostile spirits and sending them among pigs, the representatives of Jesus Christ began to preach that Rubanga was the Holy Father who created the Acholi. (62)

Let us assume that p'Bitek is right in this account, as he very well might be; then one can expect quite wide-ranging incongruities in the translation of Christian theology into the Luo language; p'Bitek, in fact, went on to illustrate this problem with the translation of the first sentence of St. John's Gospel into Luo. St. John's opening message is, of course: 'In the beginning was the Word (Logos) and the *Word* was with God, and the *Word* was God.' Now, according to p'Bitek, '(T)he Nilotes, like the early Jews, did not think metaphysically. The concept of *Logos* does not exist in Nilothic thinking; so the world *Word* as translated into *Lok* which means *news* or message. . . . And as Nilotes were not very concerned with the beginning or the end of the world, the phrase 'In the beginning' was rendered, '*Nia con ki con*,' which is, 'From long long ago.' In the upshot, the Luo translation read as follows: '*Nia con kicon Lok onongo tye, Lok tye bot Lubange, Lod aye ceng Lubanga*,' which, according to him, retranslates into English as 'From long long ago there was News, News was with Hunchback Spirit, News was the Hunchback Spirit' (85). One might be able to pass over this as a mere translational curiosity, for serious problems are involved here about communication across cultures.

                                                                                     (in Mudimbe, 1992: 301–32)

In any case, the use of Latin as the liturgical language in Catholicism was often mystifying, as described by Mongo Beti in his *Le Pauvre Christ de Bomba* (1956).

Briefly, in the socioeconomic and cultural reconfiguration of Africa in the nineteenth and early twentieth centuries, an *espace métissé* imposes itself against the far from peaceful ancient traditions and the newly substituted programme in colonial history. No wonder that the

IV

Acculturation
An 'Espace Métissé'

> For ideality is the equilibrium of opposites. For
> example, someone who has been motivated to crea-
> tivity by unhappiness, if he is genuinely devoted
> to ideality, will be equally inclined to write about
> happiness and about unhappiness. But silence, the
> brackets he puts around his own personality, is pre-
> cisely the condition for gaining ideality; otherwise,
> despite all precautionary measures such as setting
> the scene in Africa, etc., his one-sided performance
> will still show.
>
> Kierkegaard

A. Hastings in his *History of African Christianity 1950–1975* (1979) and
A. Shorter in *African Christian Theology* (1977) describe well a major
intellectual and spiritual transformation, in fact, a radical passage, to
use the Cameroonian Jesuit Meinrad Hebga's expression, from a 'state
of eternal juniority' to 'maturity'. Placide Tempels' *Bantu Philosophy*
opened up a new vista: the possibility of reading and exploiting
'stepping stones' of the Gospels in African cultures. Tempels had
lived with Luba people for more than ten years when he thought of
publishing his book. Perfectly acquainted with the language and the
cultural background of the Lubas, he had previously published some
anthropological articles in the journal *Kongo-Overzee*. His objective
was to rethink the equation: to convert = to Westernize:

It has repeatedly been said that evangelization . . . should be adapted. . . .
Adapted to what? We can build churches in native architecture, introduce
African melodies into the liturgy, use styles of vestments borrowed from . . .
Bedouins, but *real adaptation consists in the adaptation of our spirit to the
spirit of these people.*

(Tempels, 1959: 25, my emphasis)

In brief, (a) Tempels' conception had evolved from a negation of Bantu 'civilization' to the recognition of a 'philosophy', which he considered to be complex and elaborated, what we should strictly call a *Weltanschauung*; (b) Tempels considered this Bantu philosophy to be a *particular philosophy*, and compares its fundamentals to those of Western philosophy; but he remained convinced that Western philosophy was the *universal* and *perennial* masterpiece from which to understand all other systems; (c) 'Bantu philosophy' is, according to him, a philosophy of life. For Bantus, says Tempels, the human being (the *wezen*) is a *vital force* (*Levenskracht*).

What occurs in this book is like a miraculous delivery of a reflecting and reflected-upon body. Tempels contemplates from a supposedly neutral angle – he is, indeed, in these 1930s, an amateur, but rigorous and critical anthropologist – a 'something' that his own experience as missionary and scholar is weighing against his own thought and knowledge. As an observer, Tempels attempts to measure himself against this 'something', this body – or *corpus* of Luba experience, the Luba *Weltanschauung* – that his wavering awareness has been perceiving in its own proximity. Is this *corpus*, in its reality, a simple illusion, asks Tempels? In fact, two 'things' seem to structure independently their autonomous identities; yet they are intertwined like the dialogue of consciousness with itself. The Luba *Weltanschauung* seems like a concrete body actualizing itself as narrative. To the observing gaze, does it not appear real, organized, and having its own substance? If, in its 'being-there' as 'seen', this Luba *corpus* is not necessarily part of the field – where the knowledge of Tempels' gaze and observation might be inscribed in the tension between knowledge and non-knowledge, philosophy and un-philosophy; furthermore, if we are entitled to say that Tempels' gaze and observation constitute the metaphor of a thought – (and as such designate themselves equally as a *corpus* which, like the Luba, resounds also as a 'being-in-itself') – then we cannot forget nor can we negate that the Luba experience and *Weltanschauung* exist here for us as a 'philosophy'. This philosophy is thanks to a critical process: Tempels' perception and awareness that, indeed, he is perceiving and analysing a body; transferring it to knowledge – that is, critically organizing, restructuring and metaphorizing this perceived *corpus*, translating it and reflecting it into a new narrative that could account for the *Weltanschauung* or 'something' which was or still is out there. In any case, why could the result of the process not reverberate and impact the original something?

Insofar as *Bantu Philosophy* is concerned, we can thus distinguish three radically different issues that generally get confused in discussions about the book. First, the explicit process of a self-critical thought – dwelling on 'something' and, in a systematic manner, moving from a reflection on the being of the 'something' perceived to a reflection on valid modalities for vocalizing and describing the 'something' itself – is indeed philosophical. In this sense, Tempels is a philosopher and, should one wish, could be qualified in perfectly good taste – but perhaps in bad faith? – as a respectable 'Bantu', or 'Luba' philosopher. Second, the problem with Tempels is that, instead of assuming 'Bantu Philosophy' as his own – thus transplanting into an objective space his dream of being and feeling at least once like a *Muntu-Luba* – he modestly pretends that his treatise is a translation and a simple clarification of a 'philosophy', more precisely, of an implicit and unsystematic 'ontology' witnessing to the dynamics of a vital force and its complex unfolding in the practice of Luba everyday life and *Weltanschauung*. In this negation of a liberty and its implications, we can see and name the genesis of ethnophilosophy and ethnotheology. Third, and finally, we may consequently thematize the mistake of ethnophilosophy and ethnotheology, which resides in a confusion of two separate 'things': the thought that is *the corpus* itself (say, the *Luba Weltanschauung*, narrativized by Tempels, the Kinyarwanda experience translated by Kagame, or the Shi body analysed by Mulago), which is a philosophy; and, on the other hand, the thought which, as students of philosophy, we would like to imagine and try to express about a given body we have perceived as that 'something' – Luba, Kinyarwanda or Shi. In other words, the ethnophilosophical mistake is simply a lazy washing off of a distinction clearly represented by the genitive in such expressions as the *'thought'*, the *'philosophy'* of *Bantus*, those of *Banyarwanda*, *Bashi*, or whatsoever 'something' else. The double genitive in all these forms means and renders two different concepts that should be clearly distinguished: on the one hand, the *corpus* itself as 'thought'; and, on the other hand, the 'thought' that the philosophizing subject or the enlightened amateur anthropologist searches, elaborates and describes about the *corpus*.

When expressed for the first time in the mid-1940s, Tempels' research and its ambiguities seemed revolutionary to many. It could already then be connected to the premises of P.W. Schmidt's monumental work on *Ursprung der Gottesidee* (1933–1949). The critical process of re-evaluating the relationship between conversion and Westernization and its modalities ultimately led, as we have seen, to the *incarnation* and *inculturation* programmes. Sister Antoinette Bwanga, General Superior of the Congregation of Sisters of Saint Theresa in Kinshasa, describes the *inculturation* moment as a radical conversion of both Christianity and the African believer:

Inculturation is an evangelizing process which must mark the individual in his/her profoundest roots, including the cultural ones, when (s)he meets Christ, so that (s)he could give to Christ and the Church, what is the best in him, in her, in their own culture. It is a process which witnesses both the incarnation mystery but also redemption.

(Bwanga, 1955: 20–1)

One could also bring more programmatic texts into the panorama, such as that issued under the directorship of Mercy Oduyoye from Ghana, a Deputy General Secretary of the World Council of Churches, by the 'Daughters of Africa' during their 1989 meeting in Accra, Ghana, which concerns itself with neutralizing the disdainful anti-women policies of the Church's tradition and re-elaborates the truth of the mission from the theme of God as Being-thrown-to-the-world to save all beings equally. Indeed, we could also refer to more radical statements, such as the 'Twelve Theses on Feminist Theology' issued by women scholars in Strasbourg in 1986 and that Molara Ogundipe-Leslie amplifies in a chapter of her recent book significantly entitled 'Sisters are Not Brothers in Christ' (Molara, 1994: 179–88). They all express a new era in which the usefulness of conceiving more original ways of integrating Christianity in African lives translates itself into politics of confrontation and confession (e.g. Brezault and Clavreuil, 1987; Hastings, 1979). This shift meant that the Christian theological languages moved from grids emphasizing the sameness that should be produced through the

(Lévy-Bruhl), etc. With functionalism first and structuralism second, a reversal takes place. The study of African experiences is now carried out from the perspective of the *norm, rule* and *system*; and it is accepted that each 'something' text, experience, individuality or culture can be described and understood from its own structural organization and coherence as rendered by its own norms, rules and systems. Therefore, it becomes irrelevant to speak of a non-functional organism, a deviant social formation, primitive mentalities and abnormal histories.

It is this epistemological reconversion that renewed African studies, thanks to their youth and exemplary openness, and made them capable of contributing to the disciplines. In his article on the contribution of political science to the disciplines, the American scholar Richard Sklar uses the concept of Afrocentricity (Bates and Alii, 1993). It has a well-specified meaning and refers back to the semiotics of reading that bind an expert's discourse and, say, concrete practices in everyday life. Indeed, we cannot prevent readers from linking or opposing such a technical meaning to other usages in our fields. Even less can we deny that this concept might signify for other readers a challenge to the ongoing debate about the canon. Yet, I should say that the general economy of this particular analysis, as well as its main arguments, are based on two methodological choices. The first one, at first sight, seems negative insofar as it theoretically dissociates the history (and practice) of disciplines from those of cultural traditions, and thus dramatically faces such problems as ethnocentrism and reduction from the limited viewpoint of disciplines and their relation to a given culture. The second choice, more explicitly positive, wants to understand and describe the performance of African studies from within the disciplines and, thus, how they are submitted to well-specified epistemological configurations. In this sense, the issue of canonicity is irrelevant. In fact, since the 1950s, at least in anthropology, we are not concerned with pure cultural traditions but with 'something' else. Our objective is not to respond to questions such as why the disciplines in themselves should be challenged and, still less, why one should or should not interrogate their conditions of possibility. Indeed, by the force of circumstances in the same volume, respectively about art history and African history, Suzanne Blier and Steve Feierman end up testing the very arrangement of their own discipline and how it accommodated its object to a specific historicity. We can say, in general, that though unintentionally bypassing the theoretical issues about the foundation of disciplines and focusing on the outcome of a discursive reversal and its consequences, they emphasize a major, yet very banal, point: no one speaks from nowhere. Moreover, in a variety of disciplinary discourses, we have already observed that in the 1940s and 1950s African social and religious studies were and are exemplary: they modified their methodological approaches to the configuration of positivities (using successively biological, economic and linguistic models) and, each time, rethought and reshaped their tools, conceptual norms, and means of interpretation, directly challenging and revitalizing the disciplines that made them possible. The move had a direct impact on the practice of missiology and conversion policies, making possible an evolution from *ethics of civilizing* to *ethics of inculturation*, or to refer to markers from Cardinal de Lavigerie's memoires at the end of the nineteenth century or Victor Roelens' *Notre Vieux Congo* (1891–1917) to *Les Prêtres noirs s'interrogent* (1957). To recognize the subjectivity and normativity of each society was not to return to the old ideas of a fragmented, anarchical, political structure versus a civilized 'something'. Concrete examples of methodological procedures that managed to recognize the proper historic and cultural specificities of each human group were studies in anthropology of African religions published or signed by M. Fortes (1959, 1965), John Middleton (1960), Marcel Griaule (1948) and Luc de Heusch. (1958, 1971, 1972). They taught us that an account of, and attention to, each group's cultural arbitrariness and specific history enabled us to understand that the less visible aspect of cultural transformations might perhaps be the most important from a historical perspective.

The Practice of African Social Sciences

In the history of Western sciences, the social and human sciences are relatively young. To this day, their project as sciences and their status

162   TALES OF FAITH

as rigorous disciplines treating particular objects seem quite uncertain and much debated, as illustrated by Michel Foucault's *Archaeology of Knowledge* (1970) and Pierre Bourdieu's *Theory of Practices* (1990). It is with difficulty that these sciences succeed in setting up their projects and getting them accepted as clear and definitive topics of a field which, in the manner of the exact and natural sciences, would be quantifiable and perfectly verifiable. These uncertainties can only be worrisome. They signify, directly or indirectly, that the space in which social and human sciences are promoted is inevitably a reflection of 'something' else, another space. This space adapts and reorganizes norms and rules, allowing the adoption and application of experimental models and privileges of the so-called exact sciences. Thus, the binary opposition – exact sciences versus social and human sciences – proclaims the first problem: as a function and a cause of this opposition, the social and human sciences seem to emerge as mere shadows of other, more efficient systems that haunt them. Social, human, moral and spiritual sciences, according to the German *Geisteswissenschaften*, at present as in the past, define themselves and limit the domain of their exercises and the singularity of their methods in reference to distances and proximities separating them from the rigour and laws of other disciplines. Raymond Aron, working within the humanist tradition, expressed it well in his *Essai sur la théorie de l'histoire en Allemagne contemporaine* (1938), stating that the spiritual sciences neither can nor should imitate the natural sciences, because the realities they study have a specific structure. The psychic whole is a first result of observation, as it precedes the condition of our knowing. The originality of the moral sciences, he affirmed, depends on this fundamental fact.

There is in this appeal a clear willingness to grant the moral sciences a foundation and singular substructure. Yet, several years ago, did this appeal not also signify, as we might gather in consorting with some contemporary theorists, such as Jean-Paul Sartre (1956, 1976) and Maurice Merleau-Ponty (1989), the necessity of circumscribing a clearly autonomous and well-delineated space, distant from the one inhabited by the natural sciences? Thus, the prerequisite for a difference of objects and methods curiously assumes a kind of mistrust that, in a constant state of ambiguity, both reunites and separates the domains of the natural and moral sciences. This remarkable mistrust was emphasized during the last century by Helmholtz, apropos the astonishing undertaking of Hegel against Newton: If the "scientist"'s rigour seems to issue forth from a narrow-minded outlook, the finesse of the humanists then results from a pleasant dream state. Then, what should we think of the missionary and the anthropologist's contribution?

The violence that puts the two domains against each other as two cultures in opposition is the very same that, today as in the past, gives reason to attempts at methodological conciliation. The comparison of objects and methods allows the determination of major differences and decides about the *pros* and *cons* of analogies. This opens the way for the establishment of procedures and rules likely to 'humanize' the natural sciences and, on the other hand, to give scientific respectability to the moral sciences in matters of rigour and interpretation as, for example, Claude Lévi-Strauss has tried to demonstrate in his monumental work. Perhaps one could ask to what extent, even in this case, the project unfolds as a function of the contradiction that Lachelier reduced to a radical split: the opposition of letters and sciences; that is, in essence, as he put it, the opposition of subjectivity of man and objectivity of nature. Ampère, despite the steadfastness of his unifying principle in his *Essai sur la philosophie des sciences* (1834), established two parallel types of knowledge under two significant entries, *Mundus* and *Mens*. Moreover, speaking in Foucaultian terms, the opposition indicates the vigour of a fundamental order, a positive grounding that support general theories on the order of things and on the interpretations that it calls forth. Furthermore, the very denomination of the social and human sciences leads us toward hesitations: human sciences? moral sciences? spiritual sciences? What exactly do they cover, particularly when we keep in mind an African perspective? What do they engage in, how, and just what do they study? They are said to be preoccupied with the human, and a recent formula – human sciences – seems to express this clearly. But what exactly do they deal with, and in what way are they linked to the human, and which human?

Should we really worry about the meaning of this terminological disorder and its philosophical implications? Let us at least observe that it characterizes some current Western views whose difficulties become clear when put in a contemporary general cultural context. Furthermore, they explain the justification that human medicine, human anatomy or physiology, are not human sciences, and why the practice of social sciences, instead of relating to the 'something' of everyday life and taking its reality into account, deals generally with images, representations and those manifestations that are supposedly either individual or collective. Proposed as an object of science (and therefore subjected to abstract analysis and to a purely abusive reasoning), this social phenomenon is theoretically conceived as a reality-in-itself – capable of being the object of knowledge relative to a given 'something'. But, very early on, did we not dismember and disassemble this reality into bits? Initially, history at least created a unified model, but it was at the cost of negating the possibility of any plurality of historicities. Sociology, with Le Play, for example, was organized when it became necessary to distinguish the orders of the past from those of the present, and singularly contributed to social knowledge through description of the emergence of a bourgeois order. Anthropology, once the 'savage' was thematized in eighteenth- and nineteenth-century scholarship, was able to find a role and function in the Western paradoxical quests for self. Finally, psychology and its therapeutic extensions did the same, re-evaluating their object once the value and meaning of individual and collective behaviours were understood as separated from the activity of a conscious rationality.

The arbitrary boundaries of these sciences become untenable when one attempts to assign borders to each of the disciplines, particularly in an African context: where is the line of demarcation between history and sociology, when one no longer takes into account the diachronic–synchronic dimension? What justifications can we give to the coexistence of sociology and anthropology, apart from the imperial disposition of the West which founded and launched anthropology as 'a science of communities, of groups centered on traditionalist motivations' *vis-à-vis* sociology defined as a 'discipline interested in groups centered on rationalist motivations?' How can the object of political science be fundamentally different from that of sociology? At what exact point does psychology cease to be social and become individual? Faced with what these questions imply, how can we believe and be assured that it would not be better to extend, to all social and human sciences, what G. Politzer wrote in his 1928 *Critique des fondements de la psychologie* – that the history of psychology over the past fifty years is not, as is often asserted in introductions to psychology textbooks, the history of an *organization*, but that of a *dissolution*?

The major problems of these sciences also result remarkably from this parcelling out that is often confused with technical specializations. More precisely, the attempt to establish firm boundaries signals an essential contradiction. There is, on the other hand, the incredible postulation for extending natural sciences paradigms and wishing to reduce social phenomena to a rational subject and theoretical mechanism, whose workings it would suffice to understand and whose laws it would suffice to control, in order to deduce and foresee its functioning. However, due to the failure of the very techniques of investigation and interpretation with which these sciences endowed themselves, and that they needlessly renew with regularity, it increasingly appears that the 'something' out there, say, for instance, social elements, escape these reductive procedures and their modalities of objectification. Proposing social phenomena as objects of analysis and claiming to explain them implies some kind of erasure, at any rate a radical denial of the very complexity of their nature. In this way, as R. Laing says, we 'falsify our perception in order to adjust it to our concepts' whereas, it is plain to see, even for the most mechanicist specialists of social sciences that 'human fact is irreducible to knowledge. It must be lived and produced.'

These contradictions are still those of our present-day social sciences, particularly sociology (and anthropology), whose project (borrowing an old definition from Auguste Comte that at least has the merit of being clear) is to study positively the group of fundamental laws associated with social phenomena. The use of this discipline, as well as of all the others consequent to it, is rarely innocent. The social order, whatever it might be, cannot and does not remain neutral faced with readings and interpretations on it. Furthermore, by exercising its power and by means of a complex deployment of its implicit and explicit internal regulations, any order determines, orients, and marks the general lines of possible interpretations. This occasionally raises 'problems of conscience' in the researchers, subjective tensions which, by convenience, it is customary and considered good form to inscribe modestly in the confrontation of theoretical hypotheses. If attentively analysed, this fact rapidly allows a good understanding of the doubtful links between the scholar and his/her topic of specialization in any social formation. At the same time, before presupposing a question concerning these connections, one could ask if, in any give society, the researcher's situation does not fatally stamp a singular mark on the work produced.

In an excellent book published in 1974, Benoît Verhaegen attempted a classification of sociologists based on this criterion by hypothesizing three categories – positivists, formalists and committed (*engagés*) – corresponding more or less to the 1960s social and geo-political situations. He distinguished the following: (1) an empirical, positivist research practised in 'bureaucratic or totalitarian societies' (the United States and the former Soviet Union) 'whose factual results could still be reconciled with the political order'; (2) a formalist and uncom-mitted (*désengagée*) sociology sanctioning the break between theory and practice, as in functionalism and structuralism, exercised in 'the most liberal zones of bureaucratic and totalitarian societies in Western societies of second-order status'; (3) an *engagée* sociology likely to lead to political action: 'on the periphery of the Western and Soviet scientific worlds, among the researchers whose objects of study are societies driven toward change and toward political action in order to survive, sociology would be committed politically and intellectually, knowledge would assume an increasingly stringent reduction of the distance between the subject and the object until they overlap entirely in revolutionary action.'

At first sight this classification is a bit simplistic: it presents a schema of a beautiful theoretical purity and does not seem to take into account the complex and ambiguous lines between Euro-America and the Third World. The diverse networks of economic and cultural relations that bring the two together are guarantees of an imperialism such that in new countries, the scientific norms as models – assured as paradigms of all scientific applications – are elaborated in, and reproduced from, the West (e.g. see Saïd, 1993). Thus empirico-positivist sociology, and even theology, as well as formalist research or functionalist anthropology are often, in Black Africa, images and expressions of a discrete but efficient power that good and bright students educated in 'White schools' transform into reality. At the other end of the spectrum, yet along the same lines, the violence of totalitarian and bureaucratic structures makes possible practices that are conceived as theories of praxis, as we find in the 1960s works of R. Loureau, G. Lapassade and C. Wright Mills, and more recently in the theological work of the German Eugen Drewerman.

Verhaegen's classification, however, has the merit of shedding light on what we might call possible 'missions' of those who practise social and human sciences. Thus, faced with Africa and under the auspices of the universality of science and Christianity, the discursive police has traditionally worked clearly in the past to guarantee, with remarkable orthodoxy, the shimmering links of economic dependence and the pre-eminence of a spiritual order. Benoît Verhaegen's hypothesis of classification also shows that in the case of empirical and formalist practices, often considered as 'scientifically exemplary', ideology is more or less erased. We might ask, then, how could one exclude ideology from a domain that is not only the place from which it springs, but also the ideal territory of its application: social phenomena? The very meaning of a such a petition is evocative. It indicates the function and the role of social knowledge in the social body and demonstrates a means of understanding the principle that 'knowledge is the source of power'. This principle normally has for its corollary the ignorance in which 'objects' of social knowledge and theology are something maintained, be it as a mass, a group or as individuals.

Because ideology can define itself as *ratio*, both presiding over and determining action, the social and human sciences are, at least in two regards, ideological. First, from their very reflection of a 'something' social in the sense that any social element is dialectically marked by the dominant ideology and by the ideology *in the making*; second, by their discourses that are themselves both mirrors and reflections of a given space. Everything happens, then, as if there were two parallel but complementary structures, one of which would be the base, a 'something', a social reality in the making; and the other, the surface, the discourses constructed by specialists (e.g. see Bourdieu, 1990). The problem is thus: how can the reality of this 'something' correspond to scientific or religious constructions that claim to take it into account? Furthermore, in the case of formalist and positivist researches, which 'scientific' exercises allow us to empty the ideology? One could make a comparison between the birth of social science and the emergence of a bourgeois order in the West. To add some rigour, let us join P. Lantz in pointing out that 'sociology, for example, was born of an ambiguous project: to determine the reality of society in order to adapt politics to social transformations; the goal being the substitution of the "metaphysics" of human rights with a social physiology as Saint-Simon said, that would allow us to discern pathogenetic elements both regressive and problematic – as in the case of a political and economic orientation chosen by classes passed over by history – and to substitute in the leadership elements which are recruited from the productive elements of the society' (1969: 142). Here we find and make explicit a relationship between the promotion of social science and the affirmation of class oppositions (Lazarsfeld, 1970). At the end of the nineteenth century, sociology followed in the wake of sketched-out political ideas and theses produced under the French Second Empire and developed as a science of 'order'. It became a discourse, guiding movements of social unrest towards the ideal of society embodied by a bourgeois model, which, in return, invested that ideal in analyses constraining social reality. This will for power, as expressed in its colonial expansion, assumed two *petitiones principii*: the universality of social knowledge elaborated on the model of Western societies and, as a corollary, the stratification of different societies, conceived from comparisons and analogies coming out of precise stages in European history. As already noted, these principles propelled the thesis of the Western civilizing mission which is, among other things, obligated to justify the African colonial and missionary ventures.

Western society being the society *par excellence*, Western history, the history *par excellence*, and its religion as well as its science, the norm, the West had no choice but to 'invent' the primitive, the pagan, and thus anthropology and missiology, social science being reserved for Western societies and for their tentacles, such as urban phenomena in newly organized colonies.

In the 1950s, the structuralist wave in anthropology attempted, in terms of a critique that it strived to establish in relation to the West, to be the sign of a respectful gaze on difference and, in this capacity, maintained that it studied societies that were or are different – both for themselves and in themselves. Yet, there again, the fundamental problem remains, namely, in this process, the relationship of Western culture to other cultures. As Anouar Abdel Malek says, one can affirm methodologically that the century-old refinement of the means of analysing still does not change the very nature of the analysis undertaken. In our day, just as in the Age of Enlightenment, such an analysis falls under the jurisdiction of the will to universalism, under the assumption that all social phenomena are immediately reducible to a single grid.

Based on the questions posited up to this point, one can perceive the problems that social sciences – and, indeed, missiology and theology – confronted and obviously still face in Africa. First, to pose as 'sciences' and technically credible 'discourses', then to be true 'sciences' and well-qualified 'practices'. On the other hand, must the African researcher *necessarily* be positivist, formalist, or *engagé*? Where will (s)he find the criteria and reasons for such a choice? And whatever the choice might be, will (s)he remain innocent? The alienation of the African specialist in social, human and religious sciences can run so deep that (s)he no longer senses that there is a problem, his or her problem, that of his or her society, and that of the science which he or she practises. In all good faith and with exemplary rigour, she or he might let a foreign gaze fall on Africa, and all her or his research and work could be a mere actualization of a Western ideology.

In the West, as in Africa, the problems are apparently the same, particularly in the links between social sciences and politico-economic powers. The similarity facilitates the demonstration that, both here and there, no innocence endures the practice of the social and even religious sciences. It also allows a serious examination of the levels at which the power–knowledge articulation is situated in Africa. In other respects, and to put it in a provocative manner, any Africa researcher should at least pause momentarily on the following small points in order to ponder his or her scientific or religious practice. The West created the 'pagan' in order to 'Christianize', 'underdevelopment' in order to 'develop', the 'primitive' in order to engage in 'anthropology' and

'civilize'. These banalities overlay crushing models that must either
be accepted or re-evaluated. To accept them implies notably that the
model of life, spirituality and knowledge will be a single adjustment to
Western paradigms and that the role of the social and human sciences
will be auxiliary both to this programme and to the political prospective
of African dominating classes. To reanalyse these banalities is to
choose 'adventure' against 'science', uncertainty against intellectual
and spiritual security. But is it really possible to opt for a promise
of producing a 'science from within', a discourse of self-integration
into the true complexity of African social formations, and to take them
on, not as tracings of Western history but in their cultural and historic
specificity? Would such a critical position mean conceiving Africa as
'something' other than a margin of the West? In fact, the questions
might be transformed into a project that would mean a willingness for
our disciplines to go beyond being the so-called information collectors
and in a very real way to be revealers of social dynamics and shifts,
illustrating that social and human sciences, as well as theology, can
become sites of a permanent *prise de parole* and *prise de conscience*.

Overall, sooner or later, our sciences would have to be revised from
top to bottom, first, by exploding their hermetic language for those who
are the 'objects' of their knowledge; second, by questioning themselves
on why – especially in Africa – they promote the interests of those in
power, those appointed to apply faithfully the models of dependence;
and, finally, the problem of the social and human sciences, and even
religious studies, in Africa and elsewhere, is a political problem: who
is the master?

An Order of Succession versus the 'Colonial Library'

The preceding analysis has consciously confused two orders, the
ideological and epistemological. But such was the difficult atmosphere
during the 1960s in which the discussion about African maturity took
place. It is not my objective to reinterpret a complex process in a
few pages, but I may at least indicate axes of commitment and their

meanings.

In this post-*Négritude* era in Francophone countries, one finds a new generation of highly qualified intellectuals who, apropos colonial social sciences as well as theology and the politics of mission, are facing frontally the difficult issue of the separation between the 'objective ethical' and 'subjective ethical'. We may, for illustrative purpose, think of Engelbert Mveng, a Cameroonian Jesuit, who was then completing a *Doctorat d'Etat* in Greek philology and had already published among other things a small book on religious aesthetics, *L'Art d'Afrique noire: liturgie et langage religieux* (1965). We may also recollect Alexis Kagame, a Roman Catholic priest from Rwanda who, in 1955, obtained his doctorate in philosophy from the Gregorian University in Rome and became famous with his *La Philosophie bantu-rwandaise de l'être* (1956), ironically published in Brussels by the Belgian Academy of Colonial Sciences; in theology, Vincent Mulago, who received his doctorate in 1956, also from the Gregorian University in Rome, and whose controversial *Un Visage africain du Christianisme* (a synthesis of his thesis), published in 1965 by *Présence Africaine*, very directly suscitated a questioning of both Tempel's *Bantu Philosophy's* legacy and its understanding of philosophical practice (see Crahay, 1965); finally, Joseph Kizerbo, an *Agrégé* of history, who published the first monumental reinterpretation of African history (1970) which, contrary to Sheik Anto Diop's (e.g. 1954, 1960), imposed itself as both an original and technically dependable narrative even in the most prejudiced circles.

These four intellectuals, among whom three are priests, represent and symbolize a period. A statistical survey of those Africans who were then struggling and competing for a political succession in post-colonial regimes would confirm the hyper-representativeness of a Catholic intelligentsia during this period. It had been said that most of the francophone fathers of independence and their aids were former seminarians, but that is excessive. Yet, even if partially true, would this explain the political failure so manifest today? This is a question that deserves investigation.

Such a synthesis is highly controversial if we introduce the longer and very dynamic Islamic tradition into the picture. Djenne and Tumbuktu, for example, were organized in the thirteenth and twelfth centuries, respectively. Constituted initially as commercial posts dependent on the Maghreb, they rapidly developed into scientific centres of major importance which, in the fifteenth and sixteenth centuries, were highly respected for their contribution to knowledge. The reputation of their masters was often compared to scholars of the *nec plus ultra* Al-Azhar University in Cairo. In his intellectual genealogy, Ahmed Bâbâ (1556–1627), a native of Tumbuktu and a graduate of its university, goes as far back as the end of the ninth century(!) mentioning the father of the mother of his grandfather who served as a *cadi* (judge) of Tumbuktu (Zouber, 1977). The most important fact is the solidity of a long intellectual tradition that one can observe in Islamic regions, north, east and west of the continent (Cardaire, 1954; Ki-Zerbo, 1972; Monteil, 1964) and which, in the 1950s and 1960s, constituted a serious challenge to both colonial assimilation politics and post-colonial cultural and religious quests (e.g. Dia, 1975; Kane, 1972).

In terms of succession, a distinction among the political, religious and scientific does not seem valid for most of the African intellectuals of the twentieth century discussed here: they have been acculturated and schooled according to the demands of the Western experience and spiritually marked by an emphasis on the notions of individual personality and a universal civilization. For them this meant engaging themselves totally in a new ethical discipline and actualizing accordingly their modes of existing and believing as an ethical one. Such a project does not suppress the temptation of a risk: either/or, to use Kierkegaard's expression; or more radically the *vel*, or this or that, of usage in symbolic logic, when referring to the tension represented in the opposition between paganism and Christianity or Islam, primitivity and civilization. The opposition conveys levels and tables of values discriminating between evil and good, wrong and right, a-scientific and scientific. We can thus imagine that for these intellectuals to live and to function positively they must face determinants and choose between two alternatives: an aesthetic one, that may motivate silent procedures for a failed traditional organization replaced by the new dominant culture; or the invitation to a psychological adulthood in which the Kierkegaardian 'either/or' paradigm would allow the possibility for a cultural maturation, that is, an ethical, critical, and all-embracing mode of existing. It is from this viewpoint that one should evaluate the provocative pronouncement by Engelbert Mveng in an article entitled 'From Sub-mission to Succession': 'The West agrees with us today that the way to truth passes by numerous paths, other than Aristotelian, Thomistic logic or Hegelian dialectic. But social and human sciences themselves must be decolonized' (1978: 141).

Mveng made this declaration in the 1970s. Then it signalled in its apparent violence what I might call the management of a theory and practice of anxiety or, if one prefers the Freudian metaphor, the 'wine into vinegar' image. This new spelt-out responsibility, which claimed to signify an irreversible and irrevocable separation from colonial ideology, was a new step in a long history of a struggle for a difference (Kizerbo, 1970). Thus, we can ask: was the 1950s–1960s generation of African intellectuals naively premature? Such a rigorous Freudian question does not and cannot respond to their predicament, as it cannot solve the Freudian problem of anxiety, in actuality or symbolically in our case. Can it explain repression and not the reverse? Freud linked anxiety to fear, insisting that 'anxiety has a quality of indefiniteness', and that one should use 'the word "fear" rather than anxiety' (Freud, 1955, vol. 20: 105). Indeed, one thinks immediately of the fear of being suppressed and annihilated, which is profound and pervasive in the *Négritude* writings and the African and Pan-Africanist pre-independence ideologies (e.g. Fanon, 1952). Yet, from a different perspective, Mveng's statement might seem perturbing: it fuses the religious and the social knowledge and demands a decolonization of both. The two are different, despite their ambiguous proximity and even communion in the colonial settings, particularly in Central Africa.

I have already referred to the 'colonial library', or the scientific knowledge gathered, organized and classified by the pre-colonial and the colonial experiences. It became part of African universities, which were almost all instituted between 1950 and 1960. The drive, project and organization of these institutions were European at the heart of all subjects matters, foundational principles and aims. Mveng's invitation meant their reorganization – that is, the reformulation of the organism (biology, economics or geology for example) in an African context.

Does this reconversion concern a disintegration of disciplines? To my knowledge, no sensical African intellectual thought of it as a rejection of a will to knowledge, but instead as an opportunity for revising models, and precisely as an occasion for interrogating the law and inherited sovereignty of the *signifier*. In 1970, focusing on the Belgian Congo, Jean-Louis Litt, a former member of the Jesuit Central African province, in this sense wrote:

> In so far as the barrier put up by the colonial society against the social ascension of local elite does not exist any longer, one can suppose that a lesser degree of conformism towards the values of Western civilization would be looked after by University students. Then, should not one think that the (African) university could progressively serve as a focus for the diffusion of values and behaviors which are specifically African? However, the Congolese university will remain, and probably for a long time, under the influence of a European, markedly Belgian professional corps. It is probable that there is there a permanent source of conflicts between a professional body transmitting values that it estimates universal and a student clientele that could challenge this universality.
>
> (Litt, 1970: 180–1)

Jean-Louis Litt's perspicacious analysis was right in carefully expressing and submitting an appraisal of a difficult succession. Yet, it was too prudent. The nationalist element present in Mveng's post-factum analysis decidedly seemed to ring truer: by the mid-1970s most European professors had left, and in the 1980s, as registered by Benoît Verhaeghen, a political scientist who had spent thirty years of his life in Central Africa, the university had become just a shadow of its colonial dream (Verhaeghen, 1992). On the other hand, going back to Mveng's problematics, the critical and anti-Christian work of 1950–1960 analyses that wished to demonstrate the incompatibility between Africanity and Christianity seemed to have failed, at least provisionally. Thirty years after independence, Christian churches, and Catholicism in particular, were structurally the only solid organizations in Central Africa, even more so than in the United States where they were operating (Brezault and Clavreuil, 1987).

By bringing together the domains of human and social sciences and religion, I wanted to oppose the might of the colonial library to the objective weakness of different African ideologies. In the invocation of Africanization policies, by insisting on its dream of self-sufficiency, I wanted somehow to interrogate indirectly a subjective project and its almost suicidal terms, by playing silently on a simple Lacanian tension that is represented in the difference between *death-drive* and *being-towards-death*. I mean, on the one hand, the apparent epistemological eccentricity of the African subject, such as a Mveng, Kagame, Mulago or Kizerbo who, in their projects, are divided between their ego and 'something' else – the real, symbolic and imaginary spaces of conflicting fields of sciences opposing their own articulation as historical subjects in an intellectual configuration. On the other hand, in their consciousness, the personal experience of a possible fragmentation in an *espace métissé*, as magnificently illustrated by Eboussi-Boulaga in *Christianity without Fetishes* (1981), might indicate signs and dangers for a complete collapse of individuation. Under such an interrogation, the best resoluteness leads to a rivalry of value systems or, at best, as witnessed by Mveng and Eboussi-Boulaga, to a desire projected in an unnameable future. One could thus refer to Lacan's *Ecrits*: 'Who, then, is the other to whom I am more attached than to myself, since at the heart of my assent to my own identity it is still he who agitates me' (Lacan, 1977: 172).

Of course, to meditate on this is not at all to imply a failure but to imagine the passion of 'prophets'. I am not interested in promoting or criticizing them, but in situating them in an historical context. By calling them 'prophets', I am referring to Pierre Bourdieu's reactivation (1988) of the medieval distinction between an *auctor*, a prophetic thinker exploring the margins of a social formation and interrogating a tradition and its institutions, and a *lector*, or a priestly figure whose role is to maintain the essence of a culture and its tradition. As paradoxical as it may seem, the 1960 stage made possible an incomprehensible event: the prophetic dimension emerged in the Church as well as in the university, particularly in social and human sciences. It is represented by Mveng, Kagame, Mulago and Kizerbo – scholars who have tried to reorganize the Colonial Library. Interestingly, their whole enterprise was based on the deviation from an ethnic, racial, or cultural difference, and already signified what in American studies would later on be qualified as a post-modernist ideology of regionalism.

Neoregionalism like neo-ethnic, is a specifically post-modern form of reterritorialization; it is a flight from the realities of late capitalism, a compensatory ideology, in a situation in which regions (like ethnic groups) have been fundamentally wiped out – reduced, standardized, commodified, atomized, or rationalized. The ideology of regionalism is the sentimentalization, by the short-story writers in question, of the nature of the social life and the socioeconomic system in the superstate today.

(Jameson, 1994: 148)

I have defined, in part three, the Colonial Library as a body of knowledge generalizing conceptual rules, some historical paradigms and a political project, in which the non-Western 'something' unveils itself as lacking the Western norm, and thus offers itself as an object for conversion, transmutation and standardization. The library includes, and for good reasons, everything witnessing to difference as well as the figures indicating both the necessity and ways for an evolution. Thus, the library's signs represent more than a simple reconstruction of a history and its incoherences. In its being, this library affirms the radical importance of a conversion and its consequences, and in and by itself identifies with an imperative. In fact, it incarnates the gaze of the historically most advanced consciousness and as such, in its scientific complexity, claims to lay down, in the name of a Kantian *imperator* that it actualizes, laws of both history and salvation. It describes everything, proscribing what the real African past might suggest or require in its difference, and prescribing new ways of being and behaving; and these are, sometimes – as in the post Tempels' period – issued in the ambiguous authority of the so-called Christian stepping stones symbolizing a *praeparationem evangelicam*.

In itself, the Colonial Library is not so much about preserving past or present narratives, customs and knowledge as constituting a body or bodies having in their own right a particular quality inscribed in a given history, but about bringing together these things and collapsing them in a 'primitive background' that a new universe (the colonial) and a new cosmology (conversion) can translate and transform into an advanced modernity. Such a process of reduction is not particular to this specific library. One can observe its regular recurrence even within Western history, apropos such rejected and marginal knowledges as the so-called

le savoir des simples, le savoir des gens and *la science des bonnes
femmes*. However, in what Freud considered to be a tragic essence –
that is, an absolute necessity designating itself as the only reasonable
choice and rule (as in the metaphor opposing the intransigence of
Antigone's will against the reasonableness of the well-being of the
city), it seems clear that both the Western *savoirs des simples* as well
as the African invented primitive backgrounds could be understood as
refused knowledges – that is, as the tragic necessity of an ill-known
desire whose origin comes from elsewhere.

Apropos this universe of difference and its *barbaric splendors* (T.E.
Bowdich, 1819), its *offensive manners* (J. Duncan, 1845–6) and all its
variety of *syndromes of savagery* (e.g. S. Crowther, 1854), from the
beginning, the library was conceived as a lucid statement on '*something*'
which is not mine but which, in the best cases, could be recognized as
a symbol of absolute origins. Thus, by its very existence, it stabilizes
all differences in its being as well as stipulating the rules for possible
conversions to a normative history and culture.

From an analytical viewpoint and referring to Paul Ricoeur's *Conflicts of Interpretations* (1969), at least three levels of discourses can
be distinguished in all cultures. First there is a type of zero degree
system, a basic reading and rendition of a 'something' and its insertion
in the beginnings of the culture and its progressive constitution as a
whole. Its conceptual grids are generally difficult to handle since they
belong simultaneously to mythic enunciative rules and often lie in the
epiphany of a divine voice and the emergence of God in human history.
That the Bible, the Koran, and myths of foundation in Black Africa
deploy themselves as formations of both historical and institutional
choices and presence of a divine project does not seem to be simply
a matter of opinion but indicates that they designate in their being an
obscure point from which at least two possible interpretations, and thus
attitudes, proceed towards them. They account for the mythological
networks of founding narratives and, as such, rationally belong to the
realm of impossible desires as signified by all founding legends; they
witness to an all-embracing authority that integrated itself as a guiding
principle in the human process of understanding and appropriating the
world. Thus, their message and their very own possibility display an

absolute mystery well rendered by the Christian traditional expression
of *Mysterium Fidei*, mystery of Faith: the *Kerygma*, as a constant,
divine impulse or action in the Jewish and Christian traditions; or
the permanence of God's strategies in the prophet's word order; on
immanent grounds, the authority of the Koran or that of sacred founding
ancestors. Another method for understanding the foundational narratives
would be, quite reasonably, to opt for a reading of genesis sagas that
follow, for example, Edmund Leach's *Structuralist Interpretations of
the Biblical Myth* (1983) and bring the Torah or the Bible to a series
of structural inconsequences and contradictions proper to all founding
myths, including African. The same type of operation would easily
situate the Koran on the same horizon, thus constituting it *vis-à-vis*
the Bible and other founding narratives on the basis of the same rules.
They would all unfold, structurally, as identical or opposed statements
on absolute origins, arbitrary foundations of cultures, and variations of
their own progressive transformations through time and, in this sense,
question the evolutionary paradigms and value systems incarnated by
the Colonial Library.

There is a second level of discourses in which, since the nineteenth century, disciplinary ensembles establish themselves as exegeses,
commentaries, translations or specification of the first level. These
second-order discourses define themselves – to use contemporary
concepts – as, for example, *history*, *sociology* or *theology* of the
founding events or, more often, as interpretations and renditions of
everyday life. They elaborate their methods by rationalizing the first-
level events and their problematics, overimposing on them questions of
causality and issues of location, time and evolution, transforming thus
a living experience into a logical statement. Clearly, epics, novels and
travelogues get their substance by bringing together this second level
with the first. Homer in the Greek tradition and oral performances in
Africa are magnificent illustrations. They re-enact past facts and events
as both mythological products (that is, as part of an imaginative and
creative approach to history) and, at the same time, name them and
explicitly introduce their meaning into a constraining history. Do not
all narratives lead to unveiling voices of history? Does Rabelais in
sixteenth-century France, Dostoievski in nineteenth-century Russia, or

Marcel Proust at the beginning of the twentieth century not bring together these two levels exactly as do, say, the African Amadou Hampaté Bâ or Boubou Hama? An always given of everyday life and its aberrations or marvels comes into contact with the logical abstraction of a volume that claims to formulate and vocalize it. Indeed, Rabelais, Dostoievski, Proust or, for that matter, Conrad, Birago Diop, Wole Soyihka, or James' Ngugi wa Thiongo do not only recompose imaginative sagas challenging the contradictory veracities and supposed laws about the origins and the forbidden, but they arrange and negotiate them in a manner highly similar to certain historical practices. Indeed, fiction reflects history, and the latter appears governed by exigencies of the contemporary materiality of fictionalized obsessions, and its politics of retrodiction (see e.g. de Certeau, 1988; Veyne, 1994).

While, on the one hand, travelogues and exegeses comment on the difference, the Library, on the other hand, stabilizes African narratives and performances in a new script, definitively ruining the dynamics of their alterity through two operations. The first analyses the contents of ancient narratives and demands the transformation of African interpretations into new categories: historical or mythical, sacred or profane. The second operation details formal structures according to fields and types of discursive practices in a rigorous grid that names the specificity of genres (epic, legend, story, poetry, etc.) and their presence or absence in the African context. The Library is thus not only the absolute shining power in terms of classification of beings and things but the locus in which all knowledge transmutes itself into science. The incomprehensible beginnings of human cultures and the burgeoning of a supposed universal knowledge and its gradual formulation repeats itself in this artificial locus. Questions such as does epic exist in African cultures? why did the novel as passion assert itself only recently in the West? how can we understand the logic of segmentary social structures? seem then to represent a breakthrough in a new conceptualization of the history of humankind. From this perspective, colonial sciences – taught in *colonial universities* (e.g. that of Antwerpen in Belgium) at the highest period of the European colonizing enterprises – assure both the universality and absolute validity of the Western historical experience, and hence the imperativeness of African conversion to its solidity and logic. In a remarkable semantic transformation, colonial sciences and their academies metamorphosed themselves into 'African studies' in the 1950s. Words changed, images followed them in the ambition of a Library conceived as a treasury for the application of a monumental social and cultural engineering. A new cover obscured and transformed meanings in new vocations of service and fraternity between 'developed' or 'old' and 'underdeveloped' or 'new' nation-cultures.

The stretch of meanings has not really questioned the seriousness of a conquering rhetoric. The Library's richness and apparatuses, now part of a novel ideological milieu, still serve an epistemological order even in the most heterodox interventions that it allows. John Mbiti's and Vincent Mulago's research in religious and theological domains, Placide Tempels' and Alexis Kagame's publications in philosophy, even Jan Vansina and his disciples' promotion of the notion of 'oral tradition' as a conceptual tool in the practice of a scientific history, are, in epistemology, simply unthinkable without reference to the Colonial Library, which incarnates their conditions of possibility and reflects the constitution of their intelligibility.

To the primacy of an archaeological order demonstrating and expressing the impossibility of a 'scientific' foundation outside of its boundaries, one may add another complex issue, that of translation. There is, on the one hand, the fact of distances between levels of experience and, on the other, that of interpretation, and also the apparently banal yet incredible modification of words, meanings, and their systems that are simultaneously transmuted and recreated from one language into another. Maurice Blanchot, meditating on the translation process, puts it nicely, when he notes that

for some (narratives), the translator's work is added to the initial distancing, doubles it, so that some of them gain provisionally from this supplemental aberration, but little by little the disagreement seems too little grounded in relation to the contents, and in the end disappears like an illusion. On the contrary, for other works the act of the translator annuls all interval and all distancing: transported into a foreign language, they are less foreign than they were before they were translated; they are, so to speak, translated against the current, against translation proper to the original art, a translation that, we know, must make us discover the word 'death' as the one best adapted to death, but equally strange as death, as a term put far before us and

that we have to recognize, to relearn, as if it were completely new and
first, a word forever unknown, borrowed from an inaccessible possibility of
language, although we felt the perfect aptness of it, and because of that it tends
endlessly to disappear like a sign without value. Those are works that are called
'untranslatable', but only because the translator translates them necessarily too
much and reintegrates them into everyday language, from which very little had
kept them apart.

(Blanchot, 1995: 179)

It is now possible to situate and begin to imagine the scope of
nightmarish speculations of new religious spaces in cultures, as was
the case of some Central African entities, in which there was no
exact equivalent of such major concepts as *revelation* or *religion*, or,
to refer to a concrete case, the artificiality of conceptual incoherences
brought about in the substitution of the traditional Rwandese *Imana* by
Mungu, imported by missionaries from Swahili Eastern coasts. Even if,
as demonstrated so far, these are major problems witnessing not only
the violence but also the conquering solidity of the Colonial Library, a
brute fact remains. As Claude Lévi-Strauss would have said: what can
we conclude from it? That one can neither translate nor observe?

Finally, more or less critical, explicit, and systematic in all cultures,
there is another level of interpretations that one would qualify as bearing
on languages, human experience, and its conditions. It participates in the
formation of a *Weltanschuung* which, in turn, may reproduce itself as
spectacle of this or that ensemble of choices inscribed in narratives of
genesis. Another expression of this level would be, as in the case of
the 'Greek miracle', a will to truth signifying and exhausting itself as
an endless and obsessive question about the human condition caught
between the contingency of existing and the gravity of a history,
sublimed at best as eschatological or, at any rate, theleologized *à la
Hegel*. The prophets of the recent African cultural maturity – such as
Kagame, Kizerbo, Mulago or Mveng – stand as mediators between
this level and that of confusing and confused disciplines of African
studies, which attend to the adaptation and indigenization of supposedly
universal paradigms of sciences and those of revealed religions of the
letter. The truth that gives them the right to question the pertinence of
such an immense claim is, paradoxically, the same that define them as

this or that particular subject able to produce valid and true or false statements, and to make himself or herself understood because of his or her submission to a normative and paradigmatic epistemological order and its intellectual and ethical procedures. Michel Foucault was perfectly right when, commenting on Canguilhem's understanding of what a correct scientific practice should be, he wrote:

A l'intérieur de ses limites, chaque discipline reconnaît des propositions vraies et fausses; mais elle repousse, de l'autre côté de ses marges, toute une tératologie du savoir. L'extérieur d'une science est plus ou moins peuplé qu'on ne croit : bien sûr, il y a l'expérience immédiate, les thèmes imaginaires, qui portent et reconduisent sans cesse des croyances sans mémoire; mais peut-être n'y a-t-il pas d'erreurs au sens strict, car l'erreur ne peut surgir et être décidée qu'à l'intérieur d'une pratique définie; en revanche, des monstres rôdent dont la forme change avec l'histoire du savoir. Bref, *une proposition doit remplir de complexes et lourdes exigences pour pouvoir appartenir à l'ensemble d'une discipline; avant de pouvoir être dite vraie ou fausse, elle doit être, comme dirait M. Canguilhem, 'dans le vrai'*

On s'est souvent demandé comment les botanistes ou les biologistes du XIXème siècle avaient bien pu faire pour ne pas voir que ce que Mendel disait était vrai. Mais c'est que Mendel parlait d'objets, mettait en oeuvre des méthodes, se plaçait sur un horizon théorique, qui étaient étrangers à la biologie de son époque. Sans doute Naudin, avant lui, avait-il posé la thèse que les traits héréditaires étaient discrets; cependant, aussi nouveau ou étrange que fût ce principe, il pouvait faire partie – au moins à titre d'énigme – du discours biologique. Mendel, lui, constitue le trait héréditaire comme objet biologique absolument nouveau, grâce à un filtrage qui n'avait jamais été utilisé jusque là: il le détache de l'espèce, il le détache du sexe qui le transmet; et le domaine où il l'observe est la série indéfiniment ouverte des générations où il apparaît et disparaît selon des régularités statistiques. Nouvel objet qui appelle de nouveaux instruments conceptuels, et de nouveaux fondements théoriques. *Mendel disait vrai, mais il n'était pas 'dans le vrai' du discours biologique de son époque*: ce n'était point selon de pareilles règles qu'on formait des objets et des concepts biologiques; il a fallu tout un changement d'échelle, le déploiement de tout un nouveau plan d'objets dans la biologie pour que Mendel entre dans le vrai et que ses propositions apparaissent (pour une bonne part) exactes.

Mendel était un monstre vrai, ce qui faisait que la science ne pouvait pas en parler; cependant que Schleiden, par exemple, une trentaine d'années auparavant, niant en plein XIXe siècle la sexualité végétale, mais selon les règles du discours biologique, ne formulait qu'une erreur disciplinée.

Il se peut toujours qu'on dise le vrai dans l'espace d'une extériorité sauvage; mais on n'est dans le vrai qu'en obéissant aux règles d'une 'police' discursive qu'on doit réactiver en chacun de ses discours.

(Foucault, 1971: 35–7; my emphasis)

Within its own limits, every discipline recognizes true and false propositions, but it repulses a whole teratology of learning. The exterior of a science is both more, and less, populated than one might think: certainly, there is immediate experience, imaginary themes bearing on and continually accompanying immemorial beliefs; but perhaps there are no errors in the strict sense of the term, for error can only emerge and be identified within a well-defined process; there are monsters on the prowl, however, whose forms alter with the history of knowledge. *In short, a proposition must fulfil some onerous and complex conditions before it can be admitted within a discipline; before it can be pronounced true or false it must be, as Monsieur Canguilhem might say, 'within the true'.*

People have often wondered how nineteenth-century botanists and biologists managed not to see the truth of Mendel's statements. But it was precisely because Mendel spoke of objects, employed methods and placed himself within a theoretical perspective totally alien to the biology of his time. But then, Naudin had suggested that hereditary traits constituted a separate element before him; and yet, however novel or unfamiliar the principle may have been, it was nevertheless reconcilable, if only as an enigma, with biological discourse. Mendel, on the other hand, announced that hereditary traits constituted an absolutely new biological object, thanks to a hitherto untried system of filtrage: he detached them from species, from the sex transmitting them, the field in which hereditary traits appear and disappear with statistical regularity. Here was a new object, calling for new conceptual tools, and for fresh theoretical foundations. *Mendel spoke the truth, but he was not* 'dans le vrai' *(within the true) of contemporary biological discourse*: it was simply not along such lines that objects and biological concepts were formed. A whole change in scale, the development of a totally new range of objects in biology was required before Mendel could enter into the true and his propositions could appear, for the most part, exact.

Mendel was a true monster, so much so that science could not even properly speak of him. Yet Schleiden, for example, thirty years earlier, denying, at the height of the nineteenth century, vegetable sexuality, was committing no more than a disciplined error.

It is always possible one could speak the truth in a void, one would only be in the true, however, if one obeyed the rules of some discursive 'policy' which would have to be reactivated every time one spoke.

(Foucault, 1971: 35–7; my emphasis)

One might thus acknowledge that, against the Colonial Library, any movement from sub-mission to a mission stipulated by the demand of a succession provides its own picture as true or false only within the framework of the Library, and its relative liberty as a scientific project seems limited to turning or orienting one's gaze into this same Library. The sanctity or the profanity of a discourse that may result from such an arrangement will be, strangely enough, determined by that very fundamental coherence which founded the Library in the name of science and a will to truth; and this has nothing to do with the factuality of any African references, nor with the 'respectability' or the 'mystery' of their empiricities. To clarify this issue I could refer to an eccentric Nietzsche using extreme violence in *The Antichrist* as a way of making his point. A similar attitude has been repeated endlessly in African studies confusing the complexity of the being of the Colonial Library with racial and racist politics in the development of sciences. Eugen Fink notes that in his attack on Christianity

Nietzsche battles against the Christian religion with an unparalleled fervour of hatred, and with a flood of invectives and accusations. Here the virtuosity of his attack, leaving no stone unturned, reverses itself. The lack of measure destroys the intended effect; one can't convince while foaming at the mouth. Essentially the text offers nothing new; Nietzsche collects what he has already said about the morality of pity and the psychology of the priest – but now he gives his thoughts an exorbitant, violent edge and wants to insult, to strike the tradition in the face, to 'transvalue' by valuing in an anti-Christian way.

(Fink, 24)

Now, then, we could face this strange couple, *race* and *science*, from a recent problematic, as critically actualized in the anthology edited by Sandra Harding, *The Racial Economy of Science* (1993).

Race and Science

Rhetoricali sumus, et in morem declamatorum paululum lusimus.

St Jérome

Conscious fraud is probably rare in science. It is also not very interesting, for it tells us little about the nature of scientific activity. Liars, if discovered, are excommunicated; scientists declare that their profession has properly policed itself, and they return to work, mythology unimpaired, and objectively vindicated. The prevalence of unconscious finagling, on the other hand, suggests a general conclusion about the social context of science. For if scientists can be honestly self-deluded . . . then prior prejudice may be found anywhere, even in the basics of measuring bones and toting sums.

Stephen Jay Gould

In principle, one could classify languages according to their level of noise and expressiveness. Thus, it should be possible to delimit, again in principle, such ensembles as the language of insults (cf. playing the Dozens) with their high level of noise and expressiveness, the languages of poetry versus that of social and human sciences with their variable degree of violence, and, as exemplary, the language of science which, in its most pure manifestations in logic and mathematics, explicitly aims at an absolute inexpressiveness and lack of noise and violence.

Sandra Harding's anthology, then, comes to most of us as a shock in what it illustrates and details: there would be a 'racial' (and, as a matter of fact, a 'sexual') *economy* of science. 'By racial economy,' writes Harding, 'I mean those institutions, assumptions, and practices that are responsible for disproportionately distributing along "racial" lines the benefits of Western sciences to the haves and the bad consequences to the have-nots, thereby enlarging the gap between them.' Furthermore, there is a 'racialized' history of science as well:

The problem is not Western Sciences per se but certain configurations within them, such as Eurocentrism, that need to be cut out of our institutions, assumptions, and practices. . . . We must learn to take responsibility for the sciences we have now and have had in the past, to acknowledge their limitations and flaws as we also value their indubitable strengths and achievements. But to do so requires a more realistic and objective grasp of their origins and effects 'elsewhere' as well as in the West.

(Harding, 1993: 2)

The issue might seem political. But, following Georges Canguilhem's famous injunction, 'the past of a science is a vulgar notion [as] the past of a present-day science is not the same thing as that science in the past,' should we say that Harding's investigation, and her analysis, do not concern the past of Western science? At the same time, we should perhaps note that Sandra Harding is an epistemologist. She would, I think, concede that her relation to the histories of sciences may be different from that of the scientists and that her motivation in assembling *The Racial Economy of Science* is, indeed, very particular – even contrary to the interpretative critique discursive practices in biology offered by Greg Myers in *Writing Biology* (1990). If we can agree on this, then let us face the real question as formulated by Georges Canguilhem in *Ideology and Rationality in the History of the Life Sciences*.

Since philosophical discourse does not produce knowledge, is philosophy disqualified from discussing the conditions of its production? 'Must one resolve to say nothing about the sciences unless one produces scientific knowledge?' Hardly. There is practice and there is practice. If the word is used in the sense that Descartes used it to describe how he put his method into practice to solve mathematical problems, it may seem that a productive practice of this kind is not within the philosopher's reach; if it were, he would be among those in the vanguard of scientific progress. For the epistemologist, practising a science amounts to mimicking the practice of the scientist by attempting to reconstitute the means by which knowledge is produced through studious attention to the papers in which the producer explains his behaviour.

To reconstitute the means by which knowledge is produced. Sandra Harding, could have taken this avenue to describe an 'order of conceptual progress' with its discontinuities. Instead she chose a riskier task of showing how ideological obstacles, obsolete presumptions and preconceptions survive despite epistemological ruptures and the now universally admitted fact, as Gaston Bachelard put it in *Le Matérialisme rationnel* (1953), that 'contemporary science is based on the search for true (*véritable*) facts and the synthesis of truthful (*véridique*) laws.'

Sandra Harding's anthology is divided into six different sections, each prefaced with a brief introduction by the editor. The first section on 'Early Non-Western Scientific Traditions', includes three contributions: 'Poverties and Triumphs of the Chinese Scientific Tradition' by Joseph Needham; 'Black Athena: Hostilities to Egypt in the Eighteenth Century' by Martin Bernal; and 'Early Andean Experimental Agriculture' by Jack Weatherford. One notes immediately the geographical distribution of the studies – Asia, Africa and America, and the combination of pieces set against the backdrop of Western science should, according to Sandra Harding, raise at least three issues: (1) the scientific *parallels* and *contrasts* existing in non-Western traditions; (2) the *uniqueness* of Western traditional science; and (3) 'Is Western science the only modern science *possible* and *desirable*? Do modern Westerners not define science – 'real science' – too narrowly, as Needham argues, thereby devaluing forms of scientific thought and activity simply because they were or are not the forms favoured in the sciences most useful to dominant groups in the modern West' (emphasis mine).

Beyond these three issues and the common critical perspective they imply, let us also note the three major differences between the anthologized texts. The focus of Joseph Needham's text on the history of science in China faces two a priori issues. Why is it that Asian cultures were scientifically more efficient between the second and the sixteenth centuries AD? And why did 'the mathematization of hypotheses about Nature, with all its implications for advanced technology, take its meteoric rise *only* in the West at the time of Galileo?' Martin Bernal's brief on Egypt and European scholarship in the eighteenth century is taken from the first volume of his controversial late-1980s text *Black Athena*, in which the 'Greek miracle' is accounted for by Levantine influx instead of the nineteenth-century thesis emphasizing an Aryan model. Bernal is polemical in his deconstruction of the hostilities toward Egypt in the eighteenth century: the *Aryan argument* (which prevails to the present day) was, according to him, made possible by anti-Semitism and racism between the 1890s and the 1920s. They silenced the Ancient model that had been accepted since the time of the Greeks (and by the Greeks themselves), according to which the Greek miracle was the result of an inculturated *métissage* of influxes from the Levant. Finally, Jack Weatherford's article on Andean agriculture sets out to prove that the 'science of agriculture' stretches back in time, that 'the ancient Peruvians had been among the world's greatest experimenters with agriculture.' Weatherford's text suggests an ethnology of an original knowledge for the production of potatoes, beans, corn, squashes, amaranth, etc.

In short, Joseph Needham's analysis privileges an internal analysis of Chinese history to challenge external a prioris; Martin Bernal's discernment of a Western discontinuity aims to reaffirm an ancient hypothesis, an alternative multicultural model from within the Western tradition; and, finally, Jack Weatherford illustrates a remarkable parallel to Western agricultural sciences.

Part two of Sandra Harding's anthology, 'Science Constructs Race', has seven articles dealing directly or indirectly with race. Together the articles in question explore a series of linked concerns: the scientific history of racism, science and the politics of racism, and a critique of the concept of race.

Essays by Stephen Jay Gould, Frank B. Livingstone, Gloria A. Marshall and S. L. Washburn describe how the scientific history of racism – particularly of its biological justification – is intimately linked to the history of science, to Linnaeus's classification of races in *Systema Naturae* (1758), wherein it is affirmed that *Homo Europeus est* inaugurates a new classificatory regime. The careers of Georges Cuvier in paleontology, J.F. Blumenback in craniology, Louis Agassiz or Samuel G. Morton in polygenism, chosen from among many others throughout the eighteenth, nineteenth and twentieth centuries, illustrate the congruence of science and racism. The major fact is now that one can say science makes nothing out of nothing. As Stephen Jay Gould put it, conscious fraud is probably rare in science. Yet, should we accept such a statement when we pay attention to what has been going on, for years, in sociobiology, and led a number theorists and activitists to speak, after Joe Crocker, of a 'conspiracy theory'? (Myers, 1990: 193–246).

The tension between monogenism (which posits the unity and primary genesis of all peoples) and polygenism (which postulates human races as separate biological species) may be the most indicative of the relationships between science and the politics of racism. In any case, it is at the very moment that science is defined, conceptualized as 'a sharply edged and value-neutral domain of knowledge', and more precisely as 'an apolitical, non-theological, universal, empirical, and uniquely objective form of knowledge unlike any other,' that one could identify the racial politics of science. After Darwin had established the basic typology of races and the central fact of evolution, some American polygenists employed those classifications to justify the practice of slavery, or to accommodate a hierarchy of races. Even in its most factual readings of empiricities, to the present day, science has been racially biased – partially because it did not or could not face the political nature of its language – so that it might be time to challenge the a priori and racist assumptions of certain of its models and interpretations. There are, if specific references are needed, the manipulation of intelligence quotients and, more concretely, the corruption of Alfred Binet's test whose initial function in 1905 was 'to help identify (French) children who, as matters then stood, could not profit from instruction in the regular public schools of Paris.' From the background of American history, one could ponder on the inadequacy of indexes of racial inferiority that, between 1830 and 1920, classified in similar terms African-Americans and distinguished immigrant ethnics: Eastern-Europeans, Irish or Jews (see e.g. Todd, 1994).

Facing the simple fact of wide-ranging racist assumptions in the practice of scientists, Sandra Harding formulates a simple question in her introduction to this second section: 'Is the solution to this problem to be found "outside" the sciences themselves? How entrenched have the sciences become in legitimating the dominant views of racial difference? And how is the power and authority of the sciences enhanced as a result of their serving such a legitimating role?' S.L. Washburn, commenting on the ambiguity of the very concept of race, situates the possible solution in a necessary bracketing of all a prioris:

Whether we consider intelligence, or length of life, or happiness the genetic potential of a population is only realized in a social system. . . . Human biology finds its realization in a culturally determined way of life, and the infinite variety of genetic combinations can only express themselves efficiently in a free and open society.

(1993: 132)

I might suggest another angle for theorizing and specifying this difficult problem: to reflect on the notions of void and nothing as symbols for the formulation of the mathematical concept of absence as actualized by the sign zero. The thematization of this sign as a possible determining point of reference creates a paradox insofar as zero is also and always a relative sign designating the pole of another number. There is no reason, writes Brian Rotman in his *Signifying Nothing: The Semiotics of Zero* (1993),

why a sign such as zero cannot be a relative origin, why zero cannot signify absence relative to the presence of certain signs, why, that is, zero cannot be privileged as a meta-sign with respect to other signs not so privileged. In effect, observe . . . that zero is an origin at a very primitive, parsimonious, and minimally articulated, level of sign formation. Signification codes difference, hence the need for more than one sign. How do we produce, with the minimum of *ad hoc* extra-semiotic means, two 'different' signs? Answer: let there be a sign – call it 1 – and let there be another sign – call it 0 – indicating the absence of the sign 1. Of course, such a procedure *produces* the difference it appears subsequently to describe; and the use of absence to manufacture difference in this way is a viable sign practice only through the simultaneous introduction of a syntax: a system of placing signifiers in linear relation to each other in such a way that it allows signs to be interpretable in terms of the original absence/presence signified by 0.

(Rotman, 1993: 105)

In this production of a difference, simultaneously and ambiguously *absolute* and *relative*, designating zero as an *absence*, which is also a *presence*, one can apprehend an excellent illustration of the genesis of binary oppositions and, through analogical extensions, the foundation of what Jacques Derrida calls 'logocentrism'. This locus also magnifies the simply allegorical basis for all politics of exclusion prejudice and racism:

What for Derrida sustains the traditional and misguided account of the opposition speech/writing, allowing writing to be characterized in terms of its secondarity, as the transcription of psychologically and epistemologically prior speaking, is the parallel acceptance of a whole series of oppositions – identity/difference, presence/absence, reality/image, thing/sign, literal/meta-phorical – basic to Western conceptions of the linguistic sign. In each of these oppositional categories there is assumed to be a degree zero: one of the terms is privileged as original, generic, and primary, the other subsidiary and specified in relation to it. Thus difference is the lack of a prior conceived identity, absence is non-existence of a primary presence, images represent a given and already existent reality, signs are tokens of pre-signifying 'things' which precede them, the metaphorical is a species of the more fundamental category of the non-literal.

(Rotman, 1993: 98)

I hope it is now clear why no one needs a map to move from the mathematical ambiguous tension between *zero* and *its other* (such as the sign 1) to a conceptualization of racial views thematizing, for example, the Black (or any other demonized social, cultural or racial entity), as the paradoxical *absolute* and *relative* sign of difference.

The last theme of 'Science Constructs Race' in Harding's anthology is a broad critique of the concept of race itself. Although all of the contributions are animated in some measure by this concern, articles by Nancy Leys Stephan and Sander L. Gilman on 'The Rejection of Scientific Racism' and Nancy Krieger and Mary Basset on 'Disease, Class, and Ideology of Science' are remarkable for their exemplary empiricism. Their insights are crucial; first, they describe the dangerous power of metaphor in the sciences:

Darwin would not keep control over the metaphors he introduced (such as natural selection, struggle for survival, survival of the fittest). Nearly every term he used was multivalent and was appropriated in selective and varied ways by very different groups for very different purposes. Though Darwin endeavored in later editions of *The Origin of Species* to reduce the metaphoric ambiguities of his science, his attempts failed, and until well into the twentieth century Darwinism served as a metadiscourse that opened up, rather than merely closed off, the discussion of nature. By the 1900s in the physical sciences, and by the 1920s in the biological sciences, however, the metaphors of scientific language had become much more tightly controlled. The modern scientific text had replaced the expansive scientific book, and the possibilities of multivalent meanings being created out of scientific language were thereby curtailed.

(Harding, 1993: 174–5)

Second, the discourse of science could not but signify itself as a discourse of power, re-enacting in its domain the privileges of dominant political superstructures. Stephan and Gilman wrote that the challenges mounted by the minorities . . . often made relatively little difference to mainstream science. The white male academic usually ignored the contributions of minorities to the sciences of themselves. For instance, only one of W.E.B. du Bois' many articles was published in the journal of the new profession of sociology, The American Journal of Sociology, even during the time when the journal was actively involved in the discussion of race (and even though its editors shared to some degree the antiracist outlook of Du Bois).

(1993: 187)

Third, as suggested by Krieger and Basset, one of the possible ways of transcending the racial economy of the sciences would be to pay close attention to how the dialectic between the 'analysis of the social relations of race and class can illuminate the processes involved in the social production of disease' (see also Todd, 1994).

On the whole, this second section of Harding's book is distressing – and illuminating – as it details the scandal of science submitted to preconceived assumptions. While the section is at times repetitive – many of the contributors make nearly identical points with recourse to nearly identical stories – the delimitation of the racial economy of science is worthwhile.

Part three of Harding's anthology, 'Who Gets to Do Science', seems to be the most political. 'Science,' she writes,

is supposed to be the most universal of all human products. . . . Scientific method is supposed to be powerful enough to eliminate from the results of research any social biases that may have crept into the scientific work because of the obvious social values and interests that we all have as members of historical communities. . . . Consequently, one might think that science would be more welcoming to minorities (and women) than other professions that do not so emphasize the universality of their methods.

(Harding, 1993: 197–8)

All the articles in this section prove the contrary. We can thus risk a question: was it not possible to find texts that could witness to a more positive view of who gets to do science? In fact, to withdraw science from a mystifying heaven of purity, should we not undertake to think of it in the full (and therefore contradictory) depth of our human history, its positive moments as well as its negative preconceptions about differences, instead of reducing it to the idolatrous perfection of a conceptualization situated outside of our real, empirical context? Harding's anthology pursues her thesis rather relentlessly. Thus, Ronald T. Takaki in 'Aesculapius Was a White Man: Race and the Cult of True Womanhood', comments on how professionalized medicine in America has become the monopoly of university-trained white men and 'would maintain the exclusion of blacks and remove the competition of white women from medical practice'; Shirley Malcolm, in 'Increasing the Participation of Black Women and Technology', analyses statistics to indicate the type of 'interventions that can promote participation in science and engineering careers by minority females'; whereas Eileen M. O'Brien, in 'Without More Minorities, Women, Disabled, U.S. Scientific Failure Certain, Fed Study Says', deduces, from the 1988 Federal report ('Changing America: The New Face of Science and Engineering') an agenda for the future: a stronger representation of American Indians, Blacks, Hispanics, disabled individuals, and White women in the field of sciences. Finally, Susantha Goonatilake, in 'Modern Science and the Periphery: The Characteristics of Dependent Knowledge', focuses on creativity; her central thesis argues that

this diffusion model of knowledge that operates between the centre and the periphery really leads to a colonial division of labour in the academic world, paralleling divisions in the economic and political worlds.

(Harding, 1993: 280)

Personally, I would link Susantha Goonatilake's position to that of the African philosopher Paulin Hountondji who, in a highly sophisticated analysis, noted that

scientific activity in the Third World seems to me to be characterized, globally, by its position of dependency. This dependency is of the same nature as that of the economic activity, which is to say that, put back in the context of its historical genesis, it obviously appears to be the result of the progressive integration of the Third World into the worldwide process of the production of knowledge, managed and controlled by the Northern countries. . . . The colony was, in its fashion, a consumer of science, as it was a consumer of industrial products, imported products in every case, and perceived as such; products whose origin and mode of 'fabrication' the local population knew nothing about and that, therefore, could only appear to them as surreal and not to be mastered, miraculously placed on top of their daily reality like a veneer.

(Hountondji, 1992)

Part four of the anthology dwells on 'Science's Technologies and Applications'. These are some of the most exceptional articles in the book, united by a shared topical concern as well as a certain temper of critical despair. James Jones tells of the Tuskegee syphilis experiment, during which the United States Public Health Service conducted for forty years 'a study of the effects of untreated syphilis on black men in Macon County, Alabama, in and around the country seat of Tuskegee.' Phillida Bunkle documents the international politics of Depo-Provera, or medroxyprogesterone acetate ('the three-monthly contraceptive injection'), tested in the 1960s by Upjohn Cie, banned by the FDA from the US market in 1978, but still used overseas, particularly in the Third World. Vandana Shiva's exposition of 'Colonialism and the Evolution of Masculinist Forestry' notes that

up to 50 percent of all living things – at least five million species – are estimated to live in tropical forests. . . . The unparalleled diversity of species within tropical forests means relatively few individuals of each; any forest clearance thus disrupts their life cycles and threatens them with rapid extinction. Current estimates suggest that we are losing one species of life a day from the five–ten million species believed to exist. If present trends continue, we can expect an annual rate of loss as high as 50,000 species by the year 2000.

(Harding, 1993: 304)

Shiva stresses that 'modern science and development are projects of male, Western origin, both historically and ideologically,' and that 'it is women's work that protects and conserves nature's life in forestry and in agriculture, and through such conservation work sustains human life.' Richard Levis and Richard Lewontin expound on the theme of the struggle for a revolutionary science which, evaluating 'the nature of science in the Third World,' insists on three points: (1) 'Euro-North American science', like democracy, has been marketed to much of the Third World. Its advocates praise its values, bemoan its deficiencies, and assert its superiority over all alternatives; (2) 'science came into the Third World as a rationale for domination with theories of racial superiority, of "progress", and of its own intellectual superiority'; (3) 'science entered the Third World as a form of intellectual domination. After the troops depart, the investments remain; after direct ownership is removed, managerial skills, patents, textbooks and journals remain, repeating the message that only by adopting their ways can we progress, only by going to their universities can we learn; only by emulating their universities can we teach.'

Finally, Karl Grossman's 'Environmental Racism' sounds the same note of critical despair as it describes the findings of a 1982 Commission on 'Toxic Wastes and Race in the United States,' including the fact that 'race proved to be the most influential among variables tested in association with the location of commercial hazardous waste facilities. This represented a consistent national pattern.'

Part five, 'Objectivity, Method, and Nature: Value Neutral?' questions the method and aims of science, unfolding a critique of the naïveté that qualifies science as an objective practice. The six contributions of this section are demonstrative: science seems to submit all of its concepts, analyses and projection to something else. But must this always be so? Each of the essays collected here (including texts by Donna Haraway, Robert Proctor and Jack Stander) trace an anticipatory draft, that of revolution or, as some might prefer, of negativity. But to conceive such a draft would mean to posit a reference that would transcend the real differences between the geographical centre and the periphery of our world. Sandra Harding, on the other hand, believes that 'it is no longer reasonable to regard scientific method as value neutral. Moreover, although science training has historically avoided exposing young scientists to anything but the most minimal history, philosophy and sociology of science, [the National Academy of Sciences] recommends such studies, arguing that such accounts provide important resources for scientists in learning to identify their own and their culture's values.'

The concluding part of the anthology explores just this question: Joseph Needham correlates science and democracy, concluding that 'both are on the side of union, attraction and aggregation, leading to the higher organizational levels'; an editorial included from *The Black*

Scholar begins with the statement that 'the uses of scientific knowledge cannot be separated from the society in which its uses occur'; and David Dickson, under the entry of the new politics of sciences, elaborates a challenge:

Despite the importance of both the analytical and political work carried out on such topics, however, the agenda of the radical science movement has frequently remained restricted to those issues which gave it its initial impetus in the late 1960s and 1970s. The result was a critical approach that had much to say about the need for the control of the potential health hazards of recombinant DNA research or chemical carcinogens, but less about the increased private control of scientific knowledge resulting from changes in patent laws, attempts to use controls on the dissemination of scientific knowledge as an instrument of foreign policy and capitalist expansion, the use of scientific arguments to legitimize the molding of the regulation of technology into a form compatible with the political needs of the nation's industrial leaders, or several other key issues in what I have described as the new politics of science.

This is the task that now lies ahead. . . . In particular it is necessary to concentrate on ways of politicizing the discussion in terms and conditions of access to science, the crucial intermediate position between production and application. For it is here, I suggest, that political action is now the most needed, and where the possibilities of opening science to proper democratic control are most in danger of being foreclosed.

(1993: 473)

A manifesto of the Third World Network on 'Modern Science in Crisis' closes this sixth part of the anthology with concrete proposals on science technology and natural resources, science and hazards in technology, science and racism, women and sexism, science and militarization, energy, agriculture, health, telecommunications, science education, science policy and management, and more. All these themes can be reunited in the editor's question that opens the last part of the anthology: 'Can we transform the sciences into solution for those peoples of the world who are trying to develop more democratic ways of living together?'

The history of science, says Michel Serres, does not exist. Everyone talks as if it exists, but I don't know of any. Sandra Harding knows this and that made it possible for her to conceive this provocative and timely anthology, which brings together interpretations of scandalous scientific paradigms and hypotheses. In doing so, and in advancing a political reading of scientific propositions, she was arguing sense while at the same time invoking a necessary realism in epistemology. As Canguilhem noted in his evaluation of the 'younger generation of French epistemologists': 'The production of knowledge, [Dominique] Lecourt argues, is a social practice; hence the judgment of knowledge in relation to the conditions of its production is in fact and by right a question for the theory of political praxis, that is, for Marxist materialism as reworked by Althusser and his school. If Lecourt is right, then it must be admitted that epistemologists are wrong to attempt to reconstruct the history of science without reference to the history of society.'

Sandra Harding's *Racial Economy of Science* is one of the most distressing books I have ever read. It demystifies the practice of science; at the same time, it implicitly makes a wonderful case for the urgent necessity of scientific practices whose objective should be to actualize faithfully the ambition of any science for a non-violent, inexpressive and neutral language.

Epilogue

'Gently, mortals, be discreet.'

What I like about my madness is that it has
protected me from the very beginning against
the charms of the 'élite': never have I thought
that I was the happy possessor of a 'talent'; my
sole concern has been to save myself – nothing in
my hands, nothing up my sleeve – by work and
faith. As a result, my pure choice did not raise me
above anyone. Without equipment, without tools, I
set all of me to work in order to save all of me.
If I relegate impossible Salvation to the proproom,
what remains? A whole man, composed of all men
and as good as all of them and no better than any.

Jean-Paul Sartre, *The Words*, 255

Here, in concluding what is more a reflection on myself than strict
research on African representations of *Tales of Faith*, I discover that
I personally witness to these tales. The fact that I might not believe
in God or in some kind of divine spirit has not prevented me from
facing with sympathy the complexity of their fate and modalities
of their cultural appropriations. In fact, the language I speak, the
phenomena I comment upon, and the stories I have chosen to share in
these lectures on conversion are, indeed, not only unthinkable outside
of a space circumscribed by African elements but also well determined
by anthropology and the colonial saga, as well as the practices and
missionizing of Islam and Christianity. Thus, *Tales of Faith* is about any
post-colonial individual. Even more, I would like these tales to provide
an opportunity for reconsidering the 1960s political and intellectual
exercises, which too easily negated the evidence of *métissité* and

reduced the colonial experience to a sheer parenthesis in African histories, as did Jacob F.A. Ajayi in one of the most inspiring studies in African scholarship (1969).

Is there any individual, reflecting on his or her finitude, who does not experience the sense of being or, at any rate, of belonging to an endangered species? Death, as a closure of existence in the world, sanctions the absurdity, or – if one prefers – the mystery of life and forces the observer to evaluate existence from the background of a culture and its a prioris. My sense of belonging to a group reflects a degree of my insertion into its culture, and what my death might signify when I am gone would be my ways of witnessing to the arbitrariness of my culture. The plurality of cultural a prioris is an empirical fact. That it has nothing to do with 'races' is today a matter of debate only for those who, in the wake of some nineteenth-century presuppositions, still confuse biology and culture.

The identity of any individual or human community actualizes itself as a process through three main ektases: *temporalization*, or a subjective procedure whereby an individual or a collective consciousness negotiates the norms for its duration as being, as well as those of things in the world; *reflection*, or the incredible assumption of a reflecting consciousness present in, and separated from, a consciousness reflected on; finally, the last ektasis, *being-for-others,* during which the self conflictually apprehends itself outside of itself as an object for others. These experiences of a consciousness, standing out of itself in order to grasp and comprehend its always fluctuating identity, show well the impossibility of reducing anyone, any human culture, to an immobile essence. More importantly, living, acting and believing in a world in which there is always a history – and there are already other people preceding me – whatever I do, as Sartre would have said, I accomplish it in relation to others. I mean precisely that any action is always a consequence of my *original sin*, my upsurge in a world where I am not alone: *métis*, because of my very identity, which can only be a continuous project towards a transcendence; *métis*, also, by being there and evolving in a space – simultaneously real and constructed – already circumscribed and colonized by others' history, even when these predecessors or contemporaries of mine are my people. Finally, I am a *métis* in the very consciousness of conceiving and apprehending my freedom as both lack and need actualizing itself simultaneously as a negative and positive praxis – that is, a negative, purposeful activity because it signifies in what it is the negation of a given; positive, since it is an opening in what is coming. As Sartre describes this fundamental *métissité*:

> It is from this singular situation that the notion of guilt and sin seems to be derived. It is before the Other that I am *guilty*. I am guilty first when beneath the Other's look I experience my alienation and my nakedness as a fall from grace which I must assume. This is the meaning of the famous line from Scripture: 'They knew that they were naked.' Again I am guilty when in turn I look at the Other, because by the very fact of my own self-assertation I constitute him as an object and as an instrument, and I cause him to experience that same alienation which he must now assume. Thus original sin is my upsurge in a world where there are others; and whatever may be my further relations with others, these relations will be only variations on the original theme of my guilt.
>
> (Sartre, 1956: 31)

Then, strictly speaking, who is not a *métis*? How can any culture claim the purity of an absolute and uncontaminated identity, a pure essence, if, by analogically extending the paradox of an impossible stable identity of the I to a We-subject, we accept that a pure culture-island will become a corpse-culture?

Any conciliation between a represented and its representations is a matter of permanent negotiations. The representations are political in nature, insofar as they operate as metaphors of something else, existing out there in a sociohistorical context. For example, Conrad's sophisticated play of colours in *The Heart of Darkness* illustrates well differential logics of representation in a tradition of narratives generating economies of bad faith and misreadings of sociohistorical experiences. One could, apropos this particular book, elaborate on themes, such as 'imperialism is a robbery', and 'why condemn a society and not the empire', and link them to what politically might impose itself as symbolizing 'the light' versus 'the dark', thus bringing together Marlow and Kurtz as cultural agents in a monstrous unity. It should also be possible to begin by the symbolism itself as a call, and address its factuality in a number of conflicting representations. One would oppose, for instance, the 'white souls of black people' to the 'black souls of white people' exploiting Africans, reversing the classical decisiveness of the opposition between White and Black as corresponding to good versus bad. To use a Heideggerian expression, the whole narrative could be turned into an assessment apropos the disclosedness of Being-in-the-world, taking place in the jungle as reality of truth, or in a blinding sunshine as reference to an alienation functioning under some admirable signs of the Enlightenment. Well, what is at play here is an interpretation on the incommensurability between a representation – the novel – and its represented. After all, we know that Conrad did fieldwork, as anthropologists would put it today; he visited the Congo in 1890, was in Matadi on 13 June, and went back to Europe the following November with a well-kept diary.

'Hell is other people' might sum up a dangerous extension of the *I–Thou* relation to the Europe–Africa political and cultural rapports. Yet, in their ambiguous and often violent exchanges that go back to the end of the fifteenth century, one faces forms of other radical confrontations. For instance, any Being-in-the-world can be exemplified as *Being-in-company-of-others* – that is, existing as opening up to an outside, as reaching out and exceeding one's own limits, one's difference, and *I as the Other*. . . . What a magnificent paradigm! Rimbaud's anti-Cartesian statement echoes Rousseau's unbelievable foundation of his *Confessions* (to study oneself so that he can understand humankind) and announces Lévi-Strauss' demanding ambition for an anthropology that would be critical of its own ordinary temptation, the glorious and exotic facticity of otherness.

If the final aim of anthropology is to contribute to a better knowledge of objectified thought and its mechanisms, it is in the last resort, immaterial whether in this book the thought processes of the South American Indians take shape through the medium of my thought, or whether mine takes place through the medium of theirs. What matters is that the human kind, regardless of the identity of those who happen to be giving it expression, would display an increasingly intelligible structure as a result of the doubly reflexive forward movement of two thought processes acting one upon the other, each of which can in turn provide the spark or tinder whose conjunction will shed light on both.

(Lévi-Strauss, 1969: 13)

Let us put aside here the implicit and untenable issue of the universality form of mind and rather magnify what, in the confession, turns away from the Cartesian *Cogito* and its ontological excesses. Lévi-Strauss disposes the I not only as a being among others, but as 'the weakest, the most humble of others' (1976: 39), affirming that 'to accept oneself in others, one must first deny the self in oneself' (1976: 36), and that 'man must recognize himself as a "he" before daring to lay claim to also being a "me"' (1976: 39). What might appear to be a romanticization of the exoticism of the other and its visibility (versus the invisibility and certainty of the normative I positioning itself as foundation of knowledge) is, in actuality, a revolutionary repositioning of the projection–introjection represented by the For-Itself and the For-Other. These, as Maurice Merleau-Ponty notes, 'are each the other side of the other' to the point that I could state that 'myself and the other are like two *nearly* concentric circles which can be distinguished only by a slight and mysterious slippage. . . . Nevertheless the other is not I and on that account differences arise. I make the other in my own image. . . . Am I not to the very end of the universe, am I not, by myself, coextensive with everything I see, hear, understand, or feign?' (Merleau-Ponty, 1973: 133).

Tales of Faith is about the strange constructed space I chose to inhabit so that I could think about the unthinkable: how well the predicament of Sartre's pessimism in 'Hell is other people' meets the supreme beauty of 'I am an Other'. The two positions are inseparable in this space, in which identities are always mixtures facing each other as competitive projects aimed at, to use Schlegel's language, an impossible *ars combinatoria* – I mean a universal and definitive 'logical chemistry'.

Tales of Faith is also, and perhaps mainly, about an incomprehensible miracle – that is, an extraordinary event in the world. These lectures constitute an invitation to meditate on my composite narrative, which contemplates difficult statements that are contradictory in their effects and, in any case, unbelievable for the agnostic I am. On the pagan side, here are two illustrations: 'God was not a fool to make us Masaai', say elders in the Masaai community. The second case concerns the question of Christian redemption, as articulated in an amazing obstruction that a group of Central African Mbuti opposed to a missionary. This beautiful story is narrated by Gérard Buakasa T.K.M, a Zaïrean scholar. Reacting to the death-sacrifice of Jesus, the Mbuti said to a pastor who had just finished a long campaign of evangelization: 'We have consulted each other carefully; there is no criminal among us, no one has been killed; if we knew anything about the crime, we would have avenged that death. . . . Please, go your way, where the killing has been committed' (Buakasa, s.d: 26). On the Christian side, as well as the Islamic, the mission to convert is an inescapable imperative for the faithful, and a challenge to reason.

In the beginning of these lectures, I intended to suggest a phenomenological description of religion as a political performance in theoretical and anthropological spaces, using Lévy-Bruhl's highly spatialized representations of effects from everyday life, as well as my own presentations of transcultural enterprises of conversion, adaptation and inculturation of Christianity. Now, this reflection is ending as a personal meditation on the being of a specific *métissage* between religious forms of experiences. Moreover, I should note that my meditation is grounded not only in my subjectivity but in a special locality of my experience in the world – in a Roman Catholic culture with its sensibility, which could account for my relative disinterest in African Islam. If my 'Africaness' designates a legacy and a project, indeed it also includes the *Tales of Faith* in all the possibilities of my becoming. Looking a last time at what Christianity and Islam signify, it is from the solidity of this *métissité* that I can marvel about what they still represent as intercultural challenges.

I have demonstrated, for example, that for the inculturation trend it was imperative to dissociate biblical teaching, the Word of the Prophet, from the socioeconomic programme of the missionary; that the theoretical principles differentiated on this basis should allow a better vision of the originality of Jesus Christ's message, the significance of Islam. This is well given. However, since such an intellectual position permits some theorists to appreciate the efficiency of the Bible and the pertinence of the Koran in today's ideological practices, while allowing other theorists to propose illusory appropriations of these messages, I am afraid that such a distinction does not, and cannot, integrate the complexity and power of historical representations and their frameworks. In fact, regimes of truth represented by Christianity and Islam live in historical cadres where the progress of their doctrine takes place in an organic manner. Any profound meaning of faith is organized from this perspective and implies a critical acceptance of the architecture in which God's message has been evolving. Thus, two frightening issues arise: on the one hand, how and why do we assume the alienation incarnated by a regime in its complex historical and cultural *métissage*? On the other hand, since we are dealing with systems of absolute truths, will it be possible to stand as a freedom *vis-à-vis* religious representations conveying the old totalitarian Church's maxim – *Extra Ecclesiam Nulla Salus* – so well exemplified today in fundamentalist Islam and Christianity? This, in fact, reminds us of a 'lesson': we inhabit our tradition the way we inhabit our body.

These are provocative questions. Also provocative remains an old lesson well formulated by Heidegger in his commentaries on the principle of identity: 'Whatever and however we may try to think, we think within the sphere of tradition. Tradition prevails when it frees us from thinking back to a thinking forward, which is no longer a planning. Only when we turn thoughtfully toward what has already been thought, will we be turned to use for what must still be thought' (1969: 41).

This aporia brings to an end the fabulous ambition of *Tales of Faith*.

Bibliography

Abdel Malek, Anouar (1970) 'La notion de "profondeur du champ historique" en sociologie', In *Sociologie des mutations*, Paris: Anthropos.

Abraham, Willy E. (1962) *The African Mind*, Chicago: Chicago University Press.

Abu-Lughod, Leila (1986) *Veiled Sentiments: Honor and Poetry in a Bedouin Society*, Berkeley: University of California Press.

Adler, Alfred and Zempleni, Andreas (1972) *Le Bâton de L'aveugle*, Paris: Hermann.

Ajayi, Jacob F.A. (1965) *Christian Missions in Nigeria, 1841–1891: The Making of a New Elite*, London: Longman.

—— (1969) 'Colonialism: an episode in African history', In *Colonialism in Africa 1870–1960*, ed. L. Gann and P. Duignan, Cambridge: Cambridge University Press.

Althusser, Louis (1965) *Pour Marx*, Paris: Maspero.

Ampère, André Marie (1834) *Essai sur la Philosophie des Sciences*, Paris: Bachelier.

Anselme of Canterbury, St (1964) *Fides Quaerens Intellectum*, ed. Alexandre Koyré, Paris: J. Vrin.

Appiah, Anthony (1992) *In My Father's House*, New York, Oxford: Oxford University Press.

Apter, Andrew (1992) *Black Critics and Kings: The Hermeneutics of Power in Yoruba Society*, Chicago: Chicago University Press.

Armstrong, Robert Plant (1971) *The Affecting Presence: An Essay in Humanistic Anthropology*, Urbana: University of Illinois Press.

—— (1975) *Wellspring: On the Myth and Source of Culture*, Berkeley: University of California Press.

—— (1981) *The Powers of Presence: Consciousness, Myth, and Affecting Presence*, Philadelphia: University of Pennsylvania Press.

Aron, Raymond (1938) *Essai sur la Théorie de L'histoire en Allemagne Contemporaine*, Paris: J. Vrin.

Asad, Talal (1975) *Anthropology and the Colonial Encounter*, Ithaca, New York, Humanities Press.

Augustine, St (1984) *Retractationes*, ed. Almut Mutzenbecher, Brepols: Turnholti.

Ba, Amadou Hampate (1980) *Vie et Enseignement de Tierno Bokar, le Sage de Bandiagara*, Paris: Seuil.

Bachelard, Gaston (1953) *Le Matérialisme Rationnel*, Paris: Presses Universitaires de France.

Bachman, Steven (1989) *Preach Liberty: Selections from the Bible for Progressives*, New York: Four Walls Eight Windows.

Badinter, Elisabeth and Robert (1988) *Condorcet*, Paris: Fayard.

Bahoken, J. Calvin (1967) *Clairières Métaphysiques Africaines*, Paris: Présence Africaine.

Balandier, Georges (1955) *Sociologie actuelle de l'Afrique Noire*, Paris: Presses Universitaires de France.

Barret, David B. (1968) *Schism and Renewal*, Nairobi: Oxford University Press.

—— 'AD 2000 – 350 Million Christians in Africa', *International Review of Missions* **56** (233): 39–54.

Bascom, William (1969) *Ifa Divination*, Bloomington: Indiana University Press.

Bastide, Roger (1962) 'L'homme africain à travers sa religion traditionnelle', *Présence Africaine*, **40**: 32.

Bates, Robert; O'Barr, Jean; Mudimbe, V.Y. (1993) *Africa and the Disciplines*, Chicago: Chicago University Press.

Bauman, Zygmund (1978) *Hermeneutics and Social Science*, London: Hutchinson.

Benveniste, Emile (1973) *Indo-European Language and Society*, Coral Gables: University of Miami Press.

Beti, Mongo (1956) *Le Pauvre Christ de Bomba*, Paris: Robert Laffont.

—— (1958) *Le Roi Miraculé*, Paris: Buchet Chastel.

Biaya, T. Kayembe (1992) 'Femmes, possession et christianisme au Zaïre', Ph.D. diss., Université Laval.

Blackwell, Basil (1954) *The Institutions of Primitive Society*, Oxford: Oxford University Press.

Blanchot, Maurice (1995) *The Work of Fire*, Stanford: Stanford University Press.

Blyden, Edward (1888, reprint 1967) *Christianity, Islam and the Negro Race*, London: Edinburgh Press.

Bourdieu, Pierre (1988) *Homo Academicus*, Stanford: Stanford University Press.

—— (1990) *The Logic of Practice*, Stanford: Stanford University Press.

Boto, Eza (alias Mongo Beti) (1954) *Ville Cruelle*, Paris: Présence Africaine.

Brenner, Louis (1984) *West African Sufi: The Religious Heritage and Spiritual Search of Cerno Bokar Saalif Taal*, Berkeley and Los Angeles: University of California Press.

Brezault, Alain and Clavreul, Gérard (1987) *Missions. En Afrique les Catholiques Face à l'Islam, aux Sectes, au Vatican*, Paris: Autrement.

Brunschwig, Henri (1963) *L'Avènement de l'Afrique Noire du XIXème Siècle à nos Jours*, Paris: Armand Colin.

Buakasa, Tulu Kia Mpasu (1988) *Le Zaïre Face au Développement du Sous-développement*, Kinshasa-Libreville-Munich: Presses Universitaires Africaines.

—— (1973) *L'impensé du discours*, Kinshasa: Presses Universitaires du Zaïre.

—— s.d. *Réinventer le Zaïre*, s.l. (Montréal), Canada.

Bwanga, Antoinette, Sister (1995) 'Le Synode des Evêques sur la vie consacrée et sa mission dans l'Eglise et dans le monde', *Revue de Spiritualité Africaine*, **1**: 9–22.

Canguilhem, Georges (1988) *Ideology and Rationality in the History of the Life of Sciences*, Cambridge, Mass.: MIT Press, c1988.

Cardaire, Marcel (1954) *L'Islam et le Terroir Africain*, Bamako: IFAN.

Certeau, Michel de (1984) *The Practice of Everyday Life*, Los Angeles: University of California Press.

—— (1988) *The Writing of History*, New York: Columbia University Press.

Charles, Pierre (1939) *Missiologie* (I), Louvain: Aucam.

Chasteland, Jean-Claude; Véron, Jacques; Barbiéri, Magali (1993) *Politiques de Développement et Croissance Démographique Rapide en Afrique*, Paris: Presses Universitaires de France.

Christensen, Thomas G. (1990) *An African Tree of Life*, New York: Orbis Book.

Cicero, Marcus Tullius (1967) *De Natura Deorum*, Cambridge, Mass.: Harvard University Press.

Coleman, James S. and Halisi, C.R.D. (1983) 'American political science and tropical Africa: universalism versus relativism', *African Studies Review*, **26**: 3–4.

Collingwood, Robin George (1946) *The Idea of History*, London: Oxford University Press.

Copans, Jean (1974) *Critiques et Politiques de l'Anthropologie*, Paris: Maspero.

Copans, Jean (edit.) (1975) *Anthropologie et Impérialisme*, Paris: Maspero.

Corin, Ellen and Bibeau, Gilles (1977) 'La médecine des guérisseurs entre la tradition et la modernité', *Recherches, Pédagogie, Culture*, **32**: 50.

Crahay, Frantz (1965) 'Le "décollage" conceptuel: conditions d'une philosophie africaine', *Diogène*, 52: 61–84.

Delumeau, Jean (1978) *La Peur de l'Occident, XVIème-XVIIIème siècles: une cité assiégée*, Paris: Fayard.

Devalle, Susana B.C. (1992) *Discourses of Ethnicity. Culture and Protest in Jharkland*, New Delhi: Sage.

—— (1983) 'Anthropología, ideología, colonialismo', *Estudios de Asia y Africa*, **18** (3): 337–68.

Dia, Mamadou (1975) *Islam, Sociétés Africaines et Culture Industrielle*, Dakar: Nouvelles Editions Africaines.

—— (1979) *Essais sur l'Islam II: Socio-anthropologie de l'Islam*, Dakar: Nouvelles Editions Africaines.

—— (1980) *Islam et Civilisations Négro-Africaines*, Dakar: Nouvelles Editions Africaines.

Diagne, Pathé F. (1981) *L'Europhilosophie Face à la Pensée du Négro-Africain*, Dakar: Sankoré.

Diamond, Jared (1994) 'Of the science of race', *Discover: The World of Science*, November.

Dieng, Amady Aly (1978) *Hegel, Marx, Engels et les Problèmes de l'Afrique Noire*, Dakar: Sankoré.

—— (1983) *Contribution à L'étude des Problèmes Philosophiques en Afrique Noire*, Paris: Nubia.

Dieterlen, Germaine, (ed.) (1965) *African Systems of Thought*, London: Oxford University Press.

Diop, Cheik Anta (1954) *Nations Nègres et Culture*, Paris: Présence Africaine.

—— (1960) *L'Afrique Noire Précoloniale*, Paris: Présence Africaine.

Dodson, Michael and O'Shaugnessy, Laura Nuzzi (1990) *Nicaragua's Other Revolution: Religious Faith and Political Struggle*, Chapel Hill and London: The University of North Carolina Press.

Dolphyne, Florence (1991) *The Emancipation of Women: An African Perspective*, Accra: Ghana University Press.

Dumézil, Georges (1980) *Camillus*, Berkeley and Los Angeles: University of California Press.

Eboussi-Boulaga, Fabien (1977) *La Crise du Muntu: authenticité africaine et philosophie*, Paris: Présence Africaine.

—— (1981) *Christianity without Fetishes: An African Critique and Recapture of Christianity*, New York: Orbis Books.

—— (1991) *A Contretemps: L'Enjeu de Dieu en Afrique*, Paris: Karthala.

Ela, Jean-Marc (1982) *L'Afrique des Villages*, Paris: Karthala.

—— (1983) *La Ville en Afrique noire*, Paris: Karthala.

—— (1986) *African Cry*, New York: Orbis Books.

—— (1989) *My Faith as an African*, New York and London: Orbis Books.

Ellenberger, Victor (1958) *L'Afrique avec cette Peur venue du fond des Ages: Sorcellerie, Initiation, exorcisme.*

Evans-Pritchard, E.E. (1946) 'Applied Anthropology', *Africa*, **16**.

—— (1955) 'Witchcraft', *Africa*, **8**: 4.

—— (1980) *Theories of Primitive Religion*, Oxford: The Clarendon Press.

Fabella, Virginia and Oduyoye, Mercy, (eds) (1988) *With Passion and Compassion: Third World Woman Doing Theology*, New York: Orbis.

Fanon, Frantz (1952) *Peau Noire, Masques Blancs*, Paris: Seuil.

Fink, Eugen *Nietzches Philosophie*.

Forde, Daryll (1954) *African Worlds: Studies in the Cosmological Ideas and Social Values of African People*, London: International African Institute.

Fortes, Meyer (1959) *Oedipus and Job in West African Religion*, Cambridge: Cambridge University Press.

Foucault, Michel (1970) *The Order of Things*, New York: Vintage Books.

—— (1971) *L'Ordre du Discours*, Paris: Gallimard.

—— (1972) *L'Histoire de la Folie à l'Age Classique*, Paris: Gallimard.

—— (1972) *The Archaeology of Knowledge*, New York: Pantheon.

—— (1984) 'Nietzsche, genealogy, history': *The Foucault Reader*, New York: Pantheon.

Fourche, T. and Morlighem, H. (1973) *Une Bible noire*, Brussels: Max Arnold.

Frazer, James George (1922; reprint 1963) *The Golden Bough*, New York: Collier Books.

Freud, Sigmund (1955) *The Standard Edition of the Complete Psychological Works of Sigmund Freud*, 24 vols, London: Hogarth Press.

Frobenius, Leo (1936) *Histoire de la Civilisation Africaine*, Paris: Gallimard.

Girard, René (1987) *Things Hidden since the Foundation of the World*, Stanford: Stanford University Press.

Gramsci, Antonio (1973) *Selections from the Prison Notebooks of Antonio Gramsci*, London: Lawrence and Wishart.

Gravand, Henri (1962) *Visage Africain de l'Eglise: une Expérience au Sénégal*. Paris: Orante.

Griaule, Marcel (1948) *Dieu D'Eau: Entretiens avec Ogotemmeli*, Paris: Chêne.

Groethuysen, Bernard (1980) *Anthropologie philosophique*, Paris: Gallimard.

Hacker, Andrew (1995) *Two Nations: Black and White, Separate, Hostile, Inequal*, New York: Ballantine Books.

Hammond, Dorothy and Jablow, Alta (1977) *The Myth of Africa*, New York: The Library of Social Science.

Hampate, BA. Amadou (1968) *Kaïdara*, Paris: Julliard.

Harding, Sandra (ed.) (1993) *'Racial' Economy of Science: Towards a Democratic Future*, Bloomington: Indiana University Press.

Hastings, Adrian (1979) *A History of African Christianity, 1950–1975*, Cambridge: Cambridge University Press.

Hebga, Meinrad P. (1979) *Sorcellerie, Chimère Dangereuse?*, Abidjan: Editions de l'Enades.

Heidegger, Martin (1969) *Identity and Difference*, New York: Harper and Row.

Herrestein Smith, Barbara and Plotnitsky, Arkady (eds) (1995) 'Mathematics, science and postclassical theory', *South Atlantic Quarterly*, **94**: 2.

Herzfeld, Michael (1987) *Anthropology through the Looking-Glass: Critical Ethnography in the Margins of Europe*, Cambridge, England: Cambridge University Press.

Herzlich, Claudine (1969) *Santé et Maladie. Analyse d'une Représentation Sociale*, Paris: London, New York, published in cooperation with the European Association of Experimental Psychology by Academic Press, 1973.

Heusch, Luc de (1958) *Le Symbolisme de L'Inceste Royal en Afrique*, Brussels: Université Libre de Bruxelles.

—— (1971) *Pourquoi L'Epouser et autres Essais*, Paris: Gallimard.

—— (1972) *Le Roi Ivre*, Paris: Gallimard.

Hountondji, Paulin J. (1992) 'Daily life in Black Africa: elements for a critique', In *The Surreptitious Speech*, (ed. V.Y. Mudimbe), Chicago: The University of Chicago Press.

Hulstaert, Gustave (1980) 'Le Dieu des Mongo', In *Religions Africaines et Christianisme*, Kinshasa: Faculté de théologie catholique.

Hunter, Guy (1962) *The New Society of Tropical Africa*, London: Oxford University Press.

Hurbon, Laënnec (1993) *El Barbaro Imaginario*, Mexico: Fondo de Cultura Economica.

Husserl, Edmund (1935; reprint 1970) *The Crisis of European Sciences and Transcendental Phenomenology*, Evanston: Northwestern University Press.

Idowu, E. Bolaji (1967) 'The study of religion with special reference to African traditional religion', *Orita* **1**: 1.

Jadin, Louis (1968) 'Les sectes religieuses secrètes des Antoniens', *Cahiers des Religions Africaines* **2**: 3.

Jameson, Fredric (1994) *The Seeds of Time*, New York: Columbia University Press.

Janzen, John M. (1982) *Lemba, 1650–1930: A Drum of Affliction in Africa and the New World*, New York: Garland Press.

Jay, Martin (1972) *L'Imagination Dialectique: Histoire de l'Ecole de Francfort (1923–1950)*, Paris: Payot.

Jung, Carl Gustav (1972) *Two Essays on Analytical Psychology*, Princeton: Bollingan Series, Princeton University Press.

—— (1980) *The Archetypes and the Collective Unconscious*, Princeton: Bollingan Series, Princeton University Press.

—— (1981) *The Development of Personality*, Princeton: Bollingen Series, Princeton University Press.

Ka, Mana (1992) *Foi Chrétienne, Crise Africaine et Reconstruction de l'Afrique*, Nairobi: Lomé, Yaoundé, Ceta, Haho, Cle.

Kalulambi-Pongo, Martin (1993) 'Production et signification de l'identité Kasaienne. La revue NKURUSE en tant qu'instrument et témoin, 1890–1990', PhD diss., Université Laval.

Kane, Cheik Hamidou (1972) *Ambiguous Adventure*, London: Heinemann.

Kaoze, Stefano (1907–1911) *La Psychologie des Bantus et quelques lettres*, (ed. A.J. Smet) Kinshasa: Faculté de Théologie Catholique.

Kesteloot, Lilyan (1976) *Anthologie négro-africaine*, Verviers: Marabout.

—— (1988) *Négritude et Situation Coloniale*, Paris: Silex.

Kiangu, Sindani (1992) *Préparer un Peuple Parfait: Mgr. Joseph Guffens*, Kinshasa:Saint Paul Afrique.

Kirwen, Michel C. (1988) *The Missionary and the Diviner*, New York: Orbis Books.

Ki-Zerbo, Joseph (1972) *Histoire de l'Afrique d'hier à demain*, Paris: Hatier.

Klotz, H. Pierre (1977) *L'Homme Malade*, Paris: Mercure de France.

Koyré, Alexandre (1964, Edition of St. Anselm's) *Fides Quaerens Intellectum Id est Proslogion, liber Gaunilonis Pro Insipiente, Atque Liber Apologeticus Contra Gaunilonem*, Paris: J. Vrin.

Lacan, Jacques (1977) *Ecrits: A Selection*, New York: W.W. Norton.

—— (1988) *The Seminar of Jacques Lacan*, Book I: *Freud's Papers on Technique, 1953–1954*, 1st American edn, New York: W. W. Norton.

Lactantius (1685) *Lucii Coelii Lactantii Firmiani Opera, quae extant omnia: ad fidem codicum tam impressorum, quam manu scriptorum recesita*, Cantabrigiae, Ex officina Johan Hayes, celeberrimae academiae typographi impensis Hen. Dickinson & Rich. Green, Bibiopol.

Lalande, André (1962) *Vocabulaire Technique et Critique de la Philosophie*, Paris: Presses Universitaires de France.

Lantz, Pierre (1970) 'Critique dialectique et sociologie', *L'Homme et la Société*, **13**, Paris: Anthropos.

Lapassade, Georges (1970) *Les Etats Modifiés de Conscience*, Paris: Presses Universitaires de France.

Laverdière, Lucien (1987) *L'Africain et le Missionaire*, Montréal: Editions Bellarmin.

Leclerc, Gérard (1972) *Anthropologie et Colonialisme*, Paris: Fayard.

Lévi-Strauss, Claude (1958) *Anthropologie Structurale*, Paris: Plon.

—— (1962) *La Pensée Sauvage*, Paris: Plon.

—— (1964) *Le Cru et le Cuit*, Paris: Plon.

—— (1966) *Anthropologie Structurale II*, Paris: Plon.

—— (1966) *The Savage Mind*, Chicago: The University of Chicago Press.

—— (1969) *The Raw and The Cooked*, Chicago: The University of Chicago Press.

—— (1976) *Structural Anthropology*, Vol. 2, New York: Basic Books.

—— (1977) *Tristes Topiques*, New York: Washington Square Press.

—— (1978) *The Origins of Table Manners*, New York: Harper and Row.

—— (1979) *Myth and Meaning*, New York: Schocken Books.

Lévinas, Emmanuel (1993) *Outside the Subject*, Stanford: Stanford University Press.

Lévy-Bruhl, Lucien (1928) *The Soul of the Primitive*, London: George Allen.

Liensenborghs, O. (1940) 'L'Instruction publique des indigènes du Congon belge', *Congo* **21**: 233–72.

Litt, Jean-Louis (1970) '*Analyse d'un processus d'acculturation. Les débuts de l'enseignement supérieur au Congo et la constitution d'une élite orientée vers le statut*', Mémoire de licence en sociologie, Université Catholique de Louvain.

Mair, Lucy (1936) *Native Policies in Africa*, New York: Negro Universities Press, 1969.

Makarakiza, A. (1959) *La Dialetique des Barundi*, Brussels: Académie Royale des Sciences Coloniales.

Malinowski, B. (1938) 'Modern anthropology and European rule in Africa', *Reale Academia d'Italia*, **16**.

Mangoni, T.M. (1979) 'Conception de la mort: interrogatoire du cadavre chez quelques ethnies du Zaire', *Recherches, Pédagogie et Culture* **41–2**.

Marcel, Gabriel (1956) *The Philosophy of Existentialism*, Secaucu, n.j.: The Citadel Press.

—— (1967) *Problematic Man*, New York: Herder and Herder.

Marion, Jean-Luc (1991) *God without Being*, Chicago: The University of Chicago Press.

Marx, Karl (1967) *Writings of the Young Marx on Philosophy and Society*, Garden City: Doubleday.

Masamba ma Mpolo (1971) 'Une approche pastorale de la sorcellerie', *Revue du Clergé Africain*, Kinshasa, République du Zaire: Centre Protestant d'Editions et de diffusion, 1974.

Masolo, Dismas A. (1994) *African Philosophy in Search of Identity*, Bloomington: Indiana University Press.

Maurier, Henri (1976) *Philosophie de l'Afrique noire*, St. Augustin: Anthropos.

Mbembe, Achille (1988) *Africains Indociles: Christianisme, Pouvoir et Etat en Société Postcoloniale*, Paris: Karthala.

Meester, Paul de (1991) *Université et Conscience Chrétienne*, Lubumbashi: Presses Universitaires de Lubumbashi.

Mendieta, Fray Jeronimo, de (1870; reprint 1945) *Historia Eclesiastica Indiana*, Mexico: Salvadore Chavez Hayhoe.

Merleau-Ponty, Maurice (1989) *Phenomenology of Perception*, London: Routledge.

—— (1973) *The Prose of the World*, Evanston: Northwestern University Press.

Middleton, John (1960) *Lugbara Religion: Ritual and Authority Among an East African People*, London: Oxford University Press.

—— (1967) *Gods and Rituals*, Garden City, N.Y: The Natural History Press.

Mills, C. Wright (1956) *The Power Elite*, New York: Oxford University Press.

Molara, Ogundipe-Leslie (1994) *Recreating Ourselves: African Women and Critical Transformations*, Trenton: Africa World Press.

Monteil, Vincent (1964) *L'Islam noir*, Paris: Seuil.

Mudimbe, V.Y. (1981) *Visage de la Philosophie et de la Théologie Contemporaines au Zaïre*, Brussels: CEDAF-ASDOC.

—— (1981) *Signes Thérapeutiques et Prose de la Vie en Afrique Noire*, Soc. Sci. Med. **15b**: 195–211, Pergamon Press Ltd.

—— (1988) *The Invention of Africa*, Bloomington: Indiana University Press.

—— (1991) *Parables and Fables: Exegesis, Textuality, and Politics in Central Africa*, Madison: Wisconsin University Press.

—— (edn 1992) *The Surreptitious Speech*, Chicago: The Chicago University Press.

Mulago, Vincent (1955) 'L'Union vitale bantu chez les Bashi, les banyarwanda, et les Barundi face à l'unité vitalee ecclésiale', PhD diss. Rome: Propaganda.

—— (1959) *'La théologie et ses responsabilités' Deuxième Congrès des écrivains et artistes noirs*, Paris: Présence Africaine.

—— (1965) *Un Visage Africain du Christianisme*, Paris: Présence Africaine.

—— (1973) *La Religion Traditionnelle des Bantus et leur Vision du Monde*, Kinshasa: CERA.

—— (1979) *Simbolismo Religioso Africano*, Madrid: Bibliotheca de Autores Christianos.

Mveng, Engelbert (1965) *L'Art d'Afrique Noire: Liturgie et Langage Religieux*, Paris: Mame.

—— (1983) 'Récents développements de la théologie africaine', *Bulletin of African Theology*, **5**: 9.

Myers, Greg (1990) *Writing Biology: Texts in the Social Construction of Scientific Knowledge*, Madison: The University of Wisconsin Press.

Nancy, Jean-Luc (1993) *The Birth to Presence*, Stanford: Stanford University Press.

Ndaw, Alassane (1983) *La Pensée Africaine: Recherches sur les Fondements de la Pensée Négro-Africaine*, Dakar: Les Nouvelles Editions Africaines.

Nseya, Kabangu (1979) 'Pistes pour une recherche de l'anthropologie médicale au Zaïre', In *Recherche, Pédagogie, Culture*, **41–2**: 63.

Oduyoye, Mercy Amba and Musimbi Kanyoro, R.A. (eds) (1992) *The Will to Arise: Women, Tradition and the Church in Africa*, New York: Orbis.

Omolade, Barbara (1986) 'Black Women and Feminism', In *Women and Values*, (ed. Pearsall, Marilyn) Belmont: Wadsworth Publishing.

Oppong, Christine (1986) *Sex Roles, Population and Development in West Africa*, Portsmouth: Heinemann.

Outlaw, Lucius (1992) 'On W.E.B. DuBois. "The conservation of Races,"' *Sapina Newsletter*, **4 (1)**: 13–28.

Oyono, Ferdinand (1956) *Une Vie de Boy*, Paris: Presses Pocket.

—— (1956) *Le Vieux Nègre et la Médaille*, Paris: 10/18.

—— (1960) *Chemins d'Europe*, Paris: Julliard.

Parrinder, Edward Geoffrey (1962) *African Traditional Religion*, London: S.P.C.K.

Penoukou, Efoé-Julien (1984) *Eglises d'Afrique: Propositions pour L'Avenir*, Paris: Karthala.

Piatigorsky, Alexander (1993) *Mythological Deliberations*, London: School of Oriental and African Studies.

Politzer, Georges (1928) *Critique des Fondements de la Psychologie*, Paris: Presses Universitaires de France.

Radin, Paul (1957) *Primitive Religion*, New York: Dover Publications.

Raison-Jourde, Françoise (1991) *Bible et Pouvoir à Madagascar au 19ème Siècle*, Paris: Karthala.

Retel-Laurentin, Anne (1974) *Sorcellerie et Ordalies*, Paris: Anthropos.

—— (1978) 'Esprit, magiciens et maladies.' *Recherche, Pédagogie, Culture*, **38**: 23.

Ricoeur, Paul (1969) *Le Conflit des Interprétations: Essais d'Herméneutique*, Paris: Seuil.

Rigby, Peter (1985) *Persistent Pastoralists: Nomadic Societies in Transition*, London: Zed Books.

Rombaut, Marc (1976) *La Poésie Négro-Africaine d'Expression Française*, Paris: Seghers.

Rosny, Eric de (1981) *Les Yeux de ma Chèvre*, Paris: Plon.

—— (1992) *L'Afrique des Guérisons*, Paris: Karthala.

Rotman, Brian (1993) *Signifying Nothing. The Semiotics of Zero*, Stanford: Stanford University Press.

Said, Edward (1993) *Culture and Imperialism*, New York: Alfred Knopf.

Salvaing, Bernard (1994) *Les Missionaires à la Rencontre de l'Afrique au 19ème siècle*, Paris: L'Harmattan.

Sangmpam, S.N. (1994) *Pseudocapitalism and the Overpoliticized State*, Aldershot: Avebury.

Sartre, Jean-Paul (1948) 'Orphée noir', *Les Temps Modernes*, **4**: 577–606.

—— (1956) *Being and Nothingness*, New York: Simon and Schuster.

—— (1976) *Critique of Dialectical Reason*, London: Verso.

—— (1976) *Black Orpheus*, Paris: Présence Africaine.

—— (1981) *The Words*, New York: Vintage Books.

Shorter, Aylward (1977) *African Christian Theology: Adaptation or Incarnations*, New York: Orbis.

Sow, A. (1966) *La Femme, la Vache, la Foi*, Paris: Julliard.

Spengler, Oswald (1918) *Der Untergang des Abendlandes*.

Stoetzel, J. (1960) 'La maladie, le malade et le médecin: esquisse d'une analyse psychosociale', *Population*, **15**: 613.

Sundkler, Bengt (1976) *Zulu Zion and Some Swazi Zionists*, Uppsala: Almqvist & Wiksell.

—— (1948; reprint 1961) *Bantu Prophets in South Africa*, London: Oxford University Press.

Sylla, Assane (1978) *La Philosophie morale des Wolof*, Dakar: Sankoré.

Taiwo, Oladele (1985) *Female Novelists of Modern Africa*, New York: St Martin's Press.

Taylor, John (1963) *The Primal Vision*, Philadelphia: The Fortune Press.

Tchikaya u Tamsi (1968) *Légendes Africaines*, Paris: Seghers.

Tempels, Placide (1944; reprint 1979) *Philosophie bantue*, A.J. Smet, Kinshasa: Faculté de Théologie Catholique.

Theuws, Théodore (1951) 'Philosophie bantoue et philosophie occidentale', *Civilisations I*.

Thomas, Louis-Vincent (1972) 'Une coutume africaine: l'interrogation du cadavre', *Bulletin de la Société de Thanatologie I*.

Thomas, Louis-Vincent, Luneau, René and Doneux, Jean-L. (1969) *Les Religions d'Afrique noire*, Paris: Fayard/Denoel.

Thomas, Louis-Vincent and Luneau, René (1977) *Les Sages dépossédés*, Paris: Laffont.

—— (1980) *Le Cadavre*, Bruxelles: Editions Complexe.

Thornton, John Kelly (1983) *The Kingdom of Kongo: Civil War and Transition 1641–1718*, Madison: The University of Wisconsin Press.

Todd, Emmanuel (1994) *Le Destin des Immigrés*, Paris: Seuil.

Traore, D. (1965) 'Medecine et magie africaines', *Présence Africaine* **9**.

Tshibangu, Tharcisse (1987) *La Théologie africaine*, Kinshasa: Saint Paul Afrique.

Valabrega, J.P. (1962) *La Relation thérapeutique*, Paris.

Valéry, Paul (1919) *La Crise de L'Esprit*, Paris.

Van Der Leeuw, Gerardus (1938) *Religion in Essence and Manifestation: A Study in Phenomenology*, London: George Allen & Unwin Ltd.

Vansina, Jan (1961) *De la Tradition orale: essai de méthode historique*, Tervuren: Musée Royal de l'Afrique Centrale.

Verhaegen, Benoît (1966–9) *Rébellions au Congo*, Bruxelles: Crisp.

—— (1974) *Introduction à l'histoire immédiate*, Gemblouz: Ducolot.

—— (1992) 'The African university: evaluation and perspectives', In *The Surreptitious Speech*, (ed. V.Y. Mudimbe), Chicago and London: University of Chicago Press.

Veyne, Paul (1984) *Writing History: Essay on Epistemology*, Middletown: Wesleyan University Press.

Villa-Vicencio, Charles (1988) *Trapped in Apartheid*, New York: Orbis Books.

Williamson, Lamar (1992) *Ishaku: An African Christian Between Two Worlds*, Lima, Ohio: Fairway Press.

Wiredu, J.E. (1980) *Philosophy and African Culture*, Cambridge: Cambridge University Press.

Zahan, Dominique (1970) *Religion, Spiritualité et Pensée africaine*, Paris: Payot.

Zorn, Jean-François (1993) *Le Grand Siècle d'une Mission protestante: La Mission de Paris de 1822 à 1914*, Paris: Karthala: Les Bergers et les Mages.

Zouber, Mahmoud (1977) *Ahmad Bâbâ de Tombouctou (1556–1627): sa vie, son oeuvre*, Paris: Maisonneuve et Larose.

Index